Effective
# Supervision
## for the Helping Professions

SAGE has been part of the global academic community since 1965, supporting high quality research and learning that transforms society and our understanding of individuals, groups, and cultures. SAGE is the independent, innovative, natural home for authors, editors and societies who share our commitment and passion for the social sciences.

Find out more at: **www.sagepublications.com**

Second Edition

*Effective*
# Supervision
## for the Helping Professions

## Michael Carroll

Los Angeles | London | New Delhi
Singapore | Washington DC

Los Angeles | London | New Delhi
Singapore | Washington DC

SAGE Publications Ltd
1 Oliver's Yard
55 City Road
London EC1Y 1SP

SAGE Publications Inc.
2455 Teller Road
Thousand Oaks, California 91320

SAGE Publications India Pvt Ltd
B 1/I 1 Mohan Cooperative Industrial Area
Mathura Road
New Delhi 110 044

SAGE Publications Asia-Pacific Pte Ltd
3 Church Street
#10-04 Samsung Hub
Singapore 049483

Editor: Susannah Trefgarne
Editorial assistant: Laura Walmsley
Production editor: Rachel Burrows
Copyeditor: Solveig Gardner Servian
Proofreader: Anna Gilding
Indexer: Martin Hargreaves
Marketing manager: Tamara Navaratnam
Cover design: Lisa Harper
Typeset by: C&M Digitals (P) Ltd, Chennai, India
Printed and bound by CPI Group (UK) Ltd,
Croydon, CR0 4YY

© Michael Carroll 1996, 2014

First edition titled *Counselling Supervision* published by
Continuum in 1996. Reprinted 1996, 1998, 2001, 2003.
Reprinted by SAGE Publications in 2004, 2006, 2007 (twice),
2008, 2010 (twice), 2012 (twice) and 2013
This second edition published 2014

**Library of Congress Control Number: 2013950524**

**British Library Cataloguing in Publication data**

A catalogue record for this book is available from
the British Library

MIX
Paper from
responsible sources
FSC
www.fsc.org  FSC® C013604

ISBN 978-1-4462-6992-3
ISBN 978-1-4462-6994-7 (pbk)

# Supervision as Conversation

Two people are talking. An ordinary room, ordinary people – but this is a special conversation. They are alone; yet nothing could be further from the truth. The conversation provides a platform for hundreds of other presences to move into, through and out of the room again. Their shared words are the vehicles that transport these presences into their shared worlds. The room echoes with unseen and subtle voices. There are invited and uninvited guests. Some break in, some intrude and some are dragged in. The room is filled with people from the past, from the present and from the future.

Two people face each other. Each has her own history, his own family, her own past/present/future, and his own ways of thinking, feeling and acting. They see differently, and make sense of their experiences differently.

Two people relate to each other. Their relationship creates the space between them. Others too crowd into that relationship space calling for attention and notice. Whose relationship is it? Theirs? Or a relationship created from the shadowy ghosts of the past? How many people are there, really, in this two-way conversation?

This room is part of a house, which is part of a street, which is part of a neighbourhood, which is part of a country, which is part of the world. People from all these communities also squeeze into the room and find their way unnoticed into the conversation. How does the room itself, and all these unseen occupants, affect the conversation?

Who is being talked about? How are they being talked about? What will happen to the talk afterwards? Will it remain just words? Or will the words be translated into actions that affect the persons being talked about, and the systems of which they are a part?

A simple conversation turns out to be a complicated junction where two individuals meet each other and the world. They bring their lives, their relationships, their contexts. In a structured and guided conversation they imagine themselves into a different life, perhaps into another context.

This conversation is dealing with a complex set of interpersonal and systemic transactions involving selves, families, clients, colleagues, couples, teams, organisations and systems.

This is the conversation we call supervision.

# Contents

# About the Author

Michael Carroll, PhD is a Chartered Counselling Psychologist. He is an accredited Executive Coach and an accredited Supervisor of Executive Coaches with APECS (Association for Professional Executive Coaches and Supervisors).

Michael is Visiting Industrial Professor in the Graduate School of Education, University of Bristol and the winner of the 2001 British Psychological Society Award for Distinguished Contributions to Professional Psychology.

Michael works with individuals, teams and organisations specialising in the theme of learning and wellbeing. He supervises, coaches and trains nationally and internationally and works within the private and public spheres. He runs the Centre for Supervision Training. He has written, co-written and edited 10 books.

# Acknowledgements

I would like to dedicate this book to Elizabeth and Trevor Sheean, who have been wonderful companions on our supervision training programmes in Australia. I remember with fondness our flights together, our meals in various Australian watering holes, our tours in the main Australian cities and the many ideas born of Sauvignon Blanc and Pinot Noir. I look forward to realising our vision of eventually being together in the Home for the Chronically Appalled singing Kenny Rogers songs.

Others have contributed to my personal and professional journeys throughout the years that I would like to honour and thank. Elizabeth Holloway has been and continues to be a wonderful life and work companion whom it has been a joy to know. My peer supervision group continue to support and challenge me (Bill, Carole, Charlotte, Dave, Jenifer and Phil), and our monthly meetings are full of peer nourishment from amazingly dedicated professionals. My patient and hard-working BASPR fellow organisers (Paul, Maria and Amanda) with whom I have organised the British Association for Supervision Practice and Research conference for 23 years and the many supervisees who I have worked with continue to teach me about supervision. For nearly 30 years Cathy, my wife, has been by my side, supportive and generous – I couldn't have asked for a more loving companion. More recently Sam and Louise have been part of our lives and part of our family. Discovering that the best psychological and supervision insights don't work well on a 15-year-old girl has kept my feet on the ground and has made me definitely more realistic about supervision theories and models. Thank you all for your additions to my life and through me to this book.

Thanks are also due to Kate Wharton at Sage, who has been the motivator behind this new book. She saw potential for a rebirth of the first book and enough there for a revitalisation into a second one. Great insight, Kate. Thanks also to Susannah Trefgarne and Laura Walmsley at Sage for their patient, on-going feedback and help in the final stages of completing the book.

Two other people have helped me enormously. First, Robin Shohet became a consultant to this book. He asked a favour and I asked this one in return. I am not sure if this was my unconscious way of spreading responsibility. If you don't like the book then at least I am not totally responsible for the outcome and I have someone else to blame as well as myself. See, I am still discovering the darker sides of my personality. Whatever the motivation, Robin was terrier-like in his dedication to hunting down poorly expressed ideas and to suggesting new insights. Thank you, Robin.

Finally, special thanks to John McKeever, an editing wizard. First cousins, we rediscovered each other only two years ago after a gap of some 45 years, and it has been a pleasure and joy working with his infectious enthusiasm for literature, words and stories. He has made the book accessible and readable in a way I never could have.

July 2013

# Introduction

*And those who were dancing were thought to be insane by those who could not hear the music.* (Attributed to Nietzsche)

In 1979, fresh from my counselling psychology studies in Chicago, I was asked by a family therapist to supervise her work. I was chuffed to think that after such a brief apprenticeship as a counselling psychologist I was recognised as someone who could oversee and support the therapeutic work of others. Unwittingly and unthinkingly I found myself being asked to supervise for the first time. I suspect I was more didactic and directive then than I am now – probably because deep down I was hesitant and unsure of what I was supposed to do, but arrogant and naïve enough to think that whatever it was, I could do it.

My own experiences of supervision up to that time had been limited. My brushes with it were spasmodic and usually with wise practitioners who shared their wisdom with me. I think I did the same with my first supervisee and saw myself as the wise 'other' who guided the faltering footsteps of the less experienced.

## Supervision 101

Those first initial experiences of being a supervisee and of being a supervisor taught me a few lessons I have never forgotten. The first lesson was about how inadequately prepared most of us are as supervisees. I hadn't much of a clue about what supervision was when I first engaged in it as a supervisee; I had no idea how to prepare for it or how to use the supervisory time effectively. It was part of the training package I had agreed to, and that was that. I pitched up and presented myself as a sponge or a passive pawn in a game where the supervisor was the boss, set the agenda and kept an eye on the work so that it was passable. Supervision was primarily a forum for accountability – that I was being assessed and passed by the experienced other, the supervisor, who kept an eye on my work, and ensured I did it professionally and ethically. Like most other professionals in the field I felt that once I was qualified I would no longer need supervision – it was really only for beginners to ensure that they learned their profession well. This has taught me how important it is to not take for granted that supervisees know what supervision is, and that they know automatically how to make best use of it. It was in the light of this insight, and after experience of training supervisors in prison services, that Maria Gilbert and I wrote our manual *Becoming an Effective Supervisee: Creating Learning Partnerships* (2011). Its aim was simple: how to support supervisees in making the maximum use of supervision.

— The second lesson learned was how inadequately prepared many supervisors are to be supervisors. Many have inherited the role and mantle of supervision without having any formal training for it. Like me, some have gone on to do training in supervision while others have not. I now think that training as a supervisor is a necessity and not a luxury. I am delighted to see that now there are over 80 training programmes in supervision in Britain alone (Henderson, 2009a).

The third lesson emerging from my initial supervisory experiences taught me how easy it is to collude in supervision – as in my first placement. Collusion can result in supervision not happening at all, or in reducing it to a pleasant and innocuous relationship where challenge is at a minimum. It is very easy to engage in supervision-without-teeth or supervision as a check-box experience. My later role as the director of a postgraduate training programme convinced me that many supervisors are not direct with their supervisees, and don't give honest and transparent feedback. Many of the supervisor reports I received on students were bland, unhelpful and strongly edited to make sure the supervisor said little or nothing derogatory about the supervisees. What a pity! Our supervisees deserve our honesty and our clear, focused feedback to help them learn.

## The past and the present

In the 34 years since I first became involved in supervision, and in the almost 17 years since this book first appeared, there have been amazing advances in the fields of education, neuroscience, business studies, organisational development, psychology, coaching, counselling and psychotherapy. New technology, critical methods, models and frameworks have had profound impacts on what we communicate and how we communicate. These advances have changed the way I think about supervision, learning and teaching. In this book I seek to examine these changes as they have influenced the discipline of supervision internally and externally, theoretically and practically. In particular there have been four changes in supervision over those years that I want to note:

1. *Widening supervision:* There has been a widening of the concept of supervision from a private one-to-one conversation in a dedicated supervision room to viewing supervision as a reflective systemic stance. Supervision no longer just looks inwards to help supervisees do their work better, but also helps them look outwards to the systems which they are a part of, and in which they work. Supervision is influenced by the contexts in which it takes place and

the various themes, fashions and trends that characterise those contexts. Can supervision create ever-widening circles so that a supervisory presence pervades all of life and work? We have privatised supervision for too long and limited its impact for systemic change.

2.  *Towards supervisee-led supervision:* There is a movement from supervisor-led to supervisee-led approaches. When I first started supervising it was customary for the supervisee to adapt to how the supervisor worked. The supervisor called the shots and was the conductor of the supervisory orchestra. Now I believe that approach is unhelpful and not in the best traditions of learning. I am convinced that until supervisees become the directors of their own supervision it will remain a teaching modality rather than a learning one. A good proof of this is that under the old system many supervisees felt obliged to attend supervision as opposed to eagerly engaging with its amazing potential for learning. For far too long supervisees have had to accommodate themselves to the theoretical orientation, learning style and personal approach of supervisors – even though the focus of supervision is on the learning of supervisees. Turning that on its head makes all the difference. Supervisors now adapt, accommodate and attune to the individual learning styles and personal preferences of supervisees. Today it is up to supervisees to direct the supervisory orchestra and to make supervisors accountable for the quality of the supervision they offer. *Good enough* is at times *not* good enough, and can become a lazy catchphrase for mediocrity and low expectations. Indeed, supervisees are now more alert to their rights and supervisors more accountable for who they are, and what they do, than ever before. This is as it should be.

3.  *From teaching to learning:* I have moved from thinking about supervision as a teaching modality to thinking about the supervisor as a facilitator or a mediator of personalised learning. So often the supervisor is seen as the expert, the one who knows first, who knows more, who knows better and best. While it is indeed valuable and worthwhile having skills, knowledge and experience, these are not what makes supervision beneficial, or what makes supervisors good supervisors. Most of this book focuses on *how we learn from experience through critical reflection.* This is what I now see as the central domain of supervision at its best. Facilitating reflection becomes the prime skill of supervisors. Supervisees bring their experience into a reflective dialogue and learn in and from that dialogue. From this foundation emerge a number of related questions: How do we help supervisees learn to reflect in ever deepening ways? How do supervisors learn to become facilitators of reflective practice? How do we create the kind of learning environment that supports reflective dialogue?

4.  *The supervisor as gatekeeper:* I believe that supervision holds in tension the twin functions of facilitating the development of supervisees and maintaining accountability for the quality of the supervisees' work. Supervisors do not challenge enough on the second of these functions. I would like to see supervisors

step up to the mark as the gatekeepers of professions and see part of their role as maintaining high standards for themselves, their supervisees and the organisations to which both parties belong. It is too easy to back down, to collude, to be *nice* and, in the name of good relationships, not say it as it is. It is reckoned that up to 4 per cent of those in the helping professions lack the knowledge, skills, self-awareness, empathy and so on to make them competent practitioners. Who will tell them, if not their supervisors? I do not advocate a confrontational style of supervision but I do believe in naming the elephant in the room.

These four changes in the nature and practice of supervision over my supervisory lifetime are the cornerstones of this book.

## The changing external landscape of supervision

I am also aware that much has changed on the external supervisory landscape. Initially, the profession of counselling and counselling psychology held the monopoly on supervision research, theory and practice throughout the helping professions. Since then supervision has developed in many other professions; coaching, organisational development, human resources, police services, homeopathy, medicine, pastoral ministry, and clinical and forensic psychology to mention but a few. I have migrated into some of these professions – becoming more involved in organisational settings and adding executive coaching to my portfolio. I have also found myself providing supervision consultancy to groups other than counsellors; for example, doctors, workers in palliative care, probation officers, the prison service, pastoral care workers, business executives and so on.

Being involved in each of these new professional orientations and cultures has forced me to review what I mean by supervision. I have learned not to assume that my inherited version of it (from counselling psychology) is the only true one, and applicable to all areas of supervision. As Schon (1983) pointed out, reflection is one of the methods through which we adapt theories and principles to particular situations. Reflection becomes the bridge between the lofty highlands of theory and the swampy lowlands of practice. That journey doesn't happen automatically – it needs careful planning, strategy and feedback. So, while we can agree easily on definitions of supervision, how we apply it in these new contexts will differ, and should differ.

There has also been a shift in knowledge about learning and teaching methods which has impacted the world of supervision. Old paradigms have given way to new. I am reminded of a story told by Monty Roberts (1997) about what happened when he shared with this father his new found 'gentle' method of breaking horses. After watching him demonstrate his innovative techniques his father hit him, and told him never to show him such a demonstration again. 'If I allow myself to believe what I have just seen,' he told his shocked son, 'it means my whole life has been wasted.' This was the stance of a man who couldn't accept what was clearly an improvement on traditional methods because to do so, in his eyes, meant being untrue to who he was. This is what Scharmer (2007) has called retro-learning, where we hearken back to, and stick with, old ways of learning rather than embrace new and exciting methods that build on what we already know and advance our knowledge and skills. We can move from *accommodation learning*, which reads the new through the old, to *assimilation learning*, which allows the old to change in the light of the new. What we learned in bygone days are steps to new learning. This may involve the pain of letting go of precious beliefs because they have been overtaken by more useful approaches. It is usually more difficult to unlearn than it is to learn. I have been amazed at how tenaciously we hold on to ideas and theories even when no longer valid and indeed no longer useful. I include myself in that 'we' and wonder what it is about certain beliefs and commitments that make us treat them as privileged children that must be nourished rather than simply theories that can be held or let go as needed.

## Theoretical and practical issues and themes in supervision

While deeply involved in 'nuts and bolts' supervision, I am also interested in the evolution of supervision as a discipline and a praxis. Training in supervision necessarily involves itself with both the intellectual and the pragmatic:

What is supervision?
How do I set it up?
How do I engage in it?
How do I give effective feedback and evaluation within supervision?
How do I write supervisory reports?
How do I support learning and accountability?
How do I deal with tensions in the supervisory relationships?
What forms of supervision are there, and which format is best used in which context?
What stops or hinders me being more effective as a supervisor?

It was these sorts of foundational questions that led me to do my first supervision training with Brigid Proctor at South West London College in the early 1980s. I began a supervisory journey then that has intrigued me ever since. I followed up this first training by attending courses offered from different orientations, and in the late 1980s began a PhD course on the subject of supervision. I wrote a book based on the research I did for that doctorate in 1996 (the first edition of this book) and have continued to practice supervision, teach supervision and write about supervision since then. Both supervision and my views of supervision have changed quite dramatically during that time. My domain of supervision has widened and now includes supervising coaches, HR directors, managers, psychologists, management consultants, OD consultants and others. I have had the privilege of teaching supervision in a number of countries: the UK, Ireland, Switzerland, Norway, Germany, Australia and New Zealand. These experiences have challenged and widened my vision even more and made me rethink what supervision is all about. Hence this book. It seems that it is time to gather what knowledge, information, insights and wisdom I have gleaned over the years together and see if I can collate it to so as to create a *philosophy* of supervision. I do not want to write another 'how-to' book, valuable as that may be. While practice remains my first vocation I am also deeply interested in theory and research, the *why* questions. I am good at synthesising, at translating theory into action. In this book I am trying to translate action into theory. I am more interested in what supervision *is* rather than what it *does*. While the two cannot be separated, the emphasis in this book is about making sense of supervision and documenting some of the shifts that have taken place in the practice of supervision over the years. There are many excellent 'how-to' books available to help supervisors and supervisees set up, engage in and maintain supervision (e.g., Hawkins and Shohet, 2012; Inskipp and Proctor, 1993, 1995; Bernard and Goodyear, 2014; Henderson, 2009b).

The questions above are not unimportant and new supervisors need to be inducted into their role as supervisory administrators. Administrative supervision is always necessary but it is never sufficient. For supervision to be sufficient we must look at the supervisor, the supervisee, their relationship, learning and development, and the various contexts in which supervision takes place. This book intends to take a field trip through the landscape of supervision, occasionally stopping to look in depth at key concepts. So while including *doing it* aspects of supervision, the book will also engage with the *being it* nature of supervision. Scharmer (2007: 14) asks the kinds of questions pertinent to this stance (I have adapted his questions to supervision):

Who are we?
What are we here for?
What do we want to create together?
What do we need to let go, in order to make supervision work?
What do we need to let come in, in order to make supervision effective?

These are the themes that will make up this book. What is at the heart of supervision? Who are the players involved and what are their various roles? How does learning take place within supervision? How do I work with the twin aspects of experiential learning and critical reflection? How do I come to make ethical decisions that are mature and contextual in both practice and supervision? What does organisational supervision look like?

In a chapter on integrative supervision (Carroll, 2001), I made a distinction between *functional* supervision and *spiritual* supervision. Functional supervision fixes, sorts out, makes the supervisor into an expert who tinkers with the practice of the supervisee as one would tinker with a washing machine that needs some repair. Functional supervision is a *technology* of supervision where supervisors apply remedial processes to supervisees in 'exclusively a technical intervention' (Scaife 2009: x). It could be called *outside-in* supervision because the focus of supervision is the supervisor's role. What do *I* do in supervision? Supervision is not necessarily connected with the internal world of either the supervisor or the supervisee. Spiritual supervision, by contrast, is an *inside-out* way of thinking, where supervision emerges from who the supervisor is and the supervision becomes a collaborative relationship with learning at its heart. Who am I for supervisees?

My hope is that this book is about spiritual supervision concerned with a *supervisory way of being* rather than just administrative or functional supervision. Not that the administrative side of supervision can be ignored. Administrative supervision is the foundation on which the house is built – however, none of us live in the foundations of our homes.

## Types of supervision

There are six types of supervision that will interact and weave their ways throughout this book. These are not six separate approaches to supervision, and they complement each other rather than compete. I see them as 'compasses' that keep me on a purposeful supervisory course and as 'binoculars' that help me scan the supervisory horizon to ensure that I am heading in the right direction. The six functions revolve around:

1. The quality of practice, and accountability for that practice (Normative supervision)
2. Continual and lifelong learning from practice (Formative supervision)
3. Ensuring the wellbeing and resilience of practitioners in relation to their work (Restorative supervision)
4. Placing practice in ever widening contexts which give it deeper meanings (Systemic supervision)
5. Monitoring that the learning involved is not just theoretical or espoused learning, but learning that is translatable into action and changed practice (Transformative supervision)
6. Setting up, organising and maintaining the process of supervision through effective administration and organisation (Administrative supervision)

Common to all six is *practice*, the actual work done, and that must continue to be the central core of supervision. Kathi Murphy (2009) described supervision as 'the dancing partner of our work' in her keynote address at a BASPR conference.

## About this book

In this book I want to move away from academic writing and write as if I am working face-to-face with participants on a training course to become supervisors. I will
include more examples and anecdotes from practice and begin each chapter with a
summary. I will try to keep the tone inclusive, collegial and discursive rather than
expert and dogmatic. Some perennials from the earlier book have not dimmed
with time, and I will retain these. I will build on the past rather than see it as an
unstable foundation from which to fashion the future. Hindsight reveals how many
of our theories, values and beliefs become the springboard for new learning. They
are to be cherished rather than dismissed as theoretically primitive.

The time is long gone when a single book has been able to capture all that
needs to be said about supervision. A fair few library shelves would be needed to
cover supervision comprehensively. What do I put into this book and what do I
leave out? Difficult choices have had to be made and some good ideas have had to
be deferred to produce a focused, homogenous book.

The Introduction and Chapter 1 are new, revisiting what supervision means
and presenting my philosophy of supervision. Chapter 2 is also new and considers
the key theme of voice, power and identity in supervision; supervision is a conversation, and this chapter looks in some depth at the kind of conversation it can
be. Chapters 3 to 8 discuss the six types of supervision in detail. Chapters 9 and 10
take a deep look at reflection and reflective practice. Chapter 11 is new and summarises my understanding of how supervision can help us employ learning that is
informed by advances in neuroscience. The Epilogue summarises the supervision
journey in the book and presents some final thoughts.

An appendix connects life and supervision, asking how supervision themes
integrate at times with life themes.

## Conclusion

One of the major insights for me in growing older is how much the events and
experiences of my life seem to join up and weave together into discernible patterns.
It all gets connected in some way, even if at first it's not obvious. With Kierkegaard,
I believe we live life forward and understand it backwards. Why should I be sur-
prised that the learning currents in life will also be played out at work? Why would
I be amazed that the 'early me' fashioned in my family background will emerge
in later life as vibrant and real as that *I* was back then? After all, I bring *me* to the
work I do, whether I intend to or not. *I* am one of the most important variables in
my practice; the more I try to separate myself from my practice, the more I adopt
an unreal persona. The person and the professional cannot be separate people, no
matter how much we try to make them so. The inner-person of the professional

worker is the spirit of his/her practice. (I have put this additional material in the Appendix to describe my own supervision journey, locating myself and the connecting links between me, my life, my work and my supervision. It reveals how personal themes in my life and my upbringing have integrated almost seamlessly, often unconsciously, into my supervision journey.)

So there you have it. This book is a gathering of the years: experience of being a supervisor and a supervisee, reading and writing, training supervisors in many parts of our world. Experience is life's best teacher, and I hope my experience helps you to make sense of your experience. If you find ideas, models or frameworks in this book that help you, then take them and use them in your work. Ideas don't do well when encased in ice and bought and sold as commodities. If it helps you, use what you read here. Brookfield captures this succinctly for me when he writes 'the best teachers are good burglars, contextually attended plunderers – they are always on the lookout for something they haven't tried before that, with a few adaptations, will work with their students' (2012: x). Most supervisors think in the same practical way and forage for ways that will help them work better and more effectively. Happy plundering!

# One

# What is Supervision?

**Chapter summary**

This chapter provides a comprehensive overview of what is at the heart of supervision. It looks at how supervision can go wrong and be hijacked for purposes other than learning. It offers definitions, descriptions and metaphors of supervision before zoning in on what are the essentials of supervisory practice. The benefits of supervision are reviewed, as is the foundation or anchors on which supervision is built. The learning principles of supervision are laid out as guides for further chapters.

My first experience of supervision took place during my training as a counselling psychologist 35 year ago. I spent a summer working in a counselling service for young people. Enthused by the prospects of immersing myself in an exciting placement, and warmly greeted by the Director of the centre, I was further excited when told that he would personally supervise my work. This man was highly experienced, well qualified and an excellent role model when it came to both working with young people and managing a counselling service. What could be a better start for a young, still 'wet behind the ears' trainee taking his first tentative steps into the real world of counselling? Suffice it to say, I never saw him once for supervision in the three months I spent in that wonderful setting. He would bump into me in the canteen or the corridor, or at an agency training day, and greet me warmly with words that amounted to: 'Hearing great things about your work, Michael, hope everything is going well – do contact me if you need anything.'

Supervision, for him, meant dealing with problems I couldn't manage on my own. Supervision managed emergencies and critical incidents where support or advice was needed. Clearly, from his perspective, I was doing fine and therefore didn't need supervision. At the end of three months I received a glowing supervisor's report which I dutifully took back to my training programme. The Director and I had committed a supervisory 'sin': we had colluded in avoiding supervision as I now know it. For good reasons, let it be said. He was a very busy man, and if my supervision time rose to the top of his to-do list, then it was quickly superseded by other more urgent claims to his time and attention. I wasn't having problems and I wasn't assertive enough to demand the supervision I would have loved to have had from such a skilled practitioner. A golden opportunity was lost.

## How supervision can go wrong

Golden opportunities are missed a lot in supervision. Not everything is rosy in the supervision garden all the time. I want to begin with what supervision *is not* before looking at what *it is* as a way of clearing the ground before building the supervision edifice. Supervision can become:

- *Underused:* where it becomes solely a case conference and tries to make sense of what is happening to clients (whether those clients are individuals, couples, teams or organisations). Here supervision narrows to focus on only a fraction of the whole helping system; for example, there is no focus on the organisational or systemic aspects of the work.
- *A risk assessment:* ensuring that the work is done in the 'proper' manner so that no one can be held blameworthy if anything goes wrong. Supervision that has been hijacked to focus only on risks and the means of avoiding them becomes an arena of fear where learning is sacrificed to safety. Supervision can easily come to be seen as a form of surveillance in some professions, particularly with regard to trainees in what has famously been called 'snoopavision'.
- *The realm of experts:* where the supervisor, who is an expert, guides the footsteps of another, who is a novice, or less experienced. If not careful this can result in 'cloning' the supervisor.
- *A tick-box experience:* proving that supervision has taken place because it is a requirement of a course, an audit or a human resources duty. Supervision 'has to' be done. Supervision done out of duty rarely results in transformational learning.
- *Hijacked by management:* supervision is mixed up with, and in with, management supervision. This can happen when a manager is also the appointed reflective or clinical supervisor of a worker. Where managerial and clinical supervision merge supervision can be seen as a form of control, creating docile and conforming practitioners. This has been called 'domesticating supervision' (Hunt, 2010:161) because of its tendency to ensure that the party line is followed.
- *Used as a punishment:* when someone has transgressed and been found wanting. 'Required to be in supervision' is sometimes used as a remedial sanction for practitioners who are found wanting, or who are awaiting a disciplinary outcome.
- *Interpreted as therapy or counselling:* concentrates on the personal lives of supervisees as the sole focus of supervision.

- *Imposed without consultation or consent:* while it doesn't have to be a problem that supervisees are allocated to supervisors, it does need to be talked through, and possible problems anticipated (see Carroll and Gilbert, 2011).
- *Conducted without training:* both parties can be left fumbling or stumbling to try to make sense of what supervision is. It has been known for supervisors and supervisees to trade 'atrocity stories' about managers and organisations as a sort of default way of passing the time.
- *A psychological game:* both parties avoid the real work of reflective practice by engaging in clever and collusive theorising and interpretation. These games can range from 'you and me against the organisation' through 'please be easy on me' to 'friends don't evaluate each other' and many more (see Ladany and Bradley, 2010: 41).
- *A technology of supervision:* where pre-set formula or protocols are applied to all supervisees in the same way. 'Colonised supervision' is not uncommon – it insists that supervision is a one-size-fits-all process, where personalised learning is unknown and supervisors supervise all supervisees in the same way, in all contexts.

The example below shows how supervision can focus on one part of the supervisory system.

## Example

Lizzie's supervision is pretty straightforward. She and her supervisor fill in the forms from the organisation about her work and the administrative side of what she has done. There are scoring sheets for audits that have to be finalised and signed. There are also risk assessment forms for each client to ensure that all procedures have been followed. If there are red or yellow flags indicating levels of risk or danger, then strategies have to be devised to ensure that all parties are safe. Each case is carefully scrutinised by the supervisor, making sure that policies have been implemented and administrative procedures followed. That is about all there is time for in the hour Lizzie and her supervisor have together. Supervision is a forum for monitoring that the rules have been followed.

My favourite description or definition of misunderstood supervision was from a prison officer who suggested supervision was 'being called in by your boss and given a bollocking'!

However, hijacked supervision is not what this book is about; we want to look at what supervision is and can be when it's well used and delivering at its best. We want excellent supervisors, superb supervisees and effective supervision. Is that too much to ask? Sometimes yes. Recommending excellence can be a way of avoiding the shadow side of ourselves and our work and an inability to recognise that at the end of the day we remain human, limited and wounded. Our inabilities to reach lofty heights is a down-to-earth reminder that we should indeed strive for the best and be more compassionate to our weaknesses and what lurks continually in the human shadows.

In training programmes I often ask participants to draw me up a list of words or phrases that characterise a good/effective supervisor and a poor/ineffective supervisor. Some answers are both surprising and informative:

- A good supervisor is one who turns up for supervision.
- A good supervisor is one who uses humour.
- A poor supervisor is one who gossips and doesn't hold professional boundaries.
- A poor supervisor is one who wants to make the supervisee a clone of themselves.

## So what is supervision?

'So what do we think we are doing here?' This is an expression of curiosity and continuous inquiry (Shaw, 2002: 152). It's a question worth asking again and again. We get caught in, and comfortable with, the ways we do what we do. We take for granted that we know the answer and have always known the answer. Asking this question brings us back to basics; it revisits and renews the *why* of our practice. It's a good question for supervision!

When I started training supervisors I started gathering definitions of supervision. I was intrigued by how many there were, and by the different flavour each definition brought to the supervision banquet. When the definitions/descriptions of supervision filled four typed pages I decided to stop. It was clearly an exercise that could go on forever.

I frequently ask participants working in small groups to devise a sentence or two that capture what supervision means for them. I ask them to draw a picture or symbol that represents supervision to them. The wealth of information, ideas and images from this exercise has made me realise how 'plastic' or flexible the concept of supervision is. Supervision means different things, to different people, at different times in their professional journeys. There are also the multiple ways organisations make sense of and deploy supervision. My favourite definitions have changed over time as my focus on supervision has changed. It's a bit like asking people what 'relationship' or 'love' or 'ethics' or 'research' means. You will quickly gather a bewildering array of alternative definitions and descriptions. If you asked the same people the same question every five years you would get a different set of answers. So it is with supervision. It is not a fixed or static phenomenon; it is evolving, plastic, adaptable, flexible, nuanced.

Here are five definitions, all of which show supervision in a different light:

- A group of Maoris from the helping professions came up with this definition of supervision: 'For us Maori supervision means: gathering the treasures of the past into the competencies of the present for the wellbeing of the future.'
- Another definition captures a similar philosophy of supervision: 'Supervision begins and ends with respect for self, respect for others and taking responsibility for all your actions' (Autagavaia, 2001: 47).
- From one of the prisons in Britain came this description: 'Supervision creates a safe, supportive environment where the supervisee can reflect on practice and development, with consideration of the impact of the work with the client group on personal wellbeing.'
- Sheila Ryan writes of supervision from the world of homeopathy: 'Supervision interrupts practice. It wakes us up to what we are doing. When we are alive to what we are doing, we wake up to what is, instead of falling asleep in the comfort stories of our clinical routines and daily practice ... the supervisory voice acts as an irritator interrupting repetitive stories (comfort stories) and facilitating the creation of new stories' (Ryan, 2004: 44).
- Hawkins and Smith (2007) fashion their definition from the coaching and organisational development context: 'Coaching supervision is the process by which a Coach, with the help of a Supervisor, who is not working directly with the Client, can attend to understanding better both the Client System and themselves as part of the Client–Coach system, and by so doing transform their work. It also allows the coach to discover where he or she is not currently creating the shift for the benefit of the client and client organisation.'

Those who espouse a particular way of working (e.g., psychodynamic, humanistic, CBT, existential etc.) will gear their definition of supervision in the light of the underlying personality theory and theory of change which characterises that approach (e.g., Van Deurzen and Young (2009) from the Existential school, and Tudor and Worrall (2004) from a person–centred approach). Already the presentation of just a few definitions show the multi-faceted nature of supervision and what it means.

> At the end of this chapter I will point you in the direction of moving towards your own definition/description of supervision. I believe you can't properly take ownership or authority in supervision until you have wrestled with language to express what it is to you.

## Supervision metaphors

Images/metaphors and pictures are also a good way of trying to understand what supervision means. Good pictures can succeed when words fail. De Haan draws a useful word picture of supervision from working in the garden to the 'shift' when he finishes up and comes indoors:

> Supervision is where we wipe the sweat from our brows and the dirt from our faces, look at ourselves in the mirror and get ready to become an ordinary person again, without a role or function. To do so, we need to bring our newly acquired experiences, impressions and reflections up to the surface, review them and sometimes give them a clean, and then muster up the courage to process our emotions, undertake honest reflection and integrate our recent experiences into our broader consulting practice. (2012: 1)

Holton picks up the garden image:

> Reflecting on this holding environment in the supervisory space, the garden surfaced for me as a root metaphor. Using symbols and wise collaborative conversation in the creation of what I have named 'wisdom's garden' has become the foundation of a creative approach to reflective practice in one-to-one and group supervision. (2010: 5)

Many other images come readily to mind. Maria Gilbert and I (2011:24) gathered some of the following from supervisees who finished the sentence 'For me supervision is …':

- a torch – which illuminates my work.
- a container – where I feel safe and held.
- a mirror – where I see myself and my work (the mirror is usually held by my supervisor).
- a playpen – where we play with ideas, feelings, intuitions, hunches, theories.
- a dance – where we learn how to work together in harmony.
- a classroom – which contains two learners one of which facilitates my learning.
- a courtroom – where assessments, evaluations and judgments take place.
- a journey – where we both move through stages and need to decide where we are going, what we want to take with us, and what to leave behind.
- a thermometer – to gauge temperatures (intellectual, emotional, psychological and social climates).
- a sculpture – where I am being fashioned into something yet to be.

Sometimes roles and archetypes are used: priests and confessionals; detectives and investigations; gods and goddesses; the crusader and rescuer; the strong and the weak; the over adequate and the under adequate; male and female; and many more.

One coaching supervisor described supervision as 'somewhere between a warm bath and the Spanish Inquisition …' (Woodcock, 2012). What an image!

> You might want to stop here for a moment and see if some thoughts and images come to you about what supervision means for you in the context in which it takes place.

## What is supervision in essence?

By this stage you are probably feeling a bit overwhelmed with description, definitions and images of supervision. Not surprising. Maybe it is time to pull it together, forget about trying to confine and imprison supervision in one definition and look at some of the main features involved in it.

For me the main model that best speaks to the heart of supervision is the experiential learning model (ELM) of Kolb (1984). Supervision is a form of experiential learning, of learning from practice. Supervision is *reflection-on-action*, or indeed *reflection-in-action*, to result in *reflection-for-action*. In the present moment we consider the past in order to influence the future; in supervision we recall the past through *memory*, make meaning of the past in the present through *reflection* and redesign our future work through *imagination*. Memory, reflection and imagination are the three most used human faculties in supervision.

The process is clear: the experiential learning cycle becomes the journey through which reflection on past work leads to new learning that is integrated into future practice.

Another way to view the ELM is the after action review (AAR). This learning methodology was devised by the American Military as a way of learning from doing. Garvin (2000) reports on how, before heading back to barracks after a military operation, commanders gathered their troops in small groups of 9–10 soldiers and led them briefly through the following questions:

What did we set out to do?
What happened?
What went well?
What went badly?
What have we learned?
What will we do differently?

In supervision we go through these questions step by step. In the first four questions we move into the past and look back (reflection-on-action). We declare the purpose of our work and intervention (to help this individual deal with his depression; to coach this manager in how to create a more effective team; to facilitate this organisation make a shift in its culture etc.). We keep the purpose in mind, but as an end point to guide us and as a way of assessing whether or not our interventions are helping us move towards our purpose. In the second question we leave evaluation aside as we describe what happened (I challenged her to look at her behaviour; I listened intently; I set up a team decision-making process to help them look at how they make decisions; I shared some information about myself etc.).

Next comes evaluation as we make judgements. We look at what went well (the rapport between us is excellent; the client is highly motivated; she works very well between sessions; I got my challenge just right etc.). We then turn to what went badly (my challenging was crude and far too early; I missed the depth of her feeling around the separation; I didn't mean to but the comments I made humiliated him in the team etc.). Now we move into the present and gather our learning, our reflection-in-action (from these experiences I have learned that I sometimes misjudge the pace we are going at, and I am ahead of my client – I need to slow down and go at their pace; I have learned that I need to build a solid relationship and rapport with clients before I have permission from them to challenge them; I want to suspend judgement a bit longer and listen more carefully before coming to conclusions about what I think is going on etc.).

The final question moves both supervisor and supervisee into the future (reflection-for-action) as they consider what will change in future work (I will spend more time on the relationship; I will let my clients determine the pace we go at; I will pay more attention to the process in the team rather than the individuals etc.). These shifts in practice can then be made personal for individual clients and client groups.

In learning from the past, we sit at the feet of our own experience and allow that experience to speak to us (Zachary, 2000). We are students of the work itself. In being open to the hidden voices, in preparing to listen to what might come, we prepare ourselves for surprises.

The centre of supervision is *practice*. The work done per se, and our own experience of the work done, are the beginnings of supervision. In supervision the supervisee presents his/her work practice. How that happens we will consider later when we look at how to set up appropriate supervisor environments, relationships and contracts that allow the supervisee to present their experience of their work honestly and transparently. But for now let's stick with practice as the focus point of supervision. No practice, no supervision.

What happens to the practice that is presented? It is *reflected upon*. If the focus of supervision is practice, then the method of learning used in supervision is reflection. Supervision is a forum for reflection on practice. This reflection can have *focal points* (see Hawkins and Shohet, 2012: Ch. 7, where they present their seven-eyed model of supervision) or *different lenses* (see Chapter 10 in this book).

From reflection emerges *learning* – mainly in two areas: learning to be accountable for practice (ethical maturity), and learning to be an excellent practitioner (practical wisdom). The learning that emerges from reviewing our experiences in supervision can be of many kinds:

- Skill/competency/capability/capacity
- Knowledge and theoretical learning (theories, models, frameworks)
- Self-awareness and insights
- Transformational learning
- Emotional learning
- Reflective learning
- Practical learning
- Experiential learning

From learning comes *application* (to know and not to act is not to know, as one proverb states). Aristotle saw no difference between knowing and doing. But for us there is often a gap to be bridged between the two. Knowledge and skills do not always find their ways into practice. Supervision builds a bridge between knowing and doing, and integrates our various learnings into our practice. Our imaginations take over and we design future practice in both the short term and the long term. These may be different. Our perception is not just about what we give our attention to, it also includes the possibilities we see (De Bono, 2006).

This in turn becomes tacit knowledge where we act with automaticity. A core aim of supervision is to make our knowing unconscious so that we act intuitively and with wisdom.

In summary:

1.  The focus of supervision is *practice*.
2.  The end result of supervision is *learning* (the deepest form of which is transformational learning).
3.  The method used in supervision is *reflection* (reflection, reflexivity, critical reflection and critical self-reflection).
4.  Supervisors facilitate that *process* by creating an environment and relationship that mediate learning.
5.  The *supervisory relationship* is the engine room of supervision. Supervision, in my experience, rises or falls on the quality of that relationship. Techniques, skills, strategies, contracts and the other nuts and bolts of supervision only make sense when embedded in the kind of relationship that is initiated by supervisors and co-created by all parties – a relationship of trust, fidelity and emotional connection.

In a nutshell, supervision is a relational conversation where supervisees reflect on their work and their work experiences in order to learn how to practise better.

## Supervision is based on a number of anchors/principles

From the definitions above, from our survey of the elements in supervision and from reviewing the benefits of supervision, we are ready to draw out some of the foundation stones, anchors or principles underpinning supervision:

*   Supervision is for supervisees and the main evaluation of supervision is how effective it is in helping supervisees do their work better (does it help their clients?). Supervision is for supervisees, and through them for clients, and through them for systems and organisations.
*   Supervisees must be assisted to take charge of, take over and direct their supervision so that they use it for their learning.

- Accountability is built into all aspects of supervision so that we continually hold our practice up to the light for evaluation. We recognise and acknowledge the many stakeholders in the supervision system (supervisor, supervisee, clients, patients, families, the professions, organisations, teams, systems etc.) and be prepared to show how we are being accountable for its quality.
- Supervisees do the work in supervision; their learning is the most important aspect of supervision (Carroll & Gilbert, 2011). Every supervision session should end with the words: 'What have you learned from the past hour here in supervision? What two or three learnings are you taking away with you?' An analysis of supervision taped sessions indicates that supervisors often talk twice as much as supervisees (Carroll, 1995).
- Supervisors facilitate the learning of supervisees by asking themselves and their supervisees 'How can I best supervise you?'. The emphasis on 'you' indicates that supervision is tailor-made for supervisees and recognises that each supervisee is unique in how she or he learns. As a result different supervisees are supervised differently. We must personalise or customise learning to individual supervisees.
- Learning in supervision is ultimately transformative and not just transmissive: that is, it results in a change of mind-set or behaviour rather than simply being the transfer of ideas or knowledge alone.
- The medium of learning in supervision is critical reflection. We can't assume that individual supervisees have the ability to reflect. They often need help to do so.
- Experimental learning is the heart of supervision. Supervision is about work, practice. The supervisor's requests to their supervisees are simple and profound: 'Bring me your work. Be transparent. Lay out your practice in front of me, and let us review it together.'
- Supervision interrupts practice. In supervision we stop to reflect. At times it is difficult to stop and calm the flow of thoughts and focus on our work in order to give it mindful consideration.
- Supervision aids unlearning as well as facilitating new learning.
- Supervision helps make new connections and opens up systemic thinking and perceiving.
- Supervision redesigns the future through imagination and planning.
- Learning includes finding a voice (Belenky et al. (1986) use the theme of voice to trace the stages of learning in Women's Ways of Knowing).
- Supervision is conversation-based learning.
- Supervision entails moving from 'I-learning' to 'We-learning'.
- Creativity flows from the supervisory relationship. When in doubt review and re-establish the supervisory relationship.
- In supervision the shift in the supervisee takes place in the supervision room first, and is then transferred to work (Hawkins and Smith, 2007).
- Supervisors move beyond their embarrassments and are able to admit their limitations, their not-knowing, their being lost, and be transparent and honest.

In supervision we hope for some attitudinal and values shifts on the parts of both supervisor and supervisee:

1.  From participant to observer (to see better).
2.  From reactor to pro-actor (to initiate).
3.  From passive to active (to be effective).
4.  From teaching to facilitating learning (to focus on supervisee).
5.  From instruction to co-creating (to work collaboratively).
6.  From evaluation to curiosity (to continuously inquire).

## Why supervision? What are the benefits?

Lane and Corrie (2006) summarise what they see as the benefits of supervision for counselling psychologists. In my view these benefits apply equally to all forms of supervision. In their view supervision:

- offers protection to clients (cases are reviewed);
- offers reflective space to practitioners (enabling insights for improvement);
- helps practitioners identify their strengths, weaknesses, biases and world views;
- helps learning from peers; and
- offers the opportunity to keep up to date with professional developments.

I would add to these benefits that supervision:

- alerts practitioners to ethical and professional issues in their work and creates ethical watchfulness;
- provides a forum to consider and hold the tensions that emerge from the needs of various stakeholders in a supervisee's work (the organisation, the client, the profession);
- allows practitioners to measure the impact of their work on their lives and identify their personal reactions to their professional work (a health-and-safety early warning system);
- offers a third-person perspective (feedback) from the supervisor who is not part of the client system;
- is ultimately for the welfare of, and better service to, the client;
- creates a forum/platform of accountability for all those to whom the practitioner is accountable (organisation, clients, profession etc.) in areas such as competency, knowledge and acceptable standards of work; and
- updates workers to the best in innovation, insights and research in their chosen areas of work.

## Supervision narratives

Supervisees construct stories about their practice and tell those stories in supervision. Supervision is more about *psychological* truth (i.e., the truth as seen by the supervisee) and not so much about *objective* truth, what actually happened. In looking back and recalling what happened, memory doesn't provide a historically accurate account of what took place, rather it weaves a story to make sense and explain what happened. This is the way memory works. Recognising this, supervisors are aware that they are dealing not just with facts and interpreted facts but also ways of creating stories that are particular and peculiar to the individual recounting the narrative.

### Example

Jeremy had devised a plan for working with his stressed executives. He agreed with them that their coaching session would begin with a five-minute stress-buster where they would relax, visualise a peaceful scene and from this positive position would then launch into their coaching session. His supervisor confirms that this seemed to be a helpful strategy working with executives who had many demands in their lives. At one stage Jeremy brought an audio tape of his coaching session. He and his supervisor listened to sections of it together. The beginning was as Jeremy had said – five minutes relaxing and de-stressing. Except that it wasn't quite!

Jeremy: Good to see you again. Have a seat. Ready to go. As we have agreed, we will take about five minutes to relax and get rid of some of the stresses.

Client: Yes, it's been such a stressful week. I can't tell you how difficult it's been.

Jeremy: Good, all the more reason for relaxing and letting go the tension before we start. So, just sit back and breathe deeply.

Client: [after about two deep breaths] It's been the worst week since ...

Jeremy: [interrupting the client] Let's just relax before getting into the week as we agreed.

Client: Absolutely. [Pause, and after two more deep breaths] You know the deadline for my report ...

Jeremy: [with some obvious frustration in his voice] Hugh, we really must keep to our agreement about spending some time de-stressing before we get into the session. Otherwise ...

Client: I am so sorry. You are right. It's just that my mind is full of everything ...

Jeremy: Understandable, let's try again.

What Jeremy had explained to his supervisor and what he did in reality were two different things: one was an imposed ritual; the other was a way of helping stressed executives prepare for their coaching sessions. What Jeremy thought he was doing (his espoused theory) and what he was actually doing (theory-in-use) were significantly divergent. The supervisor enabled Jeremy to see the divide between his intention and his actual behaviour. This 'cognitive dissonance' was the beginning of new awareness to stay with his experience of what was actually happening, and not just cleave to what he intended.

## Creating a learning environment in supervision

Supervisors come to supervision to facilitate learning; supervisees come to supervision to learn from their work. How do we create the conditions that make that happen? How best set up the sort of learning environment in supervision that supports learning from experience? The following principles are also good general principles of adult learning:

- Creating curiosity and being inquisitive are key stances in on-going learning. Rumi's motto could easily become a supervisee's mantra: 'Sell certainty and buy bewilderment.' What a delightful supervisory stance!
- Go internal, be self-aware and create an inner world of thinking, feeling and imagining. Reflection turns life events into life experiences and moves us from mindless to mindful action. Supporting supervisees to become more reflective creates opportunities for learning. Self-awareness is fundamental to learning that lasts.
- It's so easy to stop learning because it is too dangerous! This danger comes either when learning creates uncertainty or when learning puts us in conflict with those who would prefer us not to think for ourselves (and there are more of those than we realise.) Learning is very restricted for those who need to be certain or require fundamentalist stances in their lives. Many organisations demand non-learning conformist stances in order to continue to be part of them.
- Relationships, environments, life experience and the use of power are immensely significant in learning. Some people cannot learn because of experience of abuse as children – a trauma that leaves indelible marks on their brains and restricts their ability to reflect and learn.
- Sometimes we need others to help us learn – there are some things we cannot learn on our own. As much learning takes place 'between people' as 'within people' (Lave and Wenger, 1991).
- We often ignore one of the best means of learning: feedback. Because of our negative experiences of receiving feedback and our anxieties about giving it, we often ignore its value and importance. Ask for feedback and keep asking for feedback if you are really interested in learning.

- We wrongly equate teaching and learning. They are not necessarily connected. All learning begins from the learner's frame of reference, while teaching invites the learner into the world of the teacher.
- One size doesn't fit all in learning. We need to set up personalised or customised learning which adapts to the learning style and learning intelligence and preferred media of different individuals.
- In the learning environment called supervision, it is the supervisor who accommodates, who moves, who adapts to the individual learning needs of supervisees. Flexibility continues to be one of the most highly rated supervisor characteristics.
- Learning is as much an emotional experience as it is a cognitive or rational one.
- It is vital to ensure that shame doesn't enter the learning or supervisory arena. Of all the emotions it is the one that blocks and impedes learning most of all.

These learning variables influence the way I think about, set up and maintain supervision and have helped me move from supervisor-led supervision to supervisee-led supervision, which returns supervisees to the centre of the supervisory process.

## Conclusion

In my view, this is the most important chapter in this book. In trying to define and describe supervision we lay the foundations for what we do as supervisors and supervisees, the roles and relationships we adopt. Perhaps we create the criteria against which we evaluate whether or not supervision is actually taking place, and how effective it is. In training I invest a lot of time and effort in assisting participants to develop a 'philosophy of supervision' – getting to the heart and centre of what we actually mean when we use the term, and what we actually do when we engage in the process. At the end of this part of the training I ask participants to do the 'elevator test' on supervision. Imagine you are getting into a lift and there is one other person travelling in the lift with you. As the doors close he or she says to you: 'You are a supervisor. What exactly is supervision?' You have exactly one minute to answer the question clearly, crisply and concisely before the lift doors open again. What would you say?

### Exercises

1  Draw a line down a sheet of paper. On the top left-hand side write 'Effective Supervisor' and on the right-hand side write 'Ineffective Supervisor'. Now fill in each column with words or short phrases that characterise these two types of supervisor.

*(Continued)*

*(Continued)*

2  Try to come to your own description/definition of supervision for your profession and in your context. Share this definition with one or two others and see if they can help you refine it.

3  Think of an image/symbol/metaphor for what supervision means to you. Draw it. With others see if you can draw a communal picture that captures what supervision means for you as a group.

# Two

# Voice, Identity and Power in Supervision

**Chapter summary**

This chapter uses the image of voice to represent the supervision conversation. It looks at different types of conversations and suggests that dialogue is the most effective supervision talk. The chapter follows the voice of the supervisee as he/she moves through the stages of finding their own voice and becoming more powerful within the supervision relationship. After Belenky et al. (1986), five stages of voice are suggested: silenced voice, the received voice, the subjective voice, the critical voice and the constructed voice. Dialogue is presented as the ideal supervision conversation and is defined and described. There are also some hints and strategies of how to prepare for and engage in dialogue as an effective learning conversation.

Speaking, and its companion listening, are partners in a marriage called dialogue. This mode of conversation is the medium of the sort of relationship and the kind of learning we hope to set up in supervision. Not monologue, or discussion, or debate, or mediation, or skilful conversation, or polite talk, but dialogue. While these other forms of communication play a large part in life and in supervision, supervision hits its own learning heights when dialogue becomes the norm. In the dialogue called supervision, supervisors and supervisees see, think, reflect on and make sense of what has happened in the practice of supervisees; they also make sense of what is happening now by looking back. Language, words, tone of voice, non-verbal communication − all interweave to create this supervision conversation. Learning takes place in learning conversations. The word 'dialogue' comes from the Greek *dialogos*, which is translated as 'flow of meaning'. It is a process where we learn to think, reflect and make meaning together. Co-created reflective learning is the heart of supervision.

We choose carefully to whom we disclose our lives. It is important that we do so. Choose unwisely and the conversation can destroy. Speech can be both generative and degenerative. Criticism, put-downs, small-mindedness, hurtfulness, gossip all lead to trauma, shame and the shutdown of learning. Conversations, like relationships themselves, are for better or for worse. Both parties need to choose carefully who they appoint as significant others in relationship and in conversation. Words, as Oscar Wilde once suggested, can kill as effectively as swords. You can feel and sense the power of words when you have been attacked verbally. Who forgets the humiliation of being isolated in a classroom and ridiculed before your peers? Words pierce our hearts and our minds; wounding, hurting, destroying, shaming and killing. Words can bring life and they can kill.

Equal care should be taken about who hears about our professional practice. In sharing our work with another in the transparency and honesty of supervision, we hear ourselves speak our-practice-in-words, and we listen for the echoes and the resonances coming back to us from the other who listens. Invited observers, such as supervisors, attend with empathy and compassion to what we say, to what we don't say, to what we can't say, and to what we dare not say. They help us express it, and by doing so we learn to deal with it. Freud talked of a cure that took place through the medium of talk (the talking cure). Talking heals. Supervisees also know that, in some healing fashion, speaking their practice is a springboard for shifts in understanding and changing that practice. There is some truth in the saying, 'What we cannot say, we repress.' What cannot be said doesn't disappear, but is sent to some silent world in the unconscious. There it continues to trouble us like a sniper that cannot be seen, but can be devastatingly controlling of our lives. Repression always has a high price tag. Locking away our work in the recesses of our own minds creates cultures of silence and shame. We are afraid to ask how good we are. We are afraid to share our scared and wounded selves with others. Our supervisees ask for listening, recognition, confirmation, challenge and care. The supervisor is more than an audience, though that as well. He or she is a witness to a testimony. 'Through writing the "I" becomes "we"' (DeSalvo, 1999: 209). This is equally true of speaking. The 'we' of supervision is the relationship that will create and re-create the meaning of our work. Opening up one's work is valuable, not just in so far as the work becomes available to scrutiny, but also in that it supports collaborative learning.

## The message is the medium

Our voices are media. They are vehicles that carry whatever we want them to carry, and often what we don't want them to carry. They bring alive things that we would prefer to keep silent. At times, unbeknownst to us, and unintended, our voices find us out and let slip the inner world we would prefer to keep secret. The good listener will hear and decide how best to use the secrets we have laid in front of them. Yeats' famous line, 'Tread softly, because you tread on my dreams', is very applicable to supervision; 'Tread lightly, you tread on my work, and how I see it, and how I view myself.' Our talking places our lives in the hands of others.

It is essential that we choose carefully into whose hands, and control, we place our dreams, and our work.

Our voices speak more than words. Gottman, an expert in understanding the dynamics of married couples, can listen to a couple talking for just a few minutes and then describe with great accuracy the state and wellbeing of their relationship. (Gladwell, 2005: 21–22). Their conversation *carries* their relationship: 'all marriages have a distinctive pattern, a kind of marital DNA that surfaces in any kind of meaningful interaction,' says Gottman (Gladwell, 2005: 26). Conversation is one of our main interactions with others, and each conversation carries an individual and relational code. Our fingerprints, our DNA and our identities are all over our conversations. Our words are structured in that they follow stable and predictable patterns. Once you know the structure of how I speak you can predict pretty accurately what I will say. My words, and even my actions, will emerge from the mould of that structure. The structure of conversations between couples was what Gottman was listening for – not so much the content. Hearing and understanding the words is important; hearing and understanding the DNA behind the words is even more important. Schon captured this well: 'Professionals hold reflective conversations with the materials of their situation and thus remake part of their practice world, *revealing the usually tacit processes of world-making that underlie all their practice*' (1987: 30, my italics). Supervision is a triadic conversation: supervisees engage in a reflective conversation with their practice in the first instance, and then bring the fruits of that conversation to the second reflective conversation called supervision. Supervision is truly a conversation (supervision) about a conversation (conversation with the work) about a conversation (the conversation with clients).

## Example

Jude enjoyed coming for coaching. He found it a great place to let off steam. And he did. His first few sessions were break-neck tirades about his awful and horrendous organisation and his impossible-to-work-with colleagues. Towards the end of the second session, Susan managed to intervene when Jude stopped for breath. 'I notice that when you talk, Jude,' she interjected, 'you take quite a negative stance – I haven't heard you give compliments or say good things about your organisation, your team or your bosses.'

Susan was beginning a conversation she was to continue with Jude about the architecture of his conversation, and uncovering some of the maps underlying his way of thinking and engaging. She was picking up, from early on, the structure of his presentations in coaching, and was beginning to help him have insight into them. Over time Jude began to see what he was doing and together they started working on the thinking behind his thinking and the speech behind his speech (as Jude put it in his evaluation).

In listening carefully to the underlying structure of speech we unearth the beliefs, world views, assumptions and meaning-making perspective of the speaker. Supervisees speak their truth and reveal who they are as well as what they do, and the methods through which they make sense of what they do; supervisors listen intently and like good archaeologists, slowly and painfully unearth the hidden person beneath the words.

## On being silenced

There are many voices. Some are muted and silenced by the experiences of the past, some are angry and troubled, some are soft and broken, some loud and domineering. The voice is a vehicle for who we are. Belenky et al. (1986) choose the word 'voice' to describe what they termed 'women's ways of knowing'. They studied women coming back into education and traced the stages of their learning journeys. The image that best captured this journey for them was the image of 'voice'. Voice characterised not just speaking but also having a point of view, understanding, being heard, having power and being connected.

The first voice Belenky et al. noticed was not really a voice as such – it was the lack of a voice, a silence. Disempowered and with little sense of self, women spoke, but without 'voice'; effectively they had been silenced and eventually silenced themselves. In good Foucauldian fashion the women eventually did to themselves what others had done to them, and didn't notice that their self-surveillance silenced them. But not just individuals. Groups, teams and whole organisations can be silenced. Not being allowed to speak one's truth imprisons a person or a group in an icy world of silence where thoughts, ideas and experiences fester. Silence is the arena in which abuse thrives. Abusers force silence on their victims; being silenced disempowers and creates escape routes for those who would dominate. When the history of silence is written it will reveal how silence and abuse go hand in hand. As Whyte writes:

> The voice carries our experience from the past, our hopes and fears from the future and the emotional resonances of the moment. If it carries none of these it must be a masked voice and, having muted the voice, anyone listening knows intuitively we are not all there ... no matter what we say, we are revealed ... If the voice originates and ends its journey in the bodies of the speaker and listener, it is also true that many parts of our bodies are struck deaf or dumb from an early age. We walk through the door into the organisation every morning looking like full grown adults, but many parts of us are still playing emotional catch-up. (1994: 106)

Voice is synonymous with identity. It presents who we are and how we view the world to others, and often, surprisingly, to ourselves.

## Example

Premula is a shy retiring young woman for whom a map of compliance and obedience has been scripted. She knows it comes from her childhood and her culture. The results are a lack of confidence in presenting herself to the world. She has been taught to be silent and if she must speak then to sub-jugate her voice to the voice of others. Others know more, know better and she knows to give right of way to them, especially to authority figures. Don't think for yourself and whatever you do, don't feel what you are feeling, is a constant inner injunction. Premula's 'inner tacit processes of world making' are now finalised. She is robotic in her responses; shy, apologetic, passive and subservient. Her words reflect the script as she struggles to say the right and acceptable thing.

Sometimes we find ourselves in our own words. 'How do I know what I think till I say it?' can be very true. In supervision too. At times our insights are captured in words; at other times our words lead to insights. As our identity grows so does our voice. Supervisees often come to supervision silenced. They have no voice of their own. They engage with supervision tentatively, anxiously, worriedly: Will they be found out? Will they be exposed? Will they be embarrassed and ashamed for their lack of knowledge and experience? Are they good enough? They wait to be spoken to, they conform, they live up to expectations and they speak as they are told to speak, as they are expected to speak. So far their voice is not in the room.

## Example

Jamie sits silently with his supervisor. This is his first supervision session and he isn't quite sure what he should do. 'Bring your clients to supervision and talk about them,' he had been told. But what to say? There had been an embarrassing moment when a client had asked if she could have a coffee, and Jamie didn't know what to do. He had gone and got her a coffee, but felt guilty about it. She was energetic, intelligent and quite funny and he loved being with women who were like that. But supervision was not the place to talk about his attractions – he was now a professional, and his own feelings shouldn't interfere with his supervision. She had also held his hand a little longer than necessary for a business handshake, and thanked him, a bit too much really, for a wonderful session. 'So what would you like to talk about today? What is on your mind?' asks his supervisor. Out of Jamie's mouth comes anything but the truth. He talks about everything except the thing that he really needs to talk about.

As supervisors we begin a conversational journey to help our supervisees move from their silences; what they find difficult to say and what they find impossible to say and what they don't even know they need to say. The supervisees' unspoken question to a new supervisor is 'What will you do with what I say?' Supervisors have to create the container of safety and trust for the individual to find his or her *first* voice. How do we set up that safe environment?

1. Build in structure.
2. Contract clearly.
3. Provide rapport, warmth and openness.
4. Go slowly and tentatively (too much challenge too soon can destroy).
5. Begin to take small risks to show that it is safe.
6. Model appropriate self-disclosure and risk-taking.
7. Provide a lot of support.
8. Normalise what is happening.

Also ask yourself some questions:

What age is your voice?
Whose voice is it?
How has your voice changed over the years?
Have you found your supervisee voice?
Have you found your supervisor voice?
Can you blend your voices with others?
Whose voice is really here?

## Who is speaking?

From silence we move into inherited voices that speak with and from the identities of others. Watch what you say. Listen closely. Attend to your own voice. So often the voice points to someone else behind the mouth: your father, mother, teacher; your religion, your wisdom tradition, your political party; your abuser, your torturer, the ones who humiliated and shamed you. What comes out of our mouths or what is communicated through our hands needs analysis to discover who is the real speaker. Received or inherited voice is the second stage in Belenky et al.'s work: the voice of the other, internalised and made one's own to such an extent that the speaker believes he or she speaks for himself or herself independently. In reality there is a hidden voice and person behind what is spoken. The voice is the voice of one 'possessed' by another. Power often determines our voice. When the voices of others are loud, demanding, dominating it can be difficult to make ourselves heard. At times it is easier to subjugate our own voice to the more convincing and powerful voices of others. Whyte suggests there are times we need to befriend the 'mouse voice' and help it come out of hiding.

Our first voice will always be an inherited voice. Often, in new relationships, new jobs and new contexts we revert to adopting the voices of others. Having a powerful patron whose voice is respected and revered gives credence and credibility to us when our own voices, as yet, mean little. It suits those voices too – as Whyte says so eloquently, 'there are those who wish to make themselves a mother or father in our lives' (1994: 101). At times we oblige and allow them to do so. Supervisees can take back to their practice the words, ideas, feelings, values and voices of their supervisors. Dunnett et al. talk about 'inappropriately imposing supervisors thinking on a client' (In press: 71). Here a supervisee becomes the conduit for the thoughts, ideas and strategies of the supervisor. 'I did it because you told me to' is one of the games supervisees play. It is usually the statement of the supervisee who has not yet found his or her own voice but mediates the voice of another.

Our early experiences influence our voices and our speech. Put down and told to be silent, we oblige. Told we have nothing of substance to say, we believe we will not be listened to. Embarrassed and made fun of when we first spoke, we blush now as we share our ideas. Ridiculed for ideas that were seen as wanting, we now expect to be dismissed, even ridiculed again. Disclosing our secrets and hidden feelings can embarrass the other and we can, once again, be told to be silent. We lock ourselves up in the prison of safety where no one gets to know us (I am a rock, I am an island). No one knows us and no one will be allowed to know us. We move inside and speak inside.

## Example

Jamie meets his client. He looks across at her and for a moment gets distracted. She is gorgeous. She isn't wearing a wedding ring and hasn't talked about relationships outside work. Maybe …. oops! Wrong direction. Jamie catches himself out and immediately moves into professional mode. As she starts talking about her new role in her organisation, and the difficult relationship with her new boss, he moves inside himself to listen to the tutor in his head, and his new supervisor on his shoulder. Both of them speak to him and he hears their words come out of his mouth. 'How do you feel about that? Do you think what is happening to you now has any connections to the past?' Can't go wrong using the words of his tutor and the ideas of his supervisor! He relaxes for a moment. His professional face and voice take over.

Later, in supervision, he recounts how he is using the theoretical approach he was taught to relate to and help his client gain insights into what is happening for her. He speaks with an inherited voice far removed from his actual experience. He says nothing of his feelings and his fantasies.

## Exercises

1   How can we help supervisees recognise the many voices in their heads and from where these voices come?
2   How can we help them turn down the volume of others' voices, and begin to tune into their own voices?
3   How do we begin to listen to ourselves and trust what is happening to us?

## My voice, my voice!

Slowly, sometimes imperceptibly, our own voice begins to find the light of day. Tentative at first, our words hang in the air waiting for a response. That response will mean a lot. It will decide whether we forge ahead, fashioning a voice of our own, or we regress to the tongues of others, or even return to the arctic wastes of cold silence. If encouraged, if listened to, if respected, then our still, small voice begins to grow and blossom. We gain confidence – we speak our minds and our truths. Our own voice longs for expression and connection – it will not be denied. At first it can be loud and dominating – for the first time we have something to say that comes from head, mouth and belly – and the new voice roars. The mouse has gone; the lion emerges. Sometimes the lion-voice thinks it is the only voice that matters, and refuses to allow other voices into the conversation. It tolerates, rather than accepts, that other voices too have a right to be. It can so easily blot out even obliterate, even persecute the voices that are different or disagree.

Again, slowly, given the right relationships and environments, the budding sub-jective voice begins to connect to other voices. First *critically* then *connectedly*, and finally *constructively*, dialogue is born.

The journey of a voice moves from silence to open speech;
from the voice of others to my own voice;
from the intolerant and arrogant voice to the accepting voice;
from the critical voice to the accepting voice;
from monologue to dialogue;
from outward observation to inner attention and tuning in to self.

## Example

Jamie looks across at his supervisor. It's my client, he thinks, you have never met her, you don't relate to her, you have no idea of the tones and nuances of our relationship. He knows he was right to take over when she burst into tears and told him through sobs how horrible and unsupportive her new boss was to her. Jamie was sympathetic and very helpful. 'I have been there,' he tells her compassionately, 'I know what it's like having bosses who think they knew it all. I found the only way to work with them was ...'

How could the supervisor even hint that Jamie might be taking on the role of rescuer? She was in crisis. He knew there were times when people needed to be supported, even carried for a while. 'It's OK,' he heard himself say, 'I know this is just a temporary state of affairs. I am working with her to build up resilience so that she can challenge and change her situation.' The 'therapeutic' hug as she was leaving the room meant the world to her, he could see that. But best not say anything to the supervisor who may not understand ....

Supporting supervisees to find their own voice is often like helping teenagers learn how to speak for themselves. Suddenly we wonder what we have created. No longer the docile, compliant, adoring follower, the teenager/supervisee finds voice and feet and begins the struggle for individuality. Parents and effective supervisees know they will develop that individuality in the relational struggle with elders who support their dreams and provide emotional safety nets. How do supervisors do that? By encouraging them to speak; to stay with their feelings, to build in listening, compassion and empathy so that their voices don't exclude others; and most importantly to maintain boundaries.

## Our voices together

Our voices enter the bodies and minds of others and have the potential to affect them deeply. Relationships are formed, created, blossom and end with language, communication and occasionally communion. Words are voices and relationships in motion – air expelled hits throat, tongue, larynx and vocal cords and sounds emerge. Physically, that is all that happens. But that air is now imbued with meanings and is incredibly powerful as the words meet to begin fashioning relationships.

The final stage in the research by Belenky et al. (1986) talks of the *constructed* voice. Having come through the stages of silence, received voice and subjective voice, constructed voice is the voice of relationship and dialogue. All speak, all listen, together voices blend and work towards new insights. DeSalvo considers this in the world of writing:

Throughout her life Virginia Woolf maintained that her work – that any work – was incomplete until it was shared with readers. Readers completed the meaning of a work and echoed it back to the writer, so the writer could fully understand, perhaps for the first time, the significance of the words he or she had penned to her own life and others. (1999: 209)

The same could be said of our practice. It is incomplete until it is shared with others, and we hear the echoes back of what we have done, or not done. Just as we see and sometimes find ourselves in the eyes of others so we hear and discover ourselves in the voices of others.

Listening empathetically and with compassion to others allows them to review their own work with empathy and compassion. We know what we need to change and adapt. Others show us the gaps in our work by being with us. They help us see the patterns in our lives and in our works. Others often know us before we know ourselves.

Beneath the voices is a new budding relationship. The supervisory relationship is a significant one, one of a close psychological and emotional contact that needs the cement of words and conversations to keep it strong and stable. How do we help it grow? By using the term 'we' to show the collaborative areas; by being open to changing our point of view; by being vulnerable and allowing vulnerability in others; by allowing, and celebrating, differences.

## The supervisory dialogue – collaborative reflection

With dialogue we enter a supervisory realm open to new learning. Acknowledging that we cannot see the assumptions that guide our behaviours, knowing we have deaf, dumb and blind spots, and realising that we perceive partially rather than fully helps us to enter dialogue open to what it may bring.

Isaac (1999) talks of four fields of conversation, which are discussed below. Supervision can be seen in all fields.

### Field 1: Politeness and (shared) monologues

In this field individuals and groups do not share what they really think or feel. There is little safety or containment to help them do so. There is little reflection here and little dialogue. Field 1 supervision plays it safe. There is little challenge and often a shared collusion for safety. All is civil and polite. Differences are covered up. Problem–solving modality in supervision does this.

### Example

Joan was appointed supervisor to Jack, who was an existential counsellor. Joan thought this was airy-fairy stuff that never tackled the real problems of life but wasted time 'philosophising'. She suppressed her reaction and was polite and agreeable publically while internally staying aloof and disinterested. Jack brought his problems to supervision and together he and Joan sorted through them. But they never really met, and never really talked about their different world views.

## Field 2: Controlled discussion, or skilful conversation

This is the supervisory field of control, power and expertise. There may be little reflection and a lot of discussion. Conflict flares up and is often uncontained.

### Example

Gary is a prison officer who has worked on prison treatment programmes for almost 10 years. His new supervisor is young, new to the programmes, and a psychologist. Trying to impress, she suggests some things that Gary could do to make his presentations more dynamic. Gary is incensed that this youngster who is 'still wet behind the ears' is dictating to him when all his evaluations on his delivery of the programme have been excellent. He feels put down and unappreciated and came to supervision with smouldering resentment. He takes part, but only because he has to.

## Field 3: Reflective dialogue

Reflection begins in this field. Individuals state where they are; differences emerge and are accepted, even seen as enrichment.

### Example

Lucas and Jonah had initially found it difficult to work together as supervisor and supervisee. They came from different orientations and they couldn't be more different personality-wise. Slowly, over time, they talked and listened to each other and suspended their own 'truths'. They found they could differ strongly and still respect each other's views and values. When they finished supervision a year later they both agreed that their shared struggle to make their relationship work had resulted in one of the most creative relationships they had ever enjoyed. They had found a way of creating reflective dialogue through the enrichment of their different viewpoints.

## Field 4: Generative dialogue

Generative dialogue begins to look and think systemically, and from that stance devises strategies and interventions for action. It has been called 'flow'. From oneness issues begin to emerge, and from connectedness action begins.

> ### Example
>
> They sat quietly together, not speaking now. Words, at this stage, would not make a difference. They had struggled with Earl's dilemma. Should he speak up about the bullying he had discovered in his coaching work? He and Emilia had looked at it from every angle, from each stakeholder's point of view. Now they sat and waited. 'I have to act,' Earl said, 'I cannot let this continue. If I do, I collude and am responsible.' 'I know you do,' Emilia replied. 'I will support you all the way with this.' They both knew it was the right decision at the right time. It had emerged from their dialogue and their joint wisdom.

These four types of conversations are qualitatively different and produce different outcomes. Silence can change as it moves through the four – from awkwardness to deep connection.

## Preparing for supervision dialogues

How will we create the fields of conversation called reflective and generative dialogue in supervision? First, a 'container' or a 'vessel' – a holding place which provides psychological and emotional safety – is necessary for dialogue. Safety is provided through relationship, rapport and presence. It is the task of supervisors to initiate and offer that through their welcome, their enthusiasm for supervision, their engagement with supervisees, and the way they structure and prepare for first meetings. I send potential candidates for supervision a form which tells me about them and in particular about the way they learn. I ask them to tell me how they think I should supervise them, what I could do to facilitate their learning, and what I might do that would block their learning. I also send them a supervisory contract that we will discuss at our first meeting, and which is open to negotiation (well, some of it is!).

Supervisor and supervisee prepare themselves for supervision. While time is given to help supervisees do this (Carroll and Gilbert, 2011), there is little for supervisors to help them prepare for supervision. Many supervisors have never thought of preparing for supervision. I try to spend about 10 minutes going back over my notes of previous supervision sessions and clear my mind to be ready for the supervisee/s when she, he or they arrive.

I like to think of Isaac's four characteristics of dialogue as four templates (Figure 2.1) in my head as I wait for supervisees:

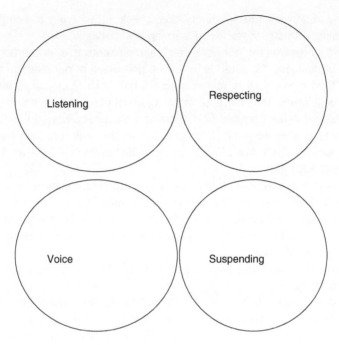

FIGURE 2.1   *Four fields of conversation (Isaac, 1999)*

- *Listening*: How can I listen more attentively? What do I find hard to hear?
- *Respecting*: Do I respect the supervisees I work with? In this respect can I say what I have to say?
- *Suspending*: Can I leave aside my own 'truth' while I engage with other truths, and remain open to what they bring?
- *Voice:* Can I hold the power of my own voice and encourage the voice of others? What voices are missing from our conversation? Can I allow them to merge with our voices (supervisor and supervisee)?
- *And finally*: How am I coming to this dialogue? What do I need to park? (Open heart, open mind, open will?)
- *Is the environment conducive to dialogue?* (Air in the room, chairs, privacy, lighting, temperature and any extras needed – tissues, recording machines?)

## Engaging in the dialogue

There are some practical actions that can encourage and facilitate the process of reflective dialogues:

- *Checking in*: Participants in supervision 'check in' as a way of being present and dealing with any obstacles to learning in supervision.
- *Listening 'to develop an inner silence'*: Isaac presents this as the first characteristic of dialogue: 'To listen is to realise that much of our reaction to others comes from memory; it is stored reaction, not fresh response at all' (1999: 92). It is listening from the past rather than listening from and into the present. When we listen from the past/memory we cannot always respond to what is happening now. We jump to conclusions all the time and then treat these conclusions as truth. We often listen from disturbance – from an emotional memory (1999: 98).
- *Respecting*: The word comes from the Latin *respicere*, meaning to look again. To observe and to honour. The second or third look. 'I see you'. It is about not intruding. Respect difference and hold the tension. We neither suppress what we think of nor advocate it with conviction. Step back a bit. With respect comes some equality of power.
- *Manufacturing uncertainty as a way of relating*: I know nothing, teach me. You are my teacher.
- *Suspending judgment*: This is always difficult to do. Suspending judgment means we don't have an already existing outcome – it may even mean leaving aside our most precious and treasured ideas and theories to meet others without conclusions already in place. We leave ourselves vulnerable to ending up in places we didn't start in, to the unknown. Some years ago I had a doorstep conversation with two people who knocked on my door and wanted to speak to me about their beliefs in God. I said I was prepared to enter the conversation with them if they were open to whatever outcome emerged from our talk. They weren't, and justified this with:

'We have the truth.'

'So no matter what I say, you are not prepared to change what you have come with?'

'That's right,' they replied.

'You would like me to be open to what you bring,' I persisted, 'and change if I find it helpful. But you are not open to what I will bring and are not prepared to change.'

'That's right,' they re-iterated their previous stance, 'Because we have the truth.'

They were not willing to suspend their truth though that is what they were asking me to do. It is extremely difficult to leave aside, just for the moment, our theories, our pet ideas, our treasured wisdom and meet someone in the space of not knowing, to begin a journey with them towards some new knowing. If you are committed to a conclusion it is very difficult to dialogue. Dialogue involves the following:

- *Allowing ambiguity, uncertainty and paradox into the conversation.*
- *Speaking from where we are*: We are honest and transparent. We speak with compassion. We move and expose ourselves. Shaw puts it well: 'We interact in ways that are aimed at preserving control, avoiding embarrassment and loss of face, seeking to preserve a sense of self-in-the-world' (2002: 131).
- Permitting ourselves to be more vulnerable. What do we not voice and why not? What are the 'un-discussables?' What can I share easily with you? What can I share with you but it will be difficult? What, just now, can I not talk to you about?

Dixon (1998: 93–95) summarises useful strategies for initiating and supporting dialogue:

- Provide others with accurate and complete information including feelings that bear upon the issue.
- Advocate one's own position.
- Make the reasoning in one's own views explicit – say how one got from the data to the conclusion.
- Invite others to comment on or inquire into one's own reasoning.
- Inquire into others' reasoning when others' views differ from one's own.
- Confirm others' personal competence when disagreeing with their reasoning.
- Design ways to test competing views.
- Regard assertions (one's own and others') as hypotheses to be tested.
- Voice the perspective of others.
- Change position when others offer convincing data and rationale.
- Illustrate and publicly test inferences.
- Back up generalisations with concrete examples.
- Acknowledge similarities in ideas as well as differences.
- Reflect critically upon presuppositions and their consequences.

## Situation variables in dialogue

- Members feel free from coercion.
- Participants have equal opportunity to participate – including the chance to challenge, question, refute and reflect and allow others do the same.
- Participants are equal in terms of such factors as personality, sex, attitudes, diverse experiences and ability.
- The context is cooperative; individuals feel safe to challenge each other and controversy is viewed as constructive.

## Other voices

As supervision progresses we note that other voices are often missing from the supervisory room. How can we include the quiet, unspoken voices, the powerless voices, the underprivileged voices, the abused voices, the hurt voices? In supervision we ask together, in dialogue and transparency:

What voices need to be heard?
What voices need to be abandoned?
What words need to be spoken?
What truth needs to be acknowledged?
What connections need to be made?
What assumptions need to be challenged?
What beliefs need to be reviewed?
What emotions need to be expressed?
What actions need to be taken?
What relationships need to be named?
What secrets need to be uncovered?
What strengths need to be seen?
What limitations need to be articulated?
What victories need to be celebrated?
What losses need to be grieved?
What mental maps need to surface?
What is the shift that needs to be enabled?
What fears am I not facing?

## Completing the dialogue

The aim of reflective dialogues is action in the world. We talk in order to act, otherwise talk becomes merely air. In order to create and build the bridge between talk and action it helps to notice the barriers to learning that are applicable to supervision. Scharmer (2007) presents four barriers:

1.  *Not to recognise what we see*: Being blind to implications or impacts of behaviour; not to trust your own perception and your own experience.
2.  *Not saying what you think*: Some organisations ask that we be silent or collude with them.
3.  *Not doing what you say*: A lot of talk, discussion and so on but putting off, procrastinating.
4.  *Not seeing what you do*: Reproducing the problems of the past.

## Conclusion

Words are more than simply vocal noises emerging as communication. They are communication. Language evolved, it is said, to help humans pass on learning in a fast and easy way. Language facilitates the learning process, not just because it enables teachers to teach, but because in our shared language we learn together in relationship.

Behind the words is a structure, an architecture of sounds that tell the world, if it can hear and listen carefully enough, how I structure my life and in particular my meaning-making. Most of us are oblivious to that underlying structural foundation and how it impacts on what emerges from our mouths, and from there into our behaviour. Schon calls this 'the usually tacit processes of world making that underlie all of practice' (1987: 30). If we could find that underground map, that anvil on which we fashion our work, if we could understand it and change it, then we would truly be 'teaching ourselves how to fish for a lifetime'.

Supervision is an arena of reflective dialogue where we use language and communication to make meaning of experience and practice.

# Three
# Managing the Supervisory Process

**Chapter summary**
This chapter offers a chronological journey through the supervision arrangements looking at the practical elements involved in each of five stages. The core of administrative supervision is not the day-to-day details of what happens but how the supervisory relationship can be set up, contracted for, monitored and serviced and how it can be clearly and cleanly ended. Within that relationship feedback and assessments take place and the chapter offers a way of connecting this to on-going development and learning.

When I first wrote this chapter in 1996, I built it around a five-stage chronological model of supervision: assessment, contracting, engaging, evaluation and termination. Two of these stages took place before supervision began (assessment and contracting), two stages took place during supervision (engaging and evaluation), and the final stage took place when the supervision was brought to a formal closure (termination). Each of those five steps was considered in some detail, with concentration on the nuts and bolts of what happened at each stage. Looking back on it now I am struck by how much my counselling orientation has influenced my supervision, and how much getting the administrative side of supervision right was foremost in my thinking. In this revised chapter, where the theme is the same, I want to move back behind the nuts and bolts of managing the supervisory process (these are still relevant and not to be ignored) to the more important relationship behind the tasks and roles. I also want to move away from a *counselling* approach to supervision and consider supervision as an educational endeavour and as a profession in its own right.

In the original chapter I got the emphasis wrong; it now seems a bit like a married couple allocating individual tasks to one another, and ignoring what they will *be* for each other, and how they will take care of their relationship. Both relationships and tasks are needed, but one is clearly of much more importance than the other. There are many excellent texts to support supervisors and supervisees to initiate, engage in, manage, service and terminate supervision (Hawkins and Shohet,

2012; Bernard and Goodyear, 2014). Here the focus will be on the supervisory relationship as the foundation stone of the supervisory process.

The five stages I will now look at are:

Stage 1: Starting the supervisory relationship
Stage 2: Consolidating the supervisory relationship
Stage 3: Engaging in the supervisory relationship
Stage 4: Servicing the supervisory relationship
Stage 5: Ending the supervisory relationship

## Stage 1: Starting the supervisory relationship – the first meeting

Starting the supervisory relationship involves: getting to know each other (the first meeting), sharing supervision histories (if appropriate), understanding contexts, defining roles and responsibilities, sharing necessary information (e.g., criteria for evaluation) and practicalities (when to meet, where to meet, fees etc.).

### The first meeting (getting to know each other)

The first meeting in supervision is vital: it sets the tone and the texture for the relationship that will unfold. In these early moments the foundations of what will happen are already being cemented. Negotiations are taking place long before formal negotiations even begin, and implicit psychological contracts are being fashioned beneath consciousness almost before the first words are spoken. Huge amounts of information are being exchanged intentionally and unintentionally in the first stages of supervision relationships. As the two strangers begin their relationship issues of power, trust, equality, respect, safety and vulnerability are already in the air and being worked out. New relationships are entered with a mixture of feelings; there is cautiousness, reserve and tentativeness, along with excitement and wonder; there can be defensiveness, and even attack. Relationship dynamics are being formed and expectations are being met or destroyed from the start. The first meeting is a highly charged, emotional encounter even if it doesn't appear to be so.

The first meeting can be experienced very differently for supervisor and supervisee. Supervisors become experienced at beginnings and can often take them for granted. Supervisees, usually in a less powerful and less experienced position, can bring to their first meetings lots of worries and anxieties. They have as yet many unanswered questions, such as:

How safe am I in this relationship?
What am I feeling about my first contact with this person?

Who does the supervisor remind me of and what connections am I making with relationships from the past?
Can I trust the other/the others in this group?
What risks will I take, and what level of vulnerability can I show here?
What early impressions am I picking up and giving?
What assumptions am I making about this person, this relationship, the context we are in?

Supervisors and supervisees circle each other; they probe, they test, they wonder, they feel, they think, they act.

## Example

Agatha comes for her first meeting with her new supervisor. She had found it difficult to find a parking space near her supervisor's home but with a few minutes to go had discovered some shops with a high-rise car park close-by. She arrived a bit breathless. Her new supervisor, Joan, opened the door still talking on her mobile. She smiled warmly and gestured to Agatha to go into her sitting/consulting room. Agatha went in and was about to sit down when Joan's dog came in to greet her with tail wagging. Joan arrived a few moments later, ushered the dog out of the room and invited Agatha to take off her coat and sit down. Joan apologised for the chaotic reception and told Agatha that her daughter had to stay off school with a sore throat and she had been setting up a doctor's appointment. However, she assured Agatha that all was now well and they would have no interruptions for the next hour.

Already Agatha is getting a sense of who Joan is and how organised she is. She is feeling a bit neglected in not being told about the car park, and then being met with some chaos as the door opens. She wonders how safe she will be with Joan after these first few experiences in her home.

Speedy conclusions are drawn from the initial contact. Supervisees are asking themselves three key questions, even if they don't articulate them clearly:

How safe am I here – physically, emotionally, and psychologically?
Can this person provide me with the safe space where I can be vulnerable?
Can I trust this person with myself, my work and my learning?

Agatha, in the example above, will have come to some tentative conclusions to all three of those issues. While she may not have come to a definitive conclusion, she will have already worked her way towards a possible decision. She has used her senses and her connecting limbic brain to suss out who Joan is and how she works.

## The relationship is the key

Two years ago I joined a group of managers who spent a day 'working with horses' as part of their leadership/management development. It was a fascinating experience, very different from other learning contexts which tended to be rational and cognitive. This experience was quite the opposite. Working with horses enabled the participants to test themselves on how well they could establish trust with and lead their individual horse. At the beginning of the day the leader of the programme pointed out why this exercise was taking place. 'These horses don't speak English,' I remember him saying, 'or any language. They are not the least impressed by your qualifications. They are only interested in two things: how safe you are to be around, and how well you will lead them if they follow you.' The horses introduced themselves warily with lots of sniffing, looking and testing these newcomers. They waited patiently, all senses alert for signs of lack of confidence, uncertainty and untrustworthiness. Eventually, when they learned to trust, they allowed themselves to be led. If trust and safety were not established, they held back, stood still and withdrew. When I asked if the trainer would give us feedback at the end of the day he said he wouldn't, but the horses would! And they did.

Humans do much the same in those first minutes of meeting new people. Like the horses, their safety and trust antennae are out and actively reading the verbal and non-verbal behaviour signs that come from the other. In particular, individuals are looking for signs that they might be in danger.

So it is while supervisors and supervisees are setting up their arrangements. Alongside the protocols, rituals, contacts, appointments, looking at requirements and demands around reports, evaluations, references and so on, another conversation is taking place. This conversation is implicit and more important than the words being exchanged. These sub-textual supervision conversations revolve around:

How will power be used in this relationship?
How will we engage with each other?
Is there anything I need to be wary about?
What will characterise our particular relationship?
What is negotiable in this relationship, and what do I sense is non-negotiable?
What do I have permission to be and do in this relationship?
Will this person be able to hold, contain and manage what I bring here, especially if I bring my shame, vulnerability and weaknesses?
Do I need to protect this person in front of me or is he/she strong enough and resilient enough to look after themselves?
Am I picking up any areas of vulnerability from this other person that it is best to avoid talking about?
What would I like to know about this person that would help me take some appropriate risks?
Will we be able to deal with conflict between us if it arises?
Will this new person allow and accompany me to go into areas that I/they have not been in before?

> ## Example
>
> Agatha comes for her first meeting with Joan, her new supervisor. Joan has already emailed Agatha an information sheet sharing some background about herself and outlining how she sees supervision. She included a sample contract they could discuss at their first meeting and helped with some practicalities – directions to her place, car-parking and so on. When Agatha arrives, Joan meets her at the door and shows her into her consulting room. Agatha notices the fresh flowers on the table and the glow from the electric fire. Joan takes her coat and indicates where she should sit. She asks Agatha if she is ready to start. Agatha already feels 'cared for' and begins to relax.

There are some aspects of initial meetings that cannot be arranged. Sending information in advance and preparing a suitable environment for supervision and learning can be done. Being safe to be with, creating trustworthy relationships and dependability all come with *being who you are*.

In an essay exploring his experiences in the early stages of setting up supervisory relationships with three new supervisees, Rob Watling (2012) concluded that there are certain things we should pay particular attention to:

- Being prepared intellectually, emotionally, physically and contractually.
- Arriving early into a well-prepared environment.
- Establishing rapport quickly and flexibly.
- Assuming and generating trust.
- Reinforcing this trust through an honest exchange of expectations and vulnerabilities.
- Noticing the early impressions we are making on each other and the possibility that they may include transference, counter-transference and projection on both sides.

Getting the first meeting with supervisees right, beginning as one wants to continue and creating the physical, emotional and psychological space that welcomes, contains and helps supervisees feel safe; all these take time and sensitivity. It is worth spending that time for the sake of the future relationship.

## Stage 2: Consolidating the supervisory relationship

Implicit and explicit *contracts* underpin the new relationship. There are three main types of contract: relational, practical and psychological.

## Contracting

When I first started supervision, I did so without any formal contracts. We met, we talked and we worked out some practical arrangements verbally that suited us both, and then we got on with supervision. Later I began to be more formal so that I devised and used formal written contracts with almost all my supervisees. Now I am more open around contracts; sometimes I use them and sometimes not. Sometimes talking together is enough for us to agree what is needed. So my present take on contracts is to have them if needed and not to worry about them if not needed. I don't have a 'one size fits all' approach to contracts anymore but try to be flexible about what will help in each specific supervisory relationship. Some supervisory relationships need a lot of contractual detail; others need little; others work themselves out as we go along.

Often when an organisation is involved it is helpful for all parties to have a contract to guide them, otherwise problems can arise.

### Example

Hubert was a trainee counsellor who had to set up individual supervision for himself as part of his training programme. He arranged this with Elisabeth, who was on his list of recommended supervisors. He also got permission from his placement in a GP surgery to bring his clients for supervision. It was only after supervision had begun that Elisabeth learned that she was expected to do bi-annual reports on Hubert which would be accessible to both the training programme and the Practice Manager in the GP surgery. She had worked on the assumption that she would only report back to the training programme or the GP surgery if she was seriously worried about the quality of Hubert's counselling work. She was now confused about what this meant, and whether or not she could charge for it.

This is an instance when a clear contract outlining the responsibilities of all parties would have helped clarify Elisabeth's roles and tasks. At times like this, when not clear, the unfortunate supervisees can get caught in the crossfire of different interest groups.

For me contracting is about watchfulness and sensitivity to the relational aspect of supervision in the first instance. Sills emphasises this side of the contract too: 'A contract is an agreement between two or more people concerning the type of activity or relationship they will have with each other' (2012: 94). I find that an interesting place to start – so often my contractual time with supervisors has been more on what we *do* together, about tasks and roles and responsibilities. This focus goes deeper and looks at the actual relationship as the contract. Contracts are about relationships even as they clarify what we do and what roles we adopt within those relations. What we will *be* for each other is as important as what we will *do* together.

The nuts and bolts of what a supervisory contract is, what should go into it and how it should be geared to different contexts is well documented. Proctor (2008) and Sills (2012) both have valuable models on contracts in general. Proctor uses the example of Russian dolls to illustrate how different types of contracts interweave to make up the full contract. Sills brings those five contracts together: wider world, organisational, client, sessional and moment to moment. Behind all of these is the relationship between the various parties involved.

Contracts are about promises, engagements, predictability and faithfulness. They are about 'caring for the relationship'. It's relatively easy to promise to be on time, or to keep confidentiality; it is more difficult to look at how I can be faithful and trustworthy in my supervisory relationships. That, in a sense, is the whole purpose of a contract – it's a promise of the future built on trust and reliability. What am I promising when I say I want to be faithful in my relationship with supervisees?

The supervisor's promise centres on a number of areas:

I will do what is best for my supervisee and make supervisee learning the centre of supervision.
I will be honest and direct in giving feedback.
I will be consistent and predictable in so far as I can.
I will spend time building and monitoring our relationship.
I will keep an eye on possible ruptures in our relationship and work to repair them.
I will try as best I can to set up a learning-friendly environment.

What might supervisee promises to supervision look like?

I will promise to engage in supervision as best I can.
I will prepare, turn up, and reflect on our supervision sessions together.
I will tell you honestly how I am finding supervision with you; I will give you honest feedback on you as supervisor.
I will be open to learning and try very hard not to be defensive when I hear what I don't like.
I will take responsibility for my own learning in supervision.
I too will monitor our relationships and take steps to ensure it is healthy.

It would be challenging to spend as much time on this side of our supervisory relationship as we do on the practical side, which is very important, but not the full picture.

Contracts are based on trust and make explicit what we agree to in a relationship of trust. Sometimes contracts are needed because there is no trust; when I cannot trust you to keep your side of the bargain or fulfil your roles then there is need to draw up a formal contract as a way of keeping us both honest. Should anything go wrong I wave the contract under your nose and suggest you are, wittingly or unwittingly, neglecting it. Legal contracts often stipulate that there are sanctions, including punishments, should the contract be broken. This is usually unnecessary in supervision arrangements where the ideal is that our contract is built on a committed, adult relationship of trust and fidelity to one another, and to the task at hand.

In supervision, we consider ourselves responsible for and trustworthy in the relationship, and the contract is a relational endeavour rather than a catalogue of duties. Bond talks about an ethics of trust in the helping professions which applies in supervision. He defines this type of relational stance: 'Trust is a relationship of sufficient quality and resilience to withstand the challenges arising from difference, inequality, risk and uncertainty' (2007: 436). With that kind of robust relationship, supervisors and supervisees can face the challenges of supervision no matter where they come from.

## The psychological contract

### Example

Joel was disappointed with his supervisor. He liked him, but he was disappointed. As he looked back on their six sessions together he realised he was not getting from supervision what he wanted. He had hoped for a stronger, more didactic style from this experienced supervisor – he knew he was a leader in the field of executive coaching, and he wanted more of his wisdom. He had expected that he would be more available outside their appointed meeting times, but his supervisor was quite strict that unless it was an emergency he expected Joel to deal with things himself. Joel had also hoped that his supervisor would help more with the academic side of his training programme – maybe read a first draft of an essay and give him feedback, or help him design his research proposal and so on.

This example highlights the psychological contract at work; Joel had a range of expectations of his supervisor that he had not shared with him, nor indeed had the supervisor asked him to. Had he expressed them then he and the supervisor would have reached a clear understanding about what was to take place in supervision and what was not to be expected. The supervisor saw supervision as focused directly on client work and not there to help Joel academically.

Psychological contracts are the hidden, unspoken sets of expectations (and therefore contracts) brought to all relationships. It just happens – we all bring hopes, desires, wishes and expectations to our relationships. That is as it should be. Problems arise when others don't know about these expectations and therefore become unwitting partners to them. The psychological contract is often broken when the recipient knows nothing about them and therefore has no basis for meeting them.

Psychological contracts in supervision arise from supervisees, supervisors and from other stakeholders in the supervisory arrangement. They need to be dealt with and managed, otherwise they can become problematic. It is understandable that we disappoint each other: it is part of life. Normally, the result is a more realistic approach to the person and to the business at hand. Realising I had hoped for more time from my supervisor helps me change that expectation to a more reasonable one. At their worst, broken psychological contracts can lead to complaints to professional bodies and serious breakdowns in professional and personal relationships.

Uncovering hidden psychological contacts is helped by asking:

- What are you hoping for from supervision? Ideally? Realistically?
- What do you want from me?
- What is reasonable to ask for and what are your unreasonable demands?
- Can I allow myself to get in touch with all the expectations I have of supervision no matter how reasonable or not?

We don't always realise that as supervisors we contract for certain qualities and values in supervision without even raising the terms integrity, beneficence, respect, attention and so on. In a sense, all relationships do.

## Stage 3: Engaging in the supervisory relationship

The relationship is up and running, we are aware of implicit and explicit contracts, we have a sense of our individual roles and responsibilities in supervision and now we begin the conversation. What is needed from us when we are engaged in supervision?

- Maintaining the relationship (reviews).
- Creating reflexive dialogue (see Chapter 10).
- Monitoring how power is used and abused.
- Using time.
- Presenting in the appropriate manner.
- Developing the needs of supervisors and supervisees.
- Managing parallel processes.
- Watching for external influences on both parties.

Engaging in supervision, like the first two stages, centres on the quality of the relationship. The relationship now settles into a pattern and a way of working that is unique to the people involved. We co-create the relational space to which we both subscribe and we form a collective, a relationship with its own particular DNA and reality maps. We slot into each other to create a third entity made up of us both. This relationship will become the foundation stone from which we will work together – it will give flavour to what happens between us. And while there is one relationship, there are still two people, each with their own personality, background and experiences.

We engage with that relationship mostly intuitively. We start off and get set in our ways. We establish our relational dance and often forget to change it even when it's not working well for us.

## Example

Ben and Christina had been in a supervision arrangement for over 10 years. They meet once a month for one and a half hours. The format they follow has been much the same for all their supervisor sessions. Both pastoral ministers, they start supervision with a prayer for guidance and then Ben outlines his agenda. He then presents a problem he is facing. Christina gives her opinion on what she understands to be some ways ahead, and often connecting these to some Gospel incidences. She and Ben talk these through and generally he comes away with some insights and some strate- gies for moving things forward. They end their sessions with a final prayer for guidance and for the future.

Many supervisor couples and groups can get into supervision 'ruts' where each session is the same and the relationship follows well-worn pathways of interaction and individual roles and responsibilities. This is not necessarily bad, but can some- times become a mindless relational routine with little creativity or passion.

It is helpful at times to review the supervisory relationship, especially around issues of power and engagement (Holloway, 1995). I have been amazed how much power supervisees give me, and indeed how much of my power I have given to supervisors. It's almost automatic, as if the very roles themselves dictate the power dynamics. Poole puts this well: 'In traditional supervision models, the dynamic of supervisor as dominant and supervisee as subordinate is not only expected, it may be reinforced by practices that reiterate the superiority of knowledge held by the super- visor' (2010: 61). Donning the mantle of supervisor can imperceptibly bring with it a feeling of power, a deference and compliance from supervisees, and an expectation that the supervisor is the one who manages and controls the supervisory details. If we think of power as relational, then it might help to stop and reflect on how supervision arrangements distribute and use power.

## Example

Elena is very attentive and dedicated to her learning. In supervision she takes copious notes, especially while her supervisor is speaking. She asks for his advice continually and her feedback is that she feels privileged to have such an experienced practitioner as a supervisor. He wonders how he can help Elena be less dependent on him and take back some of the power she has given him.

While supervisors cannot give up their power, they can support their supervisees to gain power and move towards 'power within', where they become authors of their own lives. This is a learning process which may involve any or all of the following:

- Stepping back and allowing supervisees more say and direction.
- Allowing alternative views into the supervision room.
- Being aware how power is exercised between supervisors and supervisees (see Chapter 2 on voice in supervision).

One way in which we engage with the relationship in supervision is through what has been called 'parallel or reflective processes'. Briefly, parallel process is what happens when supervisees play out or act out what happened to them in their work with their clients within the supervisory relationship. They usually do this unconsciously.

## Example

Pat presented her client in supervision. She read from her notes holding them close to her face. Julia, her supervisor, interrupted to ask for clarification. Pat looked irritated by the interruption but gave the information and went back to reading her notes. When Julia interrupted again, Pat looked distinctly annoyed. At this stage, Julia stopped the supervision and asked Pat to look at what was happening between them: her hiding behind her notes; her feeling irritated by Julia's questions. Pat suddenly realised she was doing to Julia what her client had done to her. He was very reluctant to allow her any access to his life and he was angry with her that she was not providing him with the easy answers he wanted to his quite complex problems. Pat and Julia realised that the client had subtly entered the room in Pat's way of relating to Julia.

What actually happens between supervisees and clients is not really the stuff of supervision. In supervision, supervisees tell the *stories* of what happened, which may or may not be similar to what *actually* took place; in supervision we get the supervisee's version of what transpired. Ellis is quite strong in interpreting the research data on this: 'Supervisees often miss, are unaware of, misinterpret, or inaccurately recall that which transpires in the therapy session .... Supervisees' perceptions (what they report, what they identify) do not reflect accurately that which transpires in a session' (2010: 105). This is where the parallel process can be helpful in monitoring the relationship between supervisor and supervisee. In the supervisory conversation we discover the hidden client and what really happened in the relationship between practitioner and client. As with Pat above, she had been unaware of how slippery her client was and how both of them were angry with each other until she acted out the parts with Julia. The supervisor recognised that Pat's unusual behaviour pointed to a problem elsewhere.

## Stage 4: Servicing the relationship (evaluation)

Stage 4 in the supervisory chronology centres around evaluation and feedback as ways of learning. It has constantly been seen as the most difficult task in supervision and one that potentially can lead to the most conflict and dissatisfaction. Here we will treat it not as a task to be performed, but as part of an on-going relationship where review is central to growth.

The areas covered here are giving feedback to each other and reviewing the supervisory relationship, dealing with emotional issues such as shame and fear, and dealing with critical moments in the relationship.

We are generally good at looking after the things in our lives – servicing our cars, insuring our houses and their contents, going to dentists and doctors when needed. Often we forget to service our relationships, with the result that they become dysfunctional through neglect.

### Example

Albert and Charlotte had been in supervision for six months. 'Can we take some time out,' suggested Albert in their sixth session, 'to look at our relationship and how it's going in this context?' 'Happy to do so,' Charlotte replied. She continued, 'While I acknowledge the obvious power difference between us, and think it's appropriate here, I have noticed that you very quickly give me ideas and suggestions for ways forward. I like that and I particularly like when you share your own work with me – especially when

*(Continued)*

*(Continued)*

you are struggling for a way forward. You are fast cognitively, and way ahead of me in reaching conclusions. I wonder, would you mind holding back a bit and letting me come to my own conclusions? I would find that better for my learning overall.' Albert smiled. 'Thank you for that feedback,' he said. 'That makes sense to me; I get involved and interested in your work, and forget to pause and let you think it through to its conclusions. I will certainly try to hold back and give you more time and space to reach your conclusions. I would like to monitor this with you over time to ensure that we have the right balance for your learning.'

Albert is facilitating their scrutiny of their supervisory relationship and Charlotte has sufficient trust in it, and in Albert, to be able to be honest with him.

Asking for and giving feedback is an essential component of supervision. It is one of our best ways of learning. There are times when others know us better than we know ourselves (Wilson, 2002). We all have blind, deaf and dumb spots. Listening to another speak into our lives through feedback, when done in the right way and with the right intention, is invaluable as a source of, and springboard for, new learning.

Relationships that are not reviewed, reflected on and examined can get into ruts and develop into unhealthy psychological games (see Ladany and Bradley, 2010: 41, 42). Supervision relationships are no different. When particular supervisory relationships are not held up to the light and examined openly and honestly, they can descend into meaningless routines.

I believe it is the responsibility of supervisors to patrol the relational boundaries and be alert to any areas that may militate against the health of the relationship. Outside influences need to be monitored too; they can assist learning and development and they can import toxic dynamics.

## Issues of shame and fear

In a TED lecture (2010), Brené Brown talks of shame as the fear of disconnection. Our shame-infused eyes see ourselves as not good enough and results in what she calls *excruciating vulnerability*. At the end of the day we are *not worthy of connection*. Cavicchia (2012: 159) presents shame as a rupture in relationships where we feel unaccepted by others, and indeed by ourselves. When we are seen as inadequate, and told we are so as children, we inherit that viewpoint and internalise it. If guilt is about *what we do*, then shame is about *who we are* as persons: just not good enough. Our shame is activated when we or others find us wanting. Shame can be activated in relationships when we feel humiliated, put-down or betrayed. Cavicchia (2012) talks of a shame-template which we use at times to interpret what happens to us. While most of us have experienced some shame in our lives, for others it is almost endemic. Coming from shame-based families or having been educated in shame-based environments ensures that individuals view their experiences through shame-tinted spectacles.

## Example

Jody looked down at her feet when Phyllis, her supervisor, gave her some feedback on her tendency to rescue others. She was embarrassed, hurt and felt like a fraud. She wondered why she thought she could be a nurse in palliative care – clearly she wasn't cut out for it! She didn't hear Phyllis say how amazingly good she was in her reaching out and relationships; all she heard was her mother's voice criticising her, telling her she was no good. Plunged back into her shame-based past, she once more began to 'beat herself up'.

It is so easy to unwittingly activate shame in ourselves and others. Feedback is one of the most powerful arenas in which it can happen. Listening to others tell us about ourselves, especially our weaknesses and limitations, can spiral us into shame. Once there we either attack ourselves, or we attack others who we believe have shamed us. Shame is one of the major blocks to learning. Learning depends on taking risks and making ourselves vulnerable – both difficult stances to take for those who have experienced shame.

There is good shame. Whitehead and Whitehead call this 'that healthy sensitivity we feel as we come close to others' (1994; 104). Shyness and modesty can be signs of healthy shame. Shame is often accompanied by fear, and just as there is good shame, there is also good fear – the fear that keeps us safe. But then there is the fear that terrorises us, that holds us back, that refuses to take risks. So many of our fears are manufactured, made-up fears that, once faced, lose their power.

## Example

Judith was always on guard. She lived with the fear of intimacy – that those who got close to her would find out what she was really like and would reject her. She was terrified of sharing her thoughts and her fantasies. Her supervisor, Miriam, was very open about herself and her vulnerabilities and had a gift of laughing at herself and her mistakes, yet without trivialising them. Judith was intrigued that this woman could reveal herself so much without worrying about rejection. Tentatively she began to open up, slowly at first. She shared her fear of rejection and intimacy, and found an acceptance and

*(Continued)*

*(Continued)*

understanding from Miriam. Her worst fears were not realised. She could allow someone to know her and rather than reject her, that someone came closer. As she looked back she wondered why fear of intimacy had been allowed to rule her life for so long. She also realised that fear, like most bullies, when faced down, usually turns and runs.

In a chapter called 'Fear and Love In and Beyond Supervision', Robin Shohet (2008) has two headings: *What are you afraid to Tell?* and *Bringing It Out.* These headings could well be adopted in supervision. Many years ago I joined a supervision group led by an experienced psychotherapist. He interviewed all potential members of the group individually and his question to me was: 'Tell me everything about you and your life that you would be afraid of coming out in the group.' I gulped and began. First of all it didn't take as long as I imagined it would, and secondly I watched intently for his negative reactions to my recounting all I was ashamed of. When I had finished, he smiled and said, 'I am delighted to tell you I would love to have you in the group. There is one person in the group who knows your secrets and your fears – you really don't have anything to worry about.' He reminded me how much our hidden fears which 'cluster around shame, fear of being judged, feeling a fraud, not being good enough' (Shohet, 2008: 203) hold us back from being vulnerable and taking risks in order to learn.

Shame and fear are common in supervision and both affect our ability to learn, remain open and move forwards.

## Critical moments in the supervisory relationship

### Example

Ruby is incensed. Her supervisor, Errol, has given her very direct feedback on her boundaries. He has expressed surprise that she had called round to see a suicidal client who had not appeared for their counselling session. Ruby works on placement in a university counselling centre and is still in her first year of a counselling psychology degree. It wasn't difficult for her to walk over to the accommodation hall when she realised her client was not going to appear. No one answered the door. Ruby later got a message saying her client had got her dates mixed up, and would like to rearrange their session. Now with Errol they are reviewing what happened. She feels Errol doesn't understand the seriousness of the situation, and her concern for her client; Errol feels she had not been able to contain her anxieties around her client's safety. He acknowledges that this is her first placement and the kind of mistake a beginner might make. Towards the end of the session, with Ruby feeling deskilled and ashamed, Errol asks how she feels about what he has said. Both know that this is a critical moment in their relationship and what happens next might make or break the supervisory relationship.

Supervisory relationships are the same as other relationships: they face challenging and critical moments that create relationship crossroads and tensions. These events arise from personalities, from events outside supervision, from within the supervisory relationship itself, and sometimes from the evaluation aspects of supervision. They inevitably heighten emotions, and if not dealt with constructively can lead to the end of the relationship, or serious lack of trust within it. Worked with well, they can strengthen, refresh and deepen the bonds between the parties.

Research on these critical moments in supervisory relationships suggest that they are unforeseen and creep up on us, that they evoke heightened emotions, or that they give rise to tensions within the relationship which engender anxiety (De Haan et al., 2010; Hitchings, 2012).

Some hints from Nelson et al. (2008) and Hitchings (2012) on how to manage such moments are:

- Realise that relationship problems and dilemmas are part and parcel of supervision – expect them.
- Do not apologise too quickly. Do not attack or defend positions.
- Deal with all parties' feelings.
- Believe in and want resolution, and say so.
- See if this is a parallel process, unique to the supervision relationship, or both.
- Be patient, flexible and work together to resolve the issue.
- Look at how both can learn from this event.

Appropriate humour can also help. Seeing ruptures or difficult moments in supervisory relationships as challenges to meet rather than obstacles to avoid helps both supervisors and supervisees to learn. Staying with these moments, talking about them and learning from them not only models what supervision is about, but also reminds us that relationships are never static – they are continually pushing us to new depths and fresh challenges.

## Stage 5: Ending the supervisory relationship

Some of the areas that help make endings complete and clean are: reviewing the relationship and learning; reviewing the work and learning objectives; looking ahead; identifying appreciations; and writing references.

'Endings are hell,' one client exclaimed during our final session together. For him they certainly were: ending supervision activated a gunpowder trail into his childhood which raised agonising issues of loss, abandonment, isolation and rejection. If not quite hell, endings can certainly be difficult for many people, and if not handled clearly and cleanly can result in unfinished business, unclear expectations, confusion and other negative emotions.

---

### Example

Harold and Edna worked right up to their final supervision session together. They had had a good supervisory relationship for two years, meeting once a month. Edna was moving home and city and had already made arrangements for her future supervision. At the door, as they shook hands, Harold wished Edna all the best for her new job and new supervision. 'I have enjoyed working with you,' he said as she stepped across the door. 'Me too,' she replied. 'Do give me a call if you ever need supervision in the future,' was his final comment as she headed down the path towards her car.

---

This ending feels somewhat unsatisfactory. There has been no review of the work together, no feedback to each other, no articulation of learning from supervision, no formal goodbyes or clarity about the future. The relationship has drifted into oblivion rather than coming to a clear and clean closure.

Endings in human relationships activate different issues for different people – growing up, growing apart, separation, abandonment, loneliness, dependency, self-worth, choice – and most of them raise issues of loss. Perhaps this is one of the reasons why we are reluctant to address termination in too much detail. Ending a supervisory relationship (one-to-one or group) brings with it a number of losses, especially if the supervisory experience has been a facilitative one. A trusted mentor is no longer there; the members of the group have disbanded.

Wall (1994) suggests that supervisees will reflect their problems with client termination in the supervisory relationship – a parallel process. He has offered some hints on what to watch out for when the parallel process is at work around termination: how termination issues are introduced into supervision and reported by supervisees; whether there are any inconsistencies or unusual behaviour by supervisees when working with termination; what timing is used to talk about termination, as in *door-handling* (when the supervisee raises the topic at the very end of the supervisory session, when it cannot be worked with sufficiently). Wall puts it succinctly:

If supervisors refrain from participating in the same dynamics as trainees and clients, but instead assist interns in recognizing the parallel process occurring in supervision, students can explore their own feelings and conflicts about terminating with clients as well as ending the field placements and supervisory relationship. (1994: 32)

And, of course, the parallel process will work both ways. When supervisor and supervisee do not deal effectively with termination in supervision, then it is highly possible that endings with clients will be affected.

Practicalities often determine termination in supervision: the training course is coming to an end, a placement in an agency is finishing, a supervision group is breaking up. Termination can be a result of the time-limited contract between supervisor and supervisee. Usually, a termination time is built into the supervisory contract and most supervisees are aware that the supervisory relationship will end at a specified time.

## Process of termination

It makes sense to build some form of evaluation of supervisees into the termination stage of supervision. This provides an opportunity to review what has happened, what learning has taken place, and whether and how learning aims and objectives have been met. It also gives the chance to acknowledge the strengths and weaknesses of the supervision arrangement – what seems to have worked, what could have been handled differently/better. Termination time can be a valuable time for evaluation of supervisors as well as of supervisees; coming to the end of the relationship is always a good time to take stock.

Part of the evaluation process is looking forwards with supervisees to their next stage of development. Termination in supervision is a golden chance to anticipate the future by considering the past. With the help of an effective supervisor, supervisees can summarise their learning and, using that as a springboard, anticipate their future learning, whether that is within a training ambience, or within supervision, or in counselling employment.

The final session is an opportunity for an appropriate form of closure to end the relationship. This can be done in a number of ways: as a celebration of the time together; as an appreciation time, when individuals recount what they have appreciated about being together and about each other; or as a goodbye gesture, a handshake, a group hug.

Whatever method is used, it is important that the ending is clear and clean, and not avoided. It is certainly worthwhile to talk about the ending of the supervisory arrangement and what that ending means to all participants.

## Particular endings

Not all endings in supervision take place by mutual agreement, and not all endings are the result of positive feelings about supervision. There are times when the supervisory relationship breaks down. Sometimes it is a result of just being the wrong people at the wrong time. It may have something to do with chemistry between the teaching style of the supervisor and the learning needs of the supervisee. Training courses should not be hasty in blaming supervisees if their supervisory arrangements do not work out and they wish to change supervisors. Nor should they be naïve in just accepting it as a fait accompli. Sometimes a three-way meeting between the training course, the supervisor and the supervisee can help resolve whatever issues are causing concern. Whatever the reason, if supervision is not working, then the participants need to talk about it, and honestly face why it is not working. Generally, it is the task of the supervisor to provide this forum and initiate this conversation. It is a wasted opportunity for learning if both supervisor and supervisee deny what is happening: sometimes relationships that do not work teach us more about relationships than ones that work well. And unsatisfactory relationships, as much as satisfactory ones, need formal closure.

Another scenario arises when a supervisor decides that they no longer wish to engage in a particular supervisory relationship because they feel that the supervisee in question should not be seeing clients. This is obviously a situation for concern, especially if there is disagreement between supervisor and supervisee. Supervisors need to be very clear about their reasons for discontinuing to supervise a particular supervisee, and should make those reasons known to supervisees. It is important that supervisees have a forum where the whole issues can be discussed.

Occasionally the unexpected/unanticipated ends the relationship, for example the death of either participant, or one member moving away. Where death ends a supervisory relationship it is essential that the remaining member of the partnership has the opportunity of dealing with this either within another supervisory relationship or within personal counselling. Within a group setting, the remaining group need to process their feelings and loss within the group. Where one party moves away, time must be set aside to deal with the reactions and issues emerging from this premature ending.

## Conclusion

Like all professional relationships, supervision has its beginning, middle and ending phases, each of which has its own characteristics. This model provides a systematic process approach to the various stages, with emphasis on how the supervisory relationship is set up, engaged in and ended well. Taking care of management, maintenance and administration issues mindfully and sensitively may be yet another way of showing care ethically, personally and professionally.

# Four

## Forming the Supervisory Relationship

**Chapter summary**

This chapter focuses on the role of the supervisor as a facilitator of learning. It presents eight key or foundational supervisory tasks that face the supervisor's formative function in supervision. Each task is considered separately and suggestions made about how supervisors can implement them effectively.

Supervisors face challenging tasks. Their overall job is to create the learning environment and a facilitative relationship that supports supervisees learning from their practice and then transferring that learning from supervision back into their work. Supervisors help supervisees build bridges between theory and practice, and mediate change in clients indirectly. Easily said, not always so easily done. 'Theory and practice are the same in theory, but not in practice' is a retake on Lewin's famous statement that 'there is nothing as practical as a good theory' (McGuire, 2013). Furthermore, supervisors have a multitude of roles to fulfil: mentor, coach, consultant, guide, counsellor, gatekeeper, evaluator, monitor, learning facilitator, judge, process chaser to name but a few. Is it any wonder supervision has been called 'the impossible profession'?

## Example

Picture two individuals coming for supervision, two supervisees. The aim of both supervision contexts is the same – to create an environment of learning and accountability, to provide a reflective dialogue where experience can be turned into practical wisdom. Both students have the same cognitive ability. Supervisee A has been sent to Supervisor A. The latter resents having to supervise and sees it as one more task amongst many in an already overburdened job. Supervisee A has been given no preparation for supervision and expects his supervisor to tell him how to do the job better, as the main

*(Continued)*

*(Continued)*

focus of supervision. Furthermore, he is anxious about being found wanting in his work, which could impact negatively on his promotion prospects, and has decided not to talk about work that he is finding difficult.

Supervisee B comes to supervision with Supervisor B. Supervisee B is eager to learn how to adapt the theory she has learned from her training programme to actual practice. She has already read up on what supervision is in a preparatory manual sent to her by Supervisor B – *Becoming an Effective Supervisee*, Carroll and Gilbert (2011) – to help her make the most of her supervisory experience. She has been allocated to Supervisor B who invests time and energy in helping her learn about supervision and how to use it. Her supervisor is enthusiastic about the work she does and is continually suggesting ways in which Supervisee B can learn and improve. Support, challenge and effective feedback are the order of the day. Supervisee B is keen to apply her skills to her new job working with depressed adolescents, where she feels she can make a real difference.

It won't be the abilities of the supervisees that will solely determine the outcome of supervision in the two instances above. No doubt their abilities will help. But it will be the relationship, environment and preparation set up by supervisors that will impact the effectiveness of supervision. Who the supervisor *is* will have a major impact on supervisory outcomes. We know there are poor supervisors, just as we know there are excellent supervisors – both will influence the supervisory process greatly.

## Supervisor tasks

As mentioned above, supervisors carry out multiple tasks ranging from creating the right environment through contracting, to giving feedback, supporting new learning and providing challenge and support. This chapter will focus on the eight underlying tasks of supervisors; those tasks which are deeply inter-related and mutually dependent. It is almost impossible to offer challenge and feedback if the relationship between supervisor and supervisee is not good. These are not by any means the only tasks, but they are *foundational* tasks. If well implemented, they support other tasks being completed. The eight are:

1   Knowing yourself and your motivation as supervisor.
2   Being present, emotionally and psychologically.
3   Creating a safe containing environment for supervisees.

4   Establishing and monitoring the relationship (personalising relationship, working with differences, understanding power).
5   Harnessing emotions as part of learning (developing emotional intelligence).
6   Facilitating reflection and learning in ever widening contexts.
7   Giving clear and focused feedback.
8   Generating hope.

## Task 1: Know thyself

Why do supervisors supervise? Otto Scharmer asks a question that he considers fundamental to outcomes for leaders which is equally applicable to supervisors: 'Where from within you does this come? – What sources are you actually operating from?' He reminds us that *knowing thyself* appears in all great wisdom traditions (2007: 164) and continues to be a valid question for engaging effectively with others. He also points out that this knowledge about the source of our actions can be a 'blind spot' and not just for individuals but for organisations too. Often we don't know why we do what we do, and as a result the outcomes get tainted. Scharmer writes:

> Bill helped me understand that what counts is not only *what* leaders do and *how* they do it but their 'interior condition', the inner place from which they operate or the *source* from which all of their actions originate … the success of an intervention depends on the interior condition of the intervener. (Italics in the original). (2007: 7)

Applied to supervision, Scharmer is emphatic that the inner condition of the supervisor affects how successful they are as supervisors. Supervision done 'out of duty' or 'in bad faith' or 'reluctantly or resentfully' taints all stakeholders involved and creates a parallel process in the supervisee's client work.

Knowing yourself means paying attention to your interior conditions and where your motivations come from. 'Bad faith' is a term coined by Sartre to indicate a divide between that which is done and the intentions with which it is done. I don't have to look too far or deep to find a classic example of bad faith in my own life: the weekly family shopping trip! Shopping drives me nuts and I do it reluctantly, resentfully and impatiently. It reached a stage where my wife suggested it would be better if I didn't come, rather than come with the attitude I had. I was there in 'bad faith'. I had a choice. I could change my attitude towards shopping which might make it a more enjoyable and a more 'chosen' activity, or I could continue to moan about having to do it and destroy the whole experience for everyone. I needed to 'become aware and change the inner place from which I was operating' (Scharmer 2007: 10). I needed to create a qualitative shift in my thinking and responding. Can I pay equal attention to *why* and *how* I do supervision?

## Why supervisors supervise

The obvious reasons for supervising are not always the real reasons. Lurking behind and alongside the given reasons there may well be other hidden reasons. Hawkins and Shohet (2012: 28) outline some of these:

- The lust for power.
- Meeting our own needs.
- The need to be liked.
- The wish to heal.

We can add others to this:

- The need to be important.
- The need to make a difference.
- The need to heal our own wounds.
- The need to control.

### Example

Jackson (2010) outlines an example of supervision within the field of pastoral ministry. A student minister comes for supervision upset because his sermon was ruined by a crying child. The child's parents did not make use of a room for crying children and the noise upset the whole congregation. Upset and dismayed, the minister wanted to talk to the parents about it. He also wanted notices put up around the church about the importance of the sermon. The supervisor listens and creates an environment where the student can reflect on his own needs in this situation. He gently helps him see a broader picture that transcends his need to have the perfect environment for his well-prepared sermon. Moving away from blame and opening up different perspectives, the supervisor enables the supervisee to see how immersed he has become in the emotions of his ruined sermon. It also helps him find the 'blind spot' within himself, from which his sermon emerged. It would not be surprising to discover that a need for praise and recognition was top of the list. No wonder he felt the way he did.

A primary task of the supervisor is to review her own interior condition and mine out her reasons for supervising others. Respect for self, for supervisees, for clients and for the professions are preconditions of supervision. The internal motivations will impact greatly on the supervisory work itself. 'Functional supervision' is a technological approach to supervision where supervisors *do something to* supervisees, in the way one processes commodities. Effective supervisors view supervision as a facilitative relationship which is treasured as a learning process, and engaged in passionately.

Close on the heels of *know thyself* is another Socratic insight: *know how little you know*. A leading politician claimed he was wiser than Socrates. Socrates replied that he (Socrates) was wiser, not because of what he knew, but because of what he knew he didn't know. For Socrates the beginning of all learning is the realisation of ignorance, or not knowing. Not a bad stance for the modern supervisor! Being liberated from the role of expert or guru is one of the best things that can happen to a supervisor. Knowing how little you know is not about denying what you do know and what your skills are; rather it's about being able to manage the embarrassment and shame that may come with recognising our limitations and realising we cannot be what the supervisee or the organisations needs us to be. Wounded healers indeed, we recognise that we are 'good enough'.

As we grow older and more experienced we can fall somewhat 'behind' in our theories and in our practice. It often happens imperceptibly. Most of us still act out of philosophies learned many years ago, and may not notice how new ideas have slipped by unnoticed. I realise that I am not as up to date with some modern therapies as I could be, yet my supervisees use these as their primary ways of working. 'Letting go' of our precious theories, frameworks and models can be a hugely challenging task for supervisors, especially as they grow older.

## Exercises

Some reflective questions for supervisors:

1   Why have I chosen to become a supervisor? Why do I continue to be a supervisor?
2   What do I need to attend to to ensure that I know and change the inner sources of my supervision work?
3   What do I need to attend to to give up power and realise that I don't need to know it all as a supervisor?
4   Where do I need to update my knowledge/theory?

## Task 2: To be present, emotionally and psychologically

A supervisee had travelled a long way to see me. Just before he arrived I opened my post and one letter there disturbed and upset me. I was still dealing with the emotions engendered from this letter when my supervisee arrived. We met and moved into the supervision room. After 10 minutes I stopped the conversation and said, 'I am sorry. I am being distracted by a letter I received and opened just before you arrived. Would you mind if I took 10 minutes out to deal with this? When I return I hope I will be able to be more present for you. I will make up the time to you.' I can still see his smile. 'Thank you for telling me that,' he said, 'I realised you weren't here with me as you usually are; I thought I was boring you.'

This taught me several important lessons: to prepare myself for my supervision sessions and avoid contentious/troubling communications/issues; to be psychologically and emotionally present for the person/s I am with; to realise how often supervisees step forward to take the blame when something goes wrong in supervision.

An African story recounts how desert guides exhibited an unusual characteristic. Occasionally, they would stop and suggest making camp even though there were several hours of daylight left which could have been used to travel further. When asked why they were stopping now, and not continuing the journey, they would often reply, 'We have to wait for our spirits to catch up'. Somewhere in the travelling they had got ahead of themselves, and now must wait for the left-behind spirits to be reunited with them. Supervision could be seen as a place where we stop to catch up with ourselves and our work. We re-collect both our work and the many strands of *ourselves*. Being present enables that to happen.

In supervision, it is the task of supervisors to ensure that they are 'all there' – not just physically but emotionally, mentally, psychologically and motivationally. People know when we are missing from the room even when our bodies are present. Supervisees deserve our presence and notice its absence. Not wanting to be there means you are not there. Being distracted means you are absent, and processing your own emotions can pull your attention away. It is not easy to re-collect the many parts of oneself in order to be totally present to supervisees. The modern world, with its many distractions, fragments us. Our bodies can be present while our minds and emotions are somewhere else – in the past and in the future, but not present in the present. The myth of multi-tasking sometimes seduces us into thinking we can do many jobs at the one time (Rock, 2007). Usually the outcome is that we do many jobs poorly and we end up fragmented and not present to the supervisee.

---

### Exercise

1   What do I need to attend to to ensure that I am present for supervisees? Emotionally? Psychologically? Motivationally?

---

## Task 3: Providing a safe container

Setting up, maintaining and sustaining a *safe container* is the supervisor's way of ensuring emotional safety for supervisees. Supervisees bring strong emotions to supervision: anxiety, embarrassment, shame, fear of failure, worries about being good enough and many others. To know that these emotions will be safely encompassed and worked with in supervision is a relief and safety valve for the supervisee

(Shohet, 2008). Sensing that supervisors will not be overcome or destroyed by their vulnerabilities leaves supervisees free to express them. In a survey of clinical psychologists in the UK, service-users prioritised this ability to contain strong emotions as the most important feature they look for in clinical psychologists. I suggest that supervisees do the same with their supervisors (Hughes and Youngson, 2009: 71).

Threat, danger and fear make learning virtually impossible. When our brain picks up signals that we are in danger, it moves us quickly into survival mode to protect and shield us from that danger. In this mode we choose from fight, flight, flock, fragment or freeze as strategies for survival. More importantly, when the brain activates survival mode as a way of coping, it limits our access to the frontal cortex from which come our reflective, creative, long-term planning and introspective gifts. In survival mode we are entering 'learning disability' territory, and the human faculties that keep us in optimum learning mode disappear or are curtailed. It is important that supervisors keep themselves out of survival mode. Full access to their prefrontal cortex and its amazing human faculties is a necessity. It is equally imperative that they recognise and manage supervisees who come to them in survival mode.

### Example

Franco comes to supervision looking dreadful: pale, dazed and remote. He had phoned Gillian, the supervisor, to ask for an emergency session, when he had learned of the suicide of one of his patients a few days before. He bursts into tears. 'How could I have missed this? I never for a moment thought he was so vulnerable. I knew it was a tough time for him but thought we were dealing with it well.' Gillian knows this is not a time to teach, plan ahead or reflect. Intuitively she knows that Franco needs her to be present to him, and allow him to experience the awfulness of what has happened. For this session Franco, traumatised by what has happened to his client, is in survival mode.

When supervisees are afraid their learning potential is reduced. We often forget, as supervisors, the fears that supervisees have. Moore lets one supervisee speak for himself:

During one of the silences in the first session (of group supervision) I became aware of my need to feel safe in this group. Can I really be open with these people? What will happen if I share a fear, concern or impact that is alien to them? What if someone in the group is there with a more closed approach or different agenda? Will this alter the dynamic? Will I be judged after the session? (2008: 24)

A key supervisor task is to provide a relationship and environment which challenges fear and helps supervisees stay sufficiently in competency mode. They need to be able to reflect deeply, plan for the future and become curious and introspective.

Supervisors must look for signs of fear because when fear enters the room transparency and honesty often make a hasty retreat! A Sufi maxim puts it poetically: 'Fear knocked on the door. Love answered and there was no-one there.'

My experience is that when supervisees are afraid or frightened they hide their work. Their fear is that they will be judged, shamed, disappoint themselves and others, and fail. Experienced practitioners fear that they will be 'found out' and so don't present client work openly and with humility.

Supervision relationships, like so many others, parallel early childhood relationships. Being and feeling safe is high on the child's survival agendas. Bowlby (1988: 4) talks of a 'sense of security' that comes with good attachment in children. The opposite happens, 'jealousy, anxiety, anger, grief and depression', if good attachment is missing. I think similar reactions happen in supervision when supervisees don't feel connected to supervisors in a way that makes them feel safe. In her research on abusive supervision, Kaberry (1995) discovered that strong negative responses by supervisors felt 'punitive' to some supervisees. As a result they didn't feel safe, and protected themselves by not sharing their real work with their supervisors.

Supervisors can unwittingly create an environment perceived as dangerous. The way feedback is given, how challenge is used, and the self-disclosure of supervisors can all contribute to less than safe environments for supervisees. This has consequences for transparency, openness and on-going learning.

## Example

Jerome was a supervisor from the old school. He felt his job was to point out areas of deficiency in his supervisees' work. He never praised what he thought was good and his feedback was always negative. The tone of supervision was deadly serious and any attempt at lightness or humour was frowned upon. His evaluation reports always emphasised what was wrong and needed to be corrected. Over time, trainees asked not to be allocated to Jerome for supervision.

## Exercises

1   How can supervisors and supervisees ensure that fear doesn't enter the supervisory room and relationship?
2   How can both parties create a safe environment?

## Task 4: Setting up and maintaining the relationship in supervision

Safe environments emerge from safe relationships. One of the key tasks of supervisors is setting up and maintaining strong relationships with supervisees. We know how important relationships are to early development and to learning (Critchley, 2010). But there is more. This relationship in supervision is special in its intensity, its depth of contact and its psychological closeness. More than a casual relationship or a business relationship, the supervisory relationship asks for profound sharing and vulnerability.

Building rapport, mutual respect and trust provides the basis of the learning experience. Relationship is the key carrier signal between the supervisor and supervisee for effecting any change or development:

> If you have a good emotional connection with the person who is trying to learn from you, you have dramatically increased the chance of them learning that thing from you. (Curran, 2008: 61)

Relationships are not one way streets, they are co-created. They become dances choreographed from the interactions of the individuals involved. Relationships are not fixed and final. The 'here and now' relationship waxes and wanes as it is being continually refashioned and remade with each interaction.

Relationships are also about caring. The word 'care' has its roots in the gothic work *kara*, meaning 'lament'. Caring means 'to grieve, to experience sorrow, to cry out with' (DeSalvo, 1999: 4). Supervisors join supervisees in the depth of their work, and with 'limbic resonance' see, feel and think with them as they re-present and re-experience their work in the safety and caring of supervision. Supervision is about 'unravelling the knots in your heart' (1999: 31).

Effective supervisors realise that each supervisee is unique, has a particular learning style, and enters the supervisory arena with his/her own way of relating and being present.

> Existential supervision cannot be done without reinventing it with every supervisee and with every new hour of practice. (Van Deurzen and Young, 2009: 12)

Not to see each individual as an individual is to treat people as billiard balls – they are the same shape and follow the same mechanistic patterns. Personalising learning for each individual supervisee is a major challenge for supervisors and distances them from the set protocols and rituals of their comfort zone. Peter Hawkins (2012b) says, 'If you are supervising all your supervisees in exactly the same way, you are probably supervising yourself'.

Supervisors, as part of their fidelity to supervisory relationships, are also good at noting and dealing with critical moments in supervision. Critical moments or notable events are usually unforeseen. They knock us off balance and create tensions. If not handled sensitively, such moments can destroy trust and damage the supervisory relationship. Supervisors should be alert to such moments and harness their learning potential for both supervisors and supervisees. Such events should deepen trust in the supervisory relationship (de Haan et al., 2010; Hitchings, 2012). See Chapter 3 on handling critical moments.

Supervisors are given a tremendous amount of power by supervisees. How we use that power means a great deal to the learning of supervisees and to the kind of relationship that emerges. We can often be unaware of how power infuses, and is worked out, in supervisory relationships. The potential for abuse of power is a significant ethical consideration in all supervisory relationships.

## Example

Ernest enjoyed supervision. He loved the moments when the 'lights came on' in the eyes of his supervisees. He relished those 'Thank you, that has been so helpful' moments when his supervisees are walking out the door. He started sharing more and more with them. Gradually his love of compliments and praise and his role as a guru was leading him to do more and more for his supervisees. It was only when he promised to rewrite the Master's thesis of one supervisee that his own 'light came on', ominously. In his own supervision he began to reflect on his use of power in supervisory relationships.

## Exercises

1   What do I need to attend to to ensure that the supervisory relationship is one of trust and strength?
2   What is my relationship style?
3   How do I use power in relationships? What would someone playing 'devil's advocate' say about my use/misuse of power?
4   Have there been any 'critical moments' I needed to be alert to and manage within supervision?

## Task 5: Supervisors and emotions

Recent insights into how the brain works has made us more aware of the role of emotion in human learning and decision making. Emotions and emotional intelligence are now being seen as crucial aspects of leadership, teaching and development within the professions. Supervisors let emotional experience lead to insight. Brown and Brown (2012) ask a question that hovers on all effective supervisors' lips: 'How can you understand, catch, use and regulate your client's emotional energy in pursuit of supervision goals?' They suggest that we all have an 'emotional patterning'. We can discover it by linking current behaviours with past experiences. This is how we discover what a person has to unlearn. Understanding a person's early patterning, and the way that has played out through life, is the key to understanding that person. From this individual emotional patterning comes the way that energy will be uniquely directed in the person's life.

One of the few academic works that focus on the role of emotions in supervision is the doctoral dissertation of Moore (2008). His dissertation begins by recounting a supervisory session with a supervisee who had been horrifically abused. The author found *himself* speechless and powerless:

> I am more aware now of the dynamics of communication that might have been played out in the room that day so long ago. It was as if her unbearable experiences had become embodied in both of us. So much of my own experience could be understood as an empathic resonance with her deeply disturbed internal world. (2008: 9)

From here Moore works out a theory of *usefulness* in supervision which examines the emotional process that takes place:

1. Clients have overwhelming emotional experiences that are brought to therapy and expressed in words and actions.
2. Therapists who engage in an empathic encounter with their clients will then experience in themselves something of the clients' feelings (this has been called 'projective identification').
3. Initially therapists can feel overwhelmed with the strength of the clients' feelings and experience an increase in their stress levels.
4. The purpose of supervision is to normalise the therapist's emotional responses (experiential knowing) by thinking of them as possible empathic resonances with the client. Making sense of the emotional impact will lower the therapists' stress.
5. As therapists' capacity to reflect increases, they can more effectively draw on the strong emotions aroused in them to gain insight into their clients' difficulties.
6. With this comes an increased capacity to reflect, it is possible to engage more creatively with the theories that underpin their practice (propositional knowing). Theoretical perspectives help make sense of the distressing experiences that often seem meaningless.

Figure 4.1 puts this process together into stages.

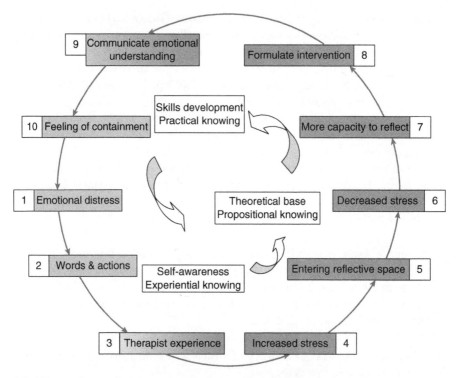

FIGURE 4.1   *Process framework for learning in supervision (Moore, 2008: 27)*

---

## Exercises

1   How can we best notice, articulate and use emotions as instruments of learning?
2   How do we help supervisees manage their emotions effectively?
3   What are the stages involved in facilitating learning from experience?

---

## Task 6: Facilitation

Chapter 8 will look at learning from experience in more detail. Here we simply mention it as a key supervisor's task.

One of the most important skills in teaching is the process of facilitation. The word 'facilitation' means *to make easy*, and the question asked by supervisors is: 'How do I make learning from experience easy for supervisees?' To do that supervisors:

- create the kind of relationship and environment that allows supervisees to be safe enough to be vulnerable and to be open to new learning;
- are themselves flexible and open learners who model what learning from experience means;

- see reflection, critical reflection and critical self-reflection as the primary means of learning from experience. They train themselves in reflective skills and coach their supervisees in the same;
- give open and honest feedback;
- present experience as a first-hand teacher that can be trusted to guide us in our learning.

## Task 7: Giving feedback

The task that is seen by supervisors as their most difficult one is evaluating supervisees and giving feedback. It is easy to see why it is so. Monitoring the work of others, helping them develop and grow, entails giving feedback on particular areas of development and limitation. It can result in supervisees feeling overwhelmed, dispirited and, at times, shamed by the realisation of imperfections and limitations. How that takes place and how it is done depends on the supervisor. When not done well it can have serious consequences. Ladany et al. (1999) found that 51 per cent of supervisees reported at least one supervisor violation of ethics. The most cited issue was related to evaluation of performance and monitoring of supervisee activities (Westefeld, 2009: 304).

### Example

Gillian was a perfectionist. She worked hard and diligently to get it right for herself and for her clients. Mark was aware of this as her supervisor. After working together for about six months and when Mark ascertained that the relationship was strong, he gave Gillian feedback on one of the features he had noticed in her work: her obsession with getting it right all the time brought an intensity and lack of empathy into some of her work. Mark shared this with her. For Gillian, it catapulted her into a shame-based place. In her eyes, she was no good, should never have thought she would make a good clinical psychologist, and wanted to run away in embarrassment. Gently, Mark helped her see how this was one aspect amongst many others and that it was normal for her to be where she was in her professional developmental. They both stayed with the pain and the learning and slowly Gillian began to integrate this learning into her work. Both realised it was not easy to take feedback and not easy to give it but that it was a great instrument for learning.

## Task 8: Generating hope

It is easy for practitioners to buckle under the stress of work, home and modern-day living. Burn-out, compassion fatigue and debilitating tiredness seem to be the order of the day in the helping professions. With fewer resources to meet increasing demands it is not surprising that many find themselves in positions of helplessness or powerlessness. Some reactions from supervisees are that they:

- Withdraw (leave me alone)
- Deny (denial can be individual or collective)
- Grieve (experience real loss)
- Experience powerlessness (apathetic, hopeless)
- Panic (work hard – an organism in pain keeps moving)
- Freeze (paralysis in the face of challenge)
- Become overwhelmed (too much data to process)
- Narrow focus to self (I will look after myself and my own)
- Project (it's them – they are to blame)
- Get angry (how could they do this to us?)
- Wait (unsure, unclear, with some hope for something to appear)
- Have optimism/hope (see problem as challenge to be overcome)
- Become curious (interest in the emerging future)

The restorative function of supervision asks supervisors to stay resilient, strong and optimistic. While some of these features can be taught, in most instances they are *caught* from supervisors. I summarise this stance under the heading of 'generating hope' because hope is optimism for the future, a positive stance in the face of the present and a constructive adoption of strategies and interventions that use what we have rather than concentrate on what is missing. Hope is the bedrock of resilience.

Supervision in organisational settings can be particularly prone to becoming environments of powerlessness and negativity (see Hawkins and Shohet, 2012: Ch. 15). Hope also contains a lightness of touch, a healthy humour where we see things in perspective and learn to laugh at ourselves.

## Conclusion

There is lots of research into what makes for an excellent supervisor. Unfortunately the end result is a series of saint-like attributes not easily found together in most humans (Carifio and Hess, 1987; Carroll and Gilbert, 2011). They range from a sense of humour to self-awareness; from structuring supervision sessions just right to giving clear feedback connected to learning; and from being trustworthy, to being open and flexible. If Alonso once referred to supervision as *the impossible profession*, then the collective features of excellent supervisors could be grouped together as *the impossible supervisor!* In this chapter we have explored some ways through which supervisors can best achieve the tasks of supervision.

# Five

## Restorative Supervision: Supporting the Supervisee

### Chapter summary

This chapter concentrates on the person behind the professional supervisee and looks at how that person can be supported and helped to take care of the 'self' that does the job in supervision. Restorative supervision is a term describing this function of the supervisor as one who offers a place and space to recoup, revitalise and re-energise oneself as supervisee. Modern work and contemporary living can be very demanding and resilience and energy are needed to meet these daily demands. The chapter argues for supervisors fulfilling this function of monitoring how well supervisees care for themselves and how much they ensure that they have the energies they need for living balanced lives in the modern world.

In his book *The Seven Habits of Highly Effective People*, Stephen Covey paints this scene:

> You come across a man in the woods working feverishly to saw down a tree. You ask him what he is doing. 'Can't you see?' comes the impatient reply. 'I'm sawing down this tree.'
>
> 'You look exhausted. How long have you been working at it?' The man replies, 'Over five hours, and I'm beat. This is very hard work.'
>
> 'Well, why don't you take a break for a few minutes and sharpen the saw. I'm sure your work would go a lot faster if your saw was sharp.'
>
> The man emphatically replies, 'I don't have time to sharpen the saw. I'm too busy sawing.' (1989: 297)

Covey's analogy applies to us all. We are not good at looking after ourselves. It is some consolation to know that we can be in the company of greats: Carl Rogers wrote 'I have always been better at caring for and looking after others than I have been in caring for myself. But in these later years, I have made some progress.' The consolation comes in knowing he was 75 when he wrote that. We are often too busy to look after the instrument that earns our living and does our work – ourselves. Skovholt, in a book aptly entitled *The Resilient Practitioner*, asks key questions of various professionals: 'How does the opera singer take care of the voice? The football player, the body? The carpenter, the tools? The professor, the mind? The photographer, the eyes? The ballerina, the legs?' (2001: ix).

To his list we add the supervisee. What does the supervisee need to look after in order to be strong, resilient and passionate about their work? Supervisees need to look after their physical, emotional, psychological and motivational selves. The consequences of not doing so have been well documented: burn out, compassion fatigue, secondary traumatisation, lack of enthusiasm and withdrawal. The price paid for not staying strong and resilient is high.

One of the major tasks facing supervisees is how to care for themselves in a physically, emotionally and psychologically demanding life and work environment. Supervisors provide the environment that supports supervisees to look after themselves – the restorative task of supervision (Inskipp and Proctor, 1993). We ask a lot of supervisees. Maybe not directly, but by implication.

The following is quite a lengthy list of supervisee tasks. As you read them, perhaps you can think of examples when you asked them from yourself as supervisee or from the supervisees you have worked alongside.

- Be honest and transparent about their practice.
- Be open to our feedback.
- Be assessed on their competencies and fitness to practice.
- Be creative about how they work.
- Be vulnerable and bring their wounds, their weaknesses and their difficulties to supervision.
- Have the courage to face up to themselves, their strengths and limitations; and be real about what they are able to do and what they cannot do.
- Be flexible and be able to experiment and move outside their comfort zones.
- Be part of an unequal relationship where supervisors have executive power and can use it for better or worse.
- Be honest about their failures and learn from them.
- Work in a fluid and uncertain area of life with people who rarely have the *right* answers and where the relationship itself is of key importance.
- Be ethically aware and sensitive, reach high standards of delivery at work and stay alert to hotspots in relationships.
- Be alert for possible issues that may impact on them, their clients and the relationships they form.
- Patrol relationship perimeters to ensure that safe environments are created and maintained for themselves and their clients.
- Look after themselves by remaining resilient and healthy and able to cope with the demands of life and work.
- Be adaptable and flexible in how they work.
- Deal with the tensions and anxieties of complex and uncertain situations.

- Be alive to the many and varied factors involved in working in the helping professions.
- Be self-aware and understand themselves sufficiently to know how they engage with others, how they use their power and how they manage relational issues.
- Have good reflection-in-action (internal supervisors) where they can make decisions as they work with their clients.
- Be able to make quick decisions based on intuition and tacit knowledge.
- Have both active and implicit processing skills enabling them to both read situations and stay in touch with underlying dynamics.
- Think individually and systemically and see the importance of contexts for behaviour, cognition and emotion.
- Work with difference and diversity in creative ways.
- Be able to adapt skills across a variety of contexts; counselling is a discrete skill but counselling someone who is actively suicidal requires creative adaptations of the core skill.

That is quite a job description! No wonder supervisees can feel overwhelmed and daunted by the prospects of supervision. While these requirements slowly emerge over time, the everyday demands on supervisees are not unsubstantial. Often these responsibilities emerge without much help in meeting them. There is not a lot of training for supervisees: 'Despite both the overt and historical importance of supervision, new supervisees often have little formal preparation for the role' (Vespia et al., 2002). This is still the norm, especially where supervision has recently entered certain professions, for example coaching and organisation development consulting. Supervisees themselves have spoken of how they feel about being in supervision:

> When I go into supervision I feel like a child being called to account for something I may or may not have done. I don't feel like I'm a colleague, more like a child fronting up a punitive parent. (Autagavaia, 2001 49)

We often forget, as supervisors, what it was like in those early days of being a supervisee. Now I ask, when training supervisors, that participants go back and re-experience what happened to them as supervisees. Many of them have had poor experiences of supervision as supervisees. So often they have felt deskilled, disempowered, criticised and shamed within supervision. In the US, 75 per cent of those surveyed said that they had had experienced inadequate supervision at some stage and 51 per cent had experienced harmful supervision (Ellis, 2010; 109). Those bad experiences leave their mark. Having time to revisit, review and repair some of these in a new supervisory relationship will go a long way to making the next experience of supervision more positive. It will also allow the supervisee to begin to take some risks in supervision, where before he or she may have been wary, in the light of their previous experiences.

## Staying strong at work

Helping supervisees stay strong and resilient throughout their training and into their qualified years is not easy. In my early days as supervisor I thought it intrusive of me to inquire about how well my supervisees were doing. Even when I noticed signs of tiredness or burnout, I felt I needed to tread gently. Supervision, I knew, focused on work – it would move it close to therapy/counselling to turn the light too intensely on the practitioner and what was happening to his life in general. Two experiences helped me change my mind on this. The first happened over time when I realised that most of the supervisees, after they had been with me for a while, started their supervision sessions by updating me on their lives in general, and not just their working lives. It was as if they learned by themselves that who they were and what was happening in their lives was important to what they did, and that supervision was about presenting the person behind the professional as much as it was about presenting the work itself. They wanted to locate their professional selves within the wider context of their overall lives. Hence they would tell me about the stresses of combining childcare or caring for aging parents while coping with demanding work schedules, in often unsupportive organisational settings. They would share the aches and pains of their health with me and the trials and tribulations of holding it all together in a complex world. Over time, I found myself reacting positively to this and beginning conversations with them about how to look after themselves. I remember one supervisee saying to me, 'When I am well, my clients are well.' My response was to ask how supervision could help her *stay* well.

The second experience involved a busy workplace counsellor requesting that I supervise her work. We met for an hour, at the end of which I said I couldn't supervise her because she wasn't looking after herself. She was the only counsellor in the organisation and she worked most days from 8.00 am to 6.00 pm or later. She carried a case load of 35 clients, most of whom she saw once a week. She was also running training programmes in stress management and mindfulness. When I asked her to describe a Friday afternoon after a busy week, she replied that she 'fantasised a lot' during those sessions. She was heading for burnout and I challenged her directly on this and related issues.

Our world is more demanding than ever on supervisees and supervision (Hawkins and Shohet, 2012: Ch. 1). There are fewer resources, more demands on the helping professions, more anxiety about the risks involved, and more accountability with accreditations, continuing professional development and evidence-based practice. Supervisees are expected to show that they are in on-going supervision and to update their skills and knowledge throughout their professional lives. More and more rigorous audits are being put in place. Some supervisees will lose control of how they work and be required to work in ways not always suited to their personality, training or style. They may be allocated to supervisors who see supervision as an onerous chore in an already overburdened workload. They will face unreasonable managers and be assessed against criteria which are not always clear. When things go wrong, they will be blamed.

## Example

Ruth has hardly a minute in her busy day. After dropping the two children at school she heads straight for the GP surgery where she is the full-time counsellor. Her workload is demanding and she can easily see five to six clients daily, many of them suffering from depression and severe anxiety. Her husband, who is a counsellor in full-time private practice, picks up the children from school while she usually calls in to see her parents who live close by when she finishes around 5.00 pm. Her mother is suffering from Alzheimer's and her father finding it increasingly difficult to cope with her at home, and Ruth needs to be there for both of them. When she gets home about 6.00 pm she makes dinner and spends some time with the children before their bedtimes. She then takes a study hour for herself to keep up with her Masters course in CBT – she has just started Year 2 of her programme. Weekends are busy ferrying her daughter to dancing lessons and horse riding while her husband takes their son to play in his football team.

Ruth and her husband Isaac are not an uncommon modern couple, with children, aging parents, busy jobs and multiple commitments demanding high energy and dedication.

Below I have listed some modern stressors, both internal and external, which are common to contemporary supervisees:

- Living complicated lives where they are required to fulfil multiple responsibilities.
- The emotional demands of dealing with the frustration, anxiety, worries, angers and depressions of everyday life. People are worried about the future, such as climate change, the environment, terrorism.
- Many people cannot turn off the racing brain or the 'internal chatter'. They become stuck in their inner worlds, inner dialogues and imaginations.
- Much of modern life is lived preparing for the future. We find it more difficult to live in and enjoy the present.
- There are high-risk jobs that bring with them the risk of emotional and psychological damage, for example working with sex-offenders, troubled families, palliative and end-of-life care.
- Some supervisees are 'toxic handlers' who stand at the interface between individuals and organisations and, at times, soak up the toxicity of difficult situations.
- Individuals often feel isolated. Many of the institutions and communities which people used to turn to are no longer accessible or relevant (extended family, neighbourhood, church, health, education, legal system).

Zuboff and Maxmin have coined the term 'psychological self-determination' to capture the challenge individuals face today: by that they mean 'A deep awareness of one's own complex individuality. Primarily the ability to assert control over your own identity' (2002).

It is not about rampant individualism but about a keen sense of 'my own identity and who I am'. Vaill coined the term 'permanent white water' to illustrate the contexts in which individuals live and work today and asks the question 'What strategies and resources do I need to stay strong and resilient in the face of these demands?' (1996).

## The forgotten supervisee

It may seem strange to say that sometimes the forgotten element in supervision is the supervisee. After all, supervision is for supervisees and, through their development and learning, for the people, teams and organisations they work with. Supervisors might feel insulted by the suggestion that the supervisee is not the central focus of supervision. What else possibly could be?

But if the supervisee is as central to supervision as is often maintained, why aren't there more publications for supervisees? Google the word 'supervision' and you will uncover millions of possible sites; trawl the supervision literature and you will find hundreds of books; attend supervision conferences and you will hear excellent addresses and workshops on multiple aspects of supervision. How many of the sites, books or workshops are specifically for supervisees? Not many. There are quite a few training programmes for supervisors in Britain, ranging from Certificates and Diplomas through to Masters and Doctorates. It won't surprise you to discover that 100 per cent of those training courses are for – you've guessed it – supervisors, not supervisees. How many people reading this chapter have engaged in supervisee training or run a training programme for supervisees? Not too many, I suspect. Hence the statement 'The forgotten factor in supervision is often the supervisee'!

My doctoral research in 1995 concluded that even after two years of being in supervision, supervisees were still unsure what supervision actually meant. They had never been properly 'inducted' into the role of being and becoming an empowered supervisee in a supervisory arrangement. This became evident to me in my early supervisory days. I was setting up a small group of three supervisees as part of a Diploma in Counselling training. I met them and explained a little about supervision and what it meant. I described supervision as the forum where they 'brought their clients and had the opportunity to talk about them and learn from that conversation.' One of the group looked puzzled and said, 'I am not sure this is going to work for me. I live in North London and could never bring my clients here to South London for supervision.' I had naïvely assumed that she would understand 'bringing your clients to supervision' was a well-known phrase, and had nothing to do with bringing them *physically* to supervision. It was an early lesson in not making assumptions; *not* assuming that supervisees know about supervision and understand its terminology.

Quite the opposite is my experience. I have repeatedly come across supervisees who are ill-prepared for the role and have had no training in either what supervision is or their part in the supervisory arrangement.

Mind you, it's not uncommon for the receiver of services to get forgotten. I had the dubious pleasure of visiting a psychiatric ward on several occasions recently – a secure, locked facility for residents with acute mental health issues and with a typical stay being approximately two months. In this psychiatric ward the needs of staff were clearly more important than the needs of the residents. Things happened if they suited the staff, but not if they didn't suit the staff. The unspoken but clear message was: bother us as little as possible, please keep quiet, if you are a problem we will 'up' your medication to quieten you down. The staff would be horrified if this was reported back to them – I'm sure they were totally unaware that their needs mattered more than those of the patients. This experience can be a powerful reminder of how easily helpers, organisations and professions forget what they are about. So often, their primary aims get corrupted and are taken over by secondary aims, unconsciously, imperceptibly and unwittingly.

The same process often happens in education. In primary schools, secondary schools and tertiary education it is so easy for the needs of students to be inferior to those of staff. How could that happen, you ask? Surely education is for students? Not always so. The needs of staff slowly take over and often students become burdens to be tolerated rather than the focus of teaching and learning. Staff can be more interested in research, in writing and attending conferences. Universities are for staff, not for students. Getting staff to teach is like asking them to visit the dentist! Again, not a conscious process, but a hijack. The same trend happens in religious environments. The abuse we hear so much about happens because the hierarchy forget that they are there to serve others. Their needs take over.

In medical circles this syndrome has a name: 'the corruption of care'. The primary aims of the caring institution are hijacked by staff needs. It's an occupational, organisational and professional hazard.

So what has this got to do with supervision and supervisees? Is it possible that supervision could also be hijacked to put the needs of supervisors before the needs of supervisees? I am reminded of the African proverb provided by my colleague, Maria Gilbert: 'Until lions have their historians, tales of the hunt will always favour the hunter'!

How can we give all of the above domains back to those whose it is by right? What would it be like if we said to supervisees, 'We are here for you, your needs are what are important, how can we meet those needs to the maximum?' How can we ensure that the supervisee becomes the centre of supervision and his/her learning the main focus of what is happening? In brief, how can we move towards the ideal of supervisee-led supervision rather than supervisor-led supervision? What is important is that staff take care of themselves in order to be better able to do their jobs where there is a balance between care of self and care of others so that neither gets emphasised to the detriment of the other.

## Learning partnerships

> Little attention is given to the development of supervisee skills and to full understanding of the purpose and process of the supervisory relationship from the perspective of the supervisee. (Barretta-Herman, 2001: 7).

This came home to me quite dramatically some years ago. I was providing supervision training to a prison service, specifically those charged with supervising treatment programmes. An ever present issue was that of motivating supervisees to come to and use supervision. Supervisors felt they had to do all the work in supervision while supervisees became passive participants in the process, and avoided supervision as much as possible. A number of times they asked me to help them provide something for supervisees that would empower them to use supervision more effectively. Two outcomes ensued. First of all, my colleague Maria Gilbert and I wrote a manual entitled *Becoming an Effective Supervisee: Creating Learning Partnerships* (2011). This was a step-by-step guide to support supervisees learning about and engaging in supervision. The second outcome was that the Prison Service began providing day-long courses with the title *Becoming an Effective Supervisee*. Both these interventions – written manual to support supervisees and day-long training to help them develop supervisee skills – have increased motivation and energy for supervision.

The manual is a step-by-step guide, a systemic do-it-yourself plan to empower and enable the supervisees to be full partners in the supervisory endeavour. The emphasis is on partnership, learning partnerships and the *induction* of supervisees into the supervisory process. Coaching is needed to do that. This manual details what supervisees can do to take charge of the supervisory arrangement and make it serve them. It suggests that they:

1. *Choose to engage in supervision*. We know from our own experience and that of others that to take part in supervision, without having chosen it, affects motivation, cooperation and involvement. The first step is for the supervisee consciously and deliberately to make a positive choice to enter the coaching relationship. Ownership by the supervisee involves them in choosing their supervisor, learning what supervision is all about and contracting for it.
2. *Spend time to understand what supervision is all about is essential if it's going to work*. Don't let's assume we all have the same understanding of supervision. There are many models, frameworks and interventions used by supervisors, some of which impose a strategy upon their unsuspecting supervisees. We want supervisees to come to supervision with a clear understanding of what it means for them and what they want from it.
3. *Create clear contracts with all parties*. Working agreements with supervisors, with managers and with organisations allows the supervisee to be clear about roles and responsibilities. Supervision is at best a three-way contract between supervisor, supervisee and the supervisee's placement or training organisation.

Having all parties signed up to the same contract helps us work together towards agreed goals (see Chapter 3).

4. *Know their learning style.* Supervision supports and helps supervisees learn from their practice. Knowing how they learn, and taking responsibility for their own learning, motivates supervisees to get the best from their supervisory relationship. Supervision then becomes personalised or individualised learning – specifically geared and tailor-made for this particular supervisee.

5. *Prepare for their supervision session.* Much supervision fails because it is not well organised and little preparation goes into it. The manual outlines ways to help supervisees prepare for supervision and come with clear agendas and specific goals.

6. *Learn how to give and receive feedback.* Feedback is one of the best ways of learning, and one of the least used. It's a key element in supervision, and supervisees who know how to give and receive feedback are in pole position to advance their learning. It's a skill that can be learned, and time spent learning it pays vast dividends in the long run.

7. *Be prepared for difficulties.* Most supervisory relationships hit roadblocks and difficulties. With so many parties involved it would be unusual not to have some problems along the way. Anticipating these, and having methods for dealing with them, allows supervisees, supervisors and organisations to be prepared in advance and to notice when action needs to be taken to resolve difficult situations.

Supervisees are at their best when:

- they take ownership of the supervision process;
- they are eager learners;
- they contract and negotiate on an on-going basis;
- they monitor and articulate their learning;
- they prepare carefully for their supervision sessions;
- they are true partners in the relationships involved;
- their organisation sees performance changes in them;
- their learning helps their organisation learn;
- they are open to on-going feedback from others.

They are at their worst when they become passive recipients or reluctant participants in arrangements they haven't chosen, and haven't been prepared for.

## Supporting supervisees in using supervision

Educational research is pretty solid in its conclusions about what helps and supports learning. Some constants keep coming through – learners (supervisees) learn best when they:

- are proactive in initiating and are actively interested in learning;
- are open to reflection, particularly critical reflection;
- are creative and prepared to think beyond where they are;
- are in a learning environment and supported by teachers/supervisors and peers who are enthusiastic about learning; and
- have the opportunity to put something into practice soon after their learning.

Besides helping supervisees become effective learners, support may also be needed to help them look after themselves. Strategies for doing so include:

- Making sure you, your team and your organisation are *not* in survival mode. In competency mode you are able to access the frontal cortex part of your brain, which allows you to engage in long-term planning, be creative and imaginative, and – above all – be reflective. Reflection is a key method of staying strong, being mindful and being able to stop and think.
- Ensuring you have energy, and different types of energy. Find your sources of energy and use them. Energy is what keeps us going – physical, emotional, mental and spiritual energy. (Table 5.1 at the end of this chapter is a handout I sometimes give my supervisees to help them monitor their energy and where it comes from).
- Moving away from fear as a motivator. So many people are driven by fear. What fears are you manufacturing that are not out there?
- Setting up support networks and systems where you can go and be yourself.
- Being self-aware – our capacity to fool ourselves is immense. Fine (2007) refers to this as the 'vain or pig-headed brain' that is wonderfully adept at hiding from you what you don't want to know.
- Using supervision as a way of monitoring your professional wellbeing, your work, your team and your organisation.
- Monitoring motivation. Look at where from within you does your work come? (Scharmer, 2007)

## Supervisees for supervision

I spend time at the beginning of supervision looking with the potential supervisee at three critical aspects of supervision:

1. What is supervision?
2. What is your learning approach/style and how can we harness that most effectively in supervision?
3. What skills/competencies do you need to get started in supervision and what skills/competencies do you need to keep going?

## Eight key skills

Eight key skills go to make up the third aspect listed above. The more these skills are learned (at times supervisors coach supervisees in these skills), the more effective supervision will be as a learning relationship.

### Skill 1: Learning how to learn

In coaching supervisees on learning how to learn, we look at:

- the learning style of individual supervisees;
- what supports their learning;
- what blocks their learning;
- the environments we need to set up to maximise learning;
- what kind of relationship is needed by them; and
- how we can personalise learning to their style and personality.

### Skill 2: Learning from experience

While learning from experience may seem to be a natural skill, many supervisees come to supervision not able to learn from their own experience. Here supervisors help them to:

- trust that their experience is good (trust themselves);
- stay with that experience as a learning springboard;
- monitor all aspects of their experience – thinking, feeling, intuitive responses;
- notice when there are differences between their experience and the theories, models and frameworks they have learned; and
- realise that experience is open to many interpretations.

### Skill 3: Learning how to give and receive feedback

A difficult part of supervision and one not always learned easily, is how to give and receive feedback. Under this skill supervisees learn how to:

- listen to feedback;
- move into a non-defensive and non-shaming place to be open to feedback;
- ask questions to make sense of feedback given;
- sift feedback to use what is best from it;
- use feedback to enhance learning; and
- give feedback that is clear, focused, specific, behavioural and helpful.

## Skill 4: Learning realistic self-evaluation

Much supervision is actually self-supervision. The relationship with the supervisor models how to:

- become an objective observer of one's own work;
- evaluate work against specific criteria;
- notice differences between espoused theory (what I think I do) and theory in action (what I actually do);
- see one's strengths and limitations;
- evaluate oneself honestly without going into a place of shame or helplessness; and
- compare and contrast one's own evaluation with that of others.

## Skill 5: Learning how to reflect

Too often we assume that supervisees bring this skill with them; experience suggests, however, that supervision assists in the processes of:

- knowing how to stop and put oneself into reflective mode;
- being able to be aware of, notice and focus on salient points from practice;
- being mindful;
- getting distance, and becoming an observer of one's own practice;
- being able to make meaning in multiple ways, and not being locked into one way of making sense of what happened;
- being aware of our individual reflective style, its strengths and weaknesses; and
- working with different reflective lenses.

## Skill 6: Learning emotional awareness

Emotional awareness can become blunt through burn out, trauma, stress and overwork. Supervision recaptures it by:

- allowing supervisees to feel whatever feelings there are;
- believing that feelings are friendly and helpful communications;
- expressing feelings appropriately;
- being able to notice, stay with and articulate the feelings of others;
- knowing what feelings one finds hard to deal with, and tracing the roots of that;
- trusting feelings; and
- believing there are no 'good or bad' feelings.

## Skill 7: Learning how to dialogue

Conversation is the heart of supervision. Supervisees skilled in conversation:

- are able to listen to what is being said;
- speak their own truth without denying the truth of others;
- respect other points of view and compare own view with that of others;
- are able to suspend own beliefs in order to listen more openly;
- change their mind if needed; and
- create the kinds of relationships that lead to dialogue.

## Skill 8: Learning how to care for self (built-in resilience)

Self-care is underpinned by the ability of the supervisee to:

- monitor energy levels and know when they are tired;
- build in strategies for looking after themselves;
- create networks of support;
- ask for help when they need it and not be afraid of being vulnerable; and
- notice the signs in their life that they are not caring for themselves.

To help monitor energy levels I sometimes ask supervisees to fill in the form in Table 5.1. I have used the work of Loehr and Schwartz (2003) to devise it, and supervisees tell me it is both helpful to them and often surprising in what it unearths when they complete it. The summaries under each of the energies are some of the sources that sustain this energy. It provides the supervisee with the information they

TABLE 5.1   *Monitoring my energy and where it comes from*

|  | **Physically** | **Emotionally** | **Mentally** | **Spiritually** |
|---|---|---|---|---|
| What energises me at work? |  |  |  |  |
| What saps my energy at work? |  |  |  |  |
| What would help energise me at work? |  |  |  |  |

*(Continued)*

TABLE 5.1    *(Continued)*

|  | **Physically** | **Emotionally** | **Mentally** | **Spiritually** |
|---|---|---|---|---|
| What do I need to change in my life to have more energy at work? | | | | |
| Sources of energy | *Eating Drinking Sleeping Physical fitness Breaks* | *Self-confidence Relationships Empathy Dealing with stress Negative emotions* | *Time management Creativity Thinking skills Challenging the brain Mental preparation* | *Commitment Enthusiasm Values Building character Purpose* |

*Source:* Loehr and Schwartz (2003)

need to build in strategies to help them care for themselves and ensure that they have the four types of energy they need to do their jobs and live their lives in a balanced manner.

## Conclusion

Central to the entire supervisory system is the supervisee. It is his/her practice that is the stuff of supervision, and his/her learning that will make the difference to that practice in the end. Helping supervisees take responsibility for their practice and for learning from experience is key to effective supervision. Time spent by both supervisor and supervisee doing just that will be time well spent, and dividends will emerge in the longer term. Often supervisees are left to learn about supervision as they go along 'on a wing and a prayer'. That seems to be far too risky an approach for such an important element of personal wellbeing and professional competence.

# Six

# Ethics and Professional Practice in Supervision

**Chapter summary**

This chapter reviews ethics, ethical awareness and ethical decision making in supervision. It makes the point that supervision is not the forum to learn about ethics or ethical codes, but it *is* the location to become ethically sensitive and ethically aware of what happens in our practices. Practical ethics is the order of the day in supervision. This chapter also makes the point that we are looking at ethical maturity in supervision rather than simply an ethics of duty. Six components of ethical maturity will be outlined and applied to supervision.

In the film *Quantum of Solace*, James Bond says, 'Right and wrong don't come into it. We act out of necessity.' Contrary to the wisdom of Bond, supervision *is* the place where right and wrong, good and bad, good and better do 'come into it'. Necessity is not the only, nor indeed the most, important criteria on which actions are evaluated as good or bad. In supervision we stop to give attention to the quality of our work and examine the ethical underpinnings of what we do. This is the *normative function* of supervision to which professional and ethical issues and matters of quality pertain. Much supervision begins with queries, questions, confusions, impasses, critical events and emotional reactions – all these indicate the sort of crossroads where ethical decisions are made about which direction to take.

While I believe that ethical training should take place in formal training programmes, supervision is often the place where we learn how to make mature ethical decisions: that is, we learn how to translate the professional codes, frameworks and ethical theories into ethical actions. Supervision is a forum for *applied* ethics – asking the question 'What is the *best* course of action to take in the circumstances I face and with the clients I am working with?' The word 'best' is in italics to show that the best is what is the goal of ethical practice; not what is our duty, nor what keeps us safe, nor what is the minimum I can do, nor what would others expect from me, nor what I can get away with without being found out. These considerations are not to be ignored, and play important parts in making ethical decisions. But in the final analysis, most practitioners want to do their best and give the best standard of service possible to clients. Coming from a position of excellence changes how we think about ethics and helps us make decisions with 'what is best' at the centre.

Heidegger (1962: 156) sees 'care' as our most fundamental stance in the world. Care has two eyes, he suggests: one is *concern*, which focuses on our relationship to objects; the other is *solicitude*, which focuses on our relationships with other people. Like care, solicitude also has two eyes or stances: 'leaping in solicitude', where we take responsibility for the other person and his/her actions, and 'leaping ahead solicitude', which facilitates the responsibility of the others to make their own choices. Ethical maturity is about accepting responsibility for who we are, the choices we make, and how to engender a 'leaping ahead solicitude' for supervisees and clients (Mitchell, 2009: 160).

Ethical issues pop up automatically in the 'swampy lowlands' of practice. This makes supervision the ideal forum for learning how to deal with them. You could say that all practice in the helping professions is, of itself, ethical. Ethics is not something added to our work or simply a way of thinking about our practice – it is more. It's built into who we are and what we do. Ethics is *always already* there; it is part and parcel of practice. Supervision becomes a 'process of ethical discernment' whereby supervisees reflect deeply on the many aspects of their practice and make decisions about what to do next. We are often faced with difficult and complex ethical situations which do not have obvious answers. We make decisions based on a whole medley of past decisions, present concerns and future hopes. Our imaginations help us fashion what we will do in the light of the past and the present. Ethical awareness weaves together the past and its influences, the present context and its demands, and the future and its requirements.

When asked how they deal with ethical issues in their work, many practitioners respond that their first port of call will be to consult their supervisor. They see supervision as the arena where they can begin to discuss, dissect and decide. These are critical moments where difficult decisions have to be made. The instinct to consult the supervisor can be motivated by either one of the following:

1.  Shifting responsibility from making a decision from self to others – outsourcing ethical decision making to one who has more knowledge or experience and who will provide some answers.
2.  Setting up a reflective dialogue with someone who facilitates that decision-making process.

Tim Bond gives an example of the first instinct:

A well-respected and internationally renowned researcher in the psychology of young people came to see me two years ago to discuss the ethics of a major project for which he had just received a large grant. 'Just tell me what I need to do ethically and let me concentrate on the research,' was his request. It was clear that he was disconcerted by the dismay on my face at his plea ... I was taken off guard by his request to be told what to do to satisfy ethical requirements. He seemed to communicate a view of ethics as merely a set of rules to be satisfied before the real work could begin. Another dimension to this brief exchange that struck me with even greater force was the contrast between his confidence and eminence as a scientist, and his willingness to become like a child dependent on parental guidance in matters of ethics. (2013: 329)

Tim Bond's experience is not unusual. Many well-qualified and well-experienced practitioners move into ethically juvenile positions when faced with moral decisions. They look outwards towards gurus, experts or external authorities who will make the decision for them. Looking outwards is not bad, and it is always useful to consult the wisdom of others, but not the best place to start when learning how to be ethically mature. All too often ethics is seen as a set of rules that will guide us rather than an attitude based on values that provide anchor points for ethical decision making. The first suggestion in working towards an ethically mature decision is to go 'inwards' to your own wisdom. This will never result in the final decision but will be the starting place for ethical excellence.

An example of the second instinct occurred in my own work several years ago. I was asked by a human resources (HR) director to give him a psychological opinion on the resilience of a manager I was coaching. I had been supporting this manager on his journey back to work after several months off with severe depression. The HR director told me that the manager was about to be made redundant but because of his recent fragility he did not want to plunge the manager back into a depressive state. Hence the request to me: did I consider this manager was strong, robust and resilient enough to hear this news? I was caught in an ethical dilemma. I was certainly the best person to give that information, having worked with the manager for about three months; yet I had no agreement from him to pass on that kind of information. Nor was it my job to tell him he was going to become redundant. I brought this issue to my own supervision group, pretty certain that I couldn't give the information asked for. However, in dialogue with them, and holding the contextual and organisational issues and what was best for my manager-client in mind, I reached a different conclusion. Despite the risk involved, I decided I would give the HR director the information he wanted so that he could then decide whether or not to proceed with the redundancy conversation at this stage. It never felt as if I was giving away my responsibility to make this ethical decision myself to my peer group. It was, however, a very helpful forum in which they raised issues I had overlooked. It was also a lesson for me about putting my client and his welfare at the centre of the ethical conversation, and moving my own safety and 'playing by the book' further down the list of important factors in making an ethically mature decision.

## Ethical decision making in supervision

One chapter will never capture the breadth, depth and sheer complexity of what ethics means and how we make ethical decisions. Volumes are written on ethical theories, ethical approaches and the features and characteristics of ethical individuals, teams and organisations. It's one of the reasons we are put off thinking too much about ethics or being involved in ethical training. At the end of the day you just don't know that the decision you made was ethically mature. A decision can be 'by the book', risk free and safe and still be ethically immature in that the client's needs were not the core issue. A decision can break the code, put the practitioner in an unsafe position and open to complaint, and yet be a fine, ethically mature decision. Kohlberg (1982) was the ethicist who reminded us that it isn't always about what you do that makes an action ethical, it's also about where it comes from within you.

The same action can emerge from many sources. For example, I can be faithful to my wife because:

- I am afraid of losing her.
- I believe it's my duty.
- I want to be true to the vows I promised.
- I may be found out and shamed.
- I may not get anyone else to live with me.
- I may lose my children.
- I am faithful to my promises.
- I love her.

Each of these actions creates a very different moral stance. Knowing why we act the way we do and knowing the sources that result in our behaviours gives wonderful insight into our level of ethical awareness and maturity. Actions, in and of themselves, do not always tell us about ethical maturity. Sometimes they do (no 'good intentions' in the world can justify some actions), but mostly we need more.

There is also a tendency to see ethical decision making as a purely logical process with reason as the main factor in decision making. Emmanuel Kant was the champion of equating the 'right thing' with the 'moral thing', basing his ethical decision making on reason and logic alone. Despite the fact that most human decisions are not made rationally, many people think that this is the best method. So we devise problem-solving, logical and rational approaches to ethics. A typical problem-solving approach to resolving ethical dilemmas follows a set procedure:

1. What exactly is the problem?
2. Look at and articulate the options you have.
3. Evaluate these options one by one (taking into account the needs of various stakeholders).

4.  Choose the best option.
5.  Implement it.

Such sequential, automaton approaches to ethical decision making rarely work, despite their popularity. They miss the impact and value of emotions and emotional responses. The relational realities are reduced to some kind of rational equation. Haidt summarises this very well: 'Trying to make children behave ethically by teaching them to reason well is like trying to make a dog happy by wagging its tail. It gets causality backwards' (2006: 165). Emotional intelligence is at the basis of ethical intelligence; our work and our lives are 'automatically coated in emotion' (Cron, 2012: Location 769 of 4021). Remove emotions from the ethical equation and you have effectively removed the relationships involved, and created an ethics involved solely with problem solving.

This chapter will take a broad-brush approach to ethical maturity within supervisory contexts. It won't tell supervisors or supervisees what to do. Nor will I look in any detail at ethical theories, ethical codes and frameworks or ethical dilemmas. Here the aim is to focus on the place of ethical decision making in supervision and how to manage that process. This chapter will present a set of foundations on which the ethical house is to be built.

## The ethical supervisor

The first consideration in ethical supervision is the ethical maturity of the supervisor. One might say that supervisees will be as ethically mature as their supervisors. Supervisees 'catch' their ethical tone from their supervisors. This should come as no surprise. We underestimate the power of 'imitation learning' – that form of learning through which we model ourselves after and imitate others. Other mammals learn entirely through imitations – watching their elders and learning from what they do. Humans have an added factor, language, through which we communicate and which we use as a method of teaching each other. It has been postulated that language developed for this very reason – that we can help each other learn rather than rely on the slower process of imitation learning: language is 'fast-track' learning. Imitation learning works with or without language. Supervisees watch supervisors intently and imitate them. Working with ethically mature supervisors will impact supervisees in how they think about ethics and how they make mature ethical decisions. Elizabeth Holloway captured this aspect of supervision well when she described supervision as 'an opportunity for the student to capture the essence of the therapeutic process *as it is articulated and modelled by the supervisor,* and to *recreate it* in the counselling relationship' (1992: my italics). The supervisee 'catches' or is infected by how the supervisor works and with true imitation learning transfers that unconscious learning to his or her work.

What are the features of the ethically mature supervisor? Ethical maturity is more of a journey than a destination. Bond describes it well:

> Maturity implies a journey from youthful exuberance to a more grounded state of being rooted in experience and reflection ... maturity is not just longevity but, in the context of ethics, suggests a quality of judgment akin to wisdom. However, maturity does not sound like a constant state which, once attained, can be secured totally forever. (2013: 9)

Some of the characteristics of ethical maturity in supervisors and supervisees include:

- being able to stop, pause, reflect and mindfully consider what has happened in their own work and in the supervision relationship;
- being able to view what has happened from a number of perspectives (client, team, systemic, professional perspectives);
- being self-aware and knowing how one typically makes decisions and how that process will translate automatically into ethical decision making (i.e., we make ethical decisions in much the same way as we make decisions in general);
- being conscious of one's own needs and how these can interfere with and influence ethical decisions;
- being alert to the power of context and how context can, in many instances, overpower ethical character;
- knowing how emotions and intuition play huge roles in ethical decision making, and not relying on logical and rational problem-solving methods alone – being emotionally aware and astute helps make ethically mature decisions;
- knowing how important it is to check things out with trusted, objective others;
- being aware of the 'relational demands' in helping and knowing that fidelity, trust and integrity are key features in ethical maturity;
- knowing that there is no one right way of making ethical decisions – making a decision will depend on a number of factors (experience, areas of expertise, context, relationships, the client's needs); and
- being aware that the ability to empathise with others and to have compassion are the bedrock of ethical maturity.

## The ethically mature supervisee

Supervisees are beginning their journey towards ethical maturity and it is unfair to ask them to speak from an experience and wisdom not yet accrued. However, supervisees can set up the environment and the relationship that sustains this journey. How can supervisors support supervisees in that journey?

One way is to help them develop the attitudes and values that underpin ethical maturity. To do this, I sometimes ask supervisees to read Gelb (1998) to help them begin to lay down the foundations of becoming ethically aware and sensitive. In that book Gelb summarises *How to Think Like Leonardo da Vinci* and presents several principles of learning:

- *Be curious:* Develop a curious approach to life and work. This is the foundation stone of all learning and creates an inquiring mind that is active, alert and sensitive.
- *Learn from experience:* For Leonardo this was the greatest teacher of all. Willingness to learn from experience and from mistakes and to question conventional wisdom is important in the journey towards maturity. Questioning conventional wisdom doesn't mean not listening intently to the theories, ideas and opinions of others – but we listen through our own experience.
- *Use your senses:* Look, notice, perceive. 'Look, look, look again' was one of Leonardo's refrains to his students. There is always more to see. What we perceive, and what we allow ourselves to perceive, limits our behaviour.
- *Be willing to embrace ambiguity, paradox and uncertainty:* 'Confusion endurance' sat well with Leonardo. Not knowing, and being able to stay with not knowing, is a strong learning position for supervisees.
- *Balance everything:* 'Both ... and' is a good principle to remember. Both logic and emotion; both intellect and imagination; both science and art.
- *Look after yourself:* Cultivate healthy ways of living.
- *Think systemically:* Keep looking for the connections. For Leonardo all things were interconnected.

Helping supervisees develop these attitudes and values places them in strong positions to deal with complex ethical issues when they arise.

### Example

Erik comes to supervision confused. He has only been coaching for a few months and has been 'thrown' by a new client, an executive. Excited by the opportunity of a referral, he set up a time to meet. The client was 15 minutes late and then chatted informally for nearly 15 minutes about current affairs. Erik wasn't sure what to do: on one hand he wanted to let the client relax, on the other hand he realised valuable time was passing and coaching was not taking place (or was it?). After half an hour the client asked if he could have a cup of coffee. Taken aback, Erik agreed and went off to find some coffee. He wondered if he should get a cup for himself as well but decided against that. Back in his consulting room, 45 minutes now having passed, he takes the plunge and asks the client what he hopes for from coaching. Erik isn't sure if he should share the contents of the chat he had

*(Continued)*

(Continued)

with the HR director who referred the executive to Erik. In that chat, the HR director had said that the client needs to work on his time-keeping skills and in particular on his people skills. He was very task oriented but now that he was leading a team he needed to communicate better. The client himself said he wanted to work on his career issues and whether or not he had a future with that company.

How might a supervisor set up a supervisory session with Erik that enables him to pause and learn from his experiences? A good start might be supporting Erik just to stop and allow himself space to feel what had happened in his coaching session. As he relaxes and monitors his feelings, Erik realises that he felt confused and out of control with his client. Rather than provide a safe and well-managed session, he relinquished control of the session over to the client. He feels trapped between wanting to stay with the client's needs and structuring the session to meet the goals of coaching – both the goals of the client and the goals of the organisation. Later, again in supervision, Erik will learn about parallel process and how the coachee's powerlessness might well be being communicated through Erik's feeling out of control.

The supervisor helps Erik stay with and trust these feelings – they come from his experience. He holds back from evaluating (Erik started by saying he had made a mess of this coaching session) and moves Erik on to a more curious stance. Why did this session unfold the way it did? Erik has a number of insights into why what took place took place. He talks about how controlling his client was, and how he was used to getting his way in his company. Now they replay the session, this time with Erik taking responsibility for the events. Towards the end of the session, the supervisor asks Erik to summarise what he has learned from the supervision session. Erik see his most important learning as 'not having to please the client by accommodating him, but having to take charge and lay a good foundation for safety and work together'.

## Components in ethical maturity

Carroll and Shaw (2012, 2013) present six components of ethical maturity that work well in supervision. These components are *not* sequential stages in a process, rather they are conditions that make for good ethical decision making. Figure 6.1 presents the six components detailed below:

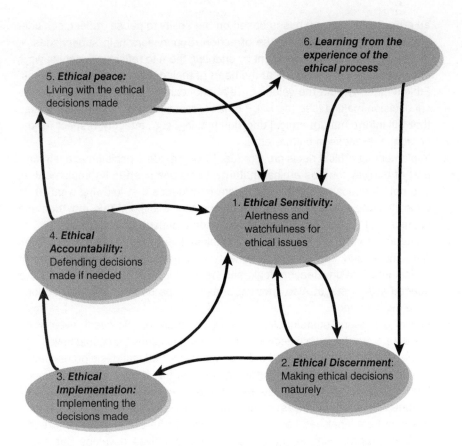

FIGURE 6.1   *The six components of mature ethical decision making*

1.  Fostering ethical sensitivity and watchfulness; creating ethical antennae that keep us alert to when ethical issues/dilemmas arise. This results in a moral compass/moral character. Ethical sensitivity provides the first alert that there is an ethical issue at stake. Not to be ethically sensitive is to miss the signs of ethical presences and abort any further stages in the ethical decision-making process. Helping supervisees develop an ethical compass is one of the first tasks of supervision and will emerge primarily from supervisors who are themselves ethically aware, and notice ethical dilemmas and problems emerging. Empathy enters the field at this stage as the primary virtue of ethical sensitivity; fostering empathy and compassion as the twin anchors of ethical sensitivity is a key supervisory role.

2.  Discerning ethical decisions and being able to make an ethical decision aligned to our ethical principles and our values. Awareness of ethical issues is only the beginning of the ethical procedure. Next comes the ability to make

an ethical decision and this is based on the ability to pause, reflect, consider and decide on a mature course of action. Supervisors help supervisees at this stage of ethical development by enabling them to reflect in widening ways and consider what values are at the heart of their decision-making processes. Ethical maturity puts the values of relational care and fidelity central to ethical decision making (see the BACP *Ethical Framework* (2010) for other values that will inform mature ethical decision making, e.g., integrity, respect for the person, awareness of culture etc.).

3.  Implementing ethical decision/s made. Having made a decision is again only part of the way towards ethical maturity. Decisions need to be implemented, and not all ethical decisions are. There is evidence that knowing what to do ethically does not always end in enacting that decision. This may demand courage and perseverance/resilience to see a difficult task completed.

4.  Being able to articulate and justify to stakeholders why the ethical decisions were made and implemented. Honesty and transparency become part of ethical justification. Reason, logic and being able to speak clearly are skills needed at this stage. Also knowing oneself helps us articulate why actions were decided upon.

5.  Ethical peace and sustainability; achieving closure on the event, even when there were other possible decisions or 'better' decisions that could have been made. Living peacefully with the consequences of ethical decision making is crucial to on-going wellbeing. Letting go of what has been and done is important in ethical closure. Supervisees learn to accept who they are, be compassionate towards themselves, be honest and make restitution when needed.

6.  Learning from what has happened and 'testing' the decision through reflection. Integrating what we have learned into our lives develops our moral character and extends our ethical wisdom and capacity. Part of the process of developing ethical maturity is learning from experience. This again takes some time in being honest with oneself and being able to trust experience even when others disagree. Emotional and social intelligence will play a large part in this.

Ultimately these six components result in ethical maturity. The six components come together in a definition or description of ethical maturity:

> Having the reflective, rational, emotional and intuitive capacity to decide if actions are right and wrong, or good and better; having the resilience and courage to implement those decisions; being accountable for ethical decisions made (publicly or privately); and being able to learn from and live with the experience. (Carroll and Shaw, 2012: 30)

Throughout life I have journeyed with a number of supervisees who have had ethical complaints taken out against them. Inevitably this has been a painful journey even when the complaints were not upheld. My experience has taught me a number of lessons; when supervisees are ethically mature they have an inner sense of what is the right way forward, even when it doesn't conform to all the rules and regulations.

Supporting supervisees develop ethical antennae is one of the most important of supervisor tasks. Ethical sensitivity produces an in-built radar that zones in on ethical dimensions almost before they emerge. At times such ethical watchfulness is missing. I remember dealing with one supervisor in an organisational setting who worked with a counsellor. Flattered to be asked by the company to take on facilitating a dysfunction team within the organisation, the supervisor shared her good news with her counsellor supervisee. The supervisee did not share her joy but reported her uneasiness with her supervisor taking on such a role as some of her own clients would be involved. The supervisor felt she could handle the boundaries; the supervisee did not think so, and felt she had 'a right of way'. They asked me to mediate their difference, and in the dialogue that followed the supervisor slowly realised that the supervisee did, indeed, have a valid point of view that she had missed. She decided, in the light of that, not to take on the work offered her by the organisation. Importantly, she learned also how to fine-tune her ethical sensibilities through her use of empathy – the gateway to seeing life from other perspectives.

Codes and frameworks are starting points for ethical decisions and not end points. They rarely tell us what to do, but do provide overarching principles to help us make decisions. Sticking only to codes results in an ethics of duty, but not always an ethics of fidelity. And it is this relational ethics of trust that is our aim. Supporting supervisees to build in this kind of relationship with their clients helps them create ethically mature practice.

---

## Exercises

1 What do we mean by ethics within supervision?
2 Can we progress from an ethics of duty and injunctions to an ethics of fidelity, care and integrity?
3 Look at the six components of ethical maturity and see how you might apply them to supervision.
4 What are you ethically responsible for as supervisor? What clinical responsibility do you hold? How do you assess risk in the work of the supervisee?
5 How do you give feedback that is clear, focused and connected to learning, especially about ethics? How do you manage ruptures and difficulties in the supervisory relationship in an ethical manner?
6 What do I need to attend to as supervisor to be ethically mature in supervision?
7 What do I need to attend to as a supervisee to be ethically mature?

## Conclusion

This chapter has looked at ethical maturity and what it might mean in the realm of supervision. In particular we are interested in how to help supervisees make ethical decisions in their practice, and also how to set up supervision as an ethical arena in its own right. I hope this chapter has not resulted in an easy answer, or formula, applicable to all ethical situations. Ethics are not problems to be solved: they are relational issues to be lived. That means the final answers to the questions asked by supervisees about making ethical decisions is 'It depends'. Sometimes we just know what to do, sometimes we wait for an answer, sometimes we use reason, sometimes emotion, often intuition. Sometimes we discern alone, often we consult others. At times codes and ethical frameworks help us, at other times they are of no use. Occasionally we rely on past experience to guide present decisions, at other times past experience leads us astray and we have to look for new pathways. Sometimes we don't know what to do and we stay with unknowing, at other times we take a risk and hope for the best. Claxton and Lucas provided a wonderful image when they imagined ethical problems as 'more like tangled fishing nets than ... mathematical equations' (2007: 80).

# Seven

## The Role of the Organisation in Supervision

### Chapter summary

In this chapter supervision is considered systemically or within the various contexts in which it occurs. Contexts give meaning but are often ignored in supervision and focus is maintained on individuals and understanding individual dynamics. Eight organisational or systemic themes are also considered.

It is relatively recently in the history of supervision that the background, context or organisations involved in the work of practitioners was allowed 'into' supervision. When I started supervising in the 1980s, it was not unusual for supervisors to ignore the organisational contexts in which practice took place. For some, supervision focused on what happened between individual practitioners and individual clients, and nothing else really mattered; other supervisors felt uncomfortable in organisational areas where they were not expert or hadn't a good working knowledge. Even supervisors that traditionally had a strong organisational background (e.g., nursing, social work or teaching) paid passing recognition to the impact of the organisation on their work. In the first edition of their book *Supervision in the Helping Professions* (1989), Hawkins and Shohet present six focus points in their process model of supervision. It is only in later editions that the seventh eye (focusing on the wider contexts in which the work happens) appears. By the time the fourth edition emerged (2012) there was a whole section of the book (Part 4) dedicated to an 'organisational approach' – showing the growing importance of factoring in the organisation when supervising. It is only from the 1990s that the organisational dimensions of supervision have become important. In my view, it was the influence of counselling in organisational settings and the rise of the systemic approach to practice that began to introduce supervision to context. Supervisors and organisations alike realised how important it was for supervisors to have some knowledge of and theories around organisational impacts on work.

## The context gives meaning

Contexts are like concentric circles with ripples of influence moving outwards and inwards. We cannot not be affected by the multiple contexts in which we live and work. It works both ways: us creating contexts, contexts creating us. Individuals are like ice-bergs: the part you see above the waterline is the individual; the main iceberg, below the waterline, is that array of relationships, connections and contexts that makes and maintains the individual. It is a fallacy to think that the small portion of the iceberg we see is all there is. We make that mistake constantly — thinking we are on our own, making our own decisions, having total free will and control over our lives and can change, if we choose, what we want to change. We often believe we are independent individuals reliant on no one else for the impor-tant challenges of life. Not so. We miss the systems part of our lives, and refuse to acknowledge its impact to our peril. There are more forces bearing on our lives and decisions than we know; acknowledging and honouring those influences puts our lives and our behaviours in some perspective. Oshry points out some of the consequences of not realising the impact of systems:

> When we don't see systems, we see individual personalities. Our explanations are personal, and our solutions are personal. Fix the individual. When we see systems, quite another world opens up to us. What we have here is not a personal problem — but a social disease — a disorder of the 'we'. (1996: 167)

Failure to take organisational and systemic awareness into account can result in making individuals alone responsible for what happens to them and exonerate the background from any responsibility. What does that mean for supervision? How do we work as supervisors with the individual in the organisation (the supervisee) and the systemic organisation as the context/environment that impacts on all par-ties? Egan and Cowan recount a telling story that partially answers this question:

> The story goes that someone walking along a river sees someone drowning. This person jumps in, pulls the victim out, and begins artificial respiration. While this is going on, another person calls for help; the rescuer jumps into the water again and pulls the second victim out. This process repeats itself several times until the rescuer gets up and walks away from the scene. A bystander approaches and asks in surprise where he is going, to which the rescuer replies, 'I am going upstream to find out who's pushing all these people in, and see if I can stop it'. (1979: 3–4)

When does an individual issue become an organisational problem?

Supervision is about gaining perspective. We stand back from our work in order to see it more objectively, and view and review it in ever widening circles, called the 'helicopter ability' (like the bigger picture perspective the rescuer took in the example above). The higher you go the more you see. Supervision too takes place in a context and is itself under the influence of contexts, many of which are organisational and invisible. This chapter looks at those contexts and how supervision can work with them effectively.

## Different organisational contexts

The organisational contexts in which supervision often finds itself are multiple. There are four main ones; I have added several references for each should you wish to follow up these areas in more detail:

- *Medical settings:* Health contexts where doctors, nurses, social workers, counsellors, psychologists and HR personnel are in supervision either individually or in teams (Henderson, 1999; Curtis Jenkins, 2001; Owen and Shohet, 2012).
- *Educational settings:* Formal learning contexts where teachers, pupils, academics, counsellors, psychologists, social workers, guidance personnel are in supervision (Tholstrup, 1999; Marzano et al., 2011).
- *Religious settings:* Pastoral care and ministry – priests, ministers, pastoral workers, youth ministry workers and laity are in supervision in teams or individually (Mann, 1999; Benefiel and Holton, 2010; Pohly, 2001).
- *Workplace settings:* Workplace contexts where managers, coaches, HR personnel, action-learning facilitators, organisation development consultants and teams are being supervised (Carroll, 1996b; De Haan and Birch, 2012; Hawkins and Smith, 2007).

Within these four organisational contexts various formats of supervision are used, similar to those taking place in supervision in general: individual supervision from internal or external supervisor; small group/team supervision again from internal or external supervisors; intervision, which involves supervision with supervisees from different professional backgrounds; and peer-group supervision (one-to-one or small group).

Organisational supervision can take place face-to-face, by telephone, audio and teleconferencing, Skype and email.

---

### Example

Anuja is a coaching supervisor who also works as a consultant to organisations. She is supervising Dave, an executive coach who in turn is working with Stephen, a director in a utilities company. Dave talks about being

*(Continued)*

*(Continued)*

stuck in his work with Stephen and not sure what to do. When Anuja asks him for any image that comes to his mind when he thinks of his work with Stephen, Dave immediately comes up with a picture of Stephen up to his waist in a swamp. Furthermore, he has tape around his mouth which effectively silences him. When Anuja asks Dave to put himself in that picture, to his surprise Dave sees himself in the same swamp up to his waist and also with taped mouth. They face one another helpless, hopeless and silenced. Making sense of this image throws Dave back into Stephen's organisation where 'being silenced' is now the order of the day. The company itself is going through major upheavals as it restructures and has already cut its workforce by one-fifth as a reaction to the current recession and global economy. The message from the top is that those who are left behind are the lucky ones but they will have to work harder and conform to the stringent cost-cutting strategies outlined by the Board. Anuja began by asking herself in what ways she too is stuck, in what ways she was being silenced, and what part she was playing in the various scenarios and relationships outlined (she and Dave, Dave and Stephen, Stephen and his organisation, the organisation and the wider world). The coachee, coach and the organisation which employs the coach as an employee weave a complicated web of relationships where parallel processes thread their way throughout the relationships. It is all interconnected and like a ball of wool can only be unravelled by paying attention to all the relationships. Anuja knows that if this cycle of paralleling with regard to silence, being stuck and helplessness is to be broken, then she needs to regain the power to speak, to move and to engender some optimism.

You may have had to read this example twice or more, or stop as you were reading and go back to make sense of the relationships involved and remind yourself of what is happening to whom. Not surprisingly. First, organisations are 'messy' places and making sense of what is happening within them is not just demanding but can be extremely confusing. That is often what makes supervising organisations and supervising those who work in organisations both fascinating and mystifying. Second, the example brings out the many stakeholders and subsystems involved, all of which find their way into supervision in visible and invisible ways. Third, the example illustrates how parallel process (leakage from one part of the system finds its way into other parts of the system) occurs. Fourth, the example points out that changing any part of the system (Anuja is now a part of the wider system) will affect the whole system.

## Some introductory comments

We are born into organisations: our journeys as social animals start the day we are born. Neuroscientists keep reminding us of how important relationships are to the social brain:

> It is life experience – and especially the way we are cared for in the first place – that provides the way the individual's brain gets organised, and a unique self starts developing. (Brown and Brown, 2012: Location 302 of 3782)

This means more than just that we born part of a system and live in systems all our lives. We are systemic by nature and from our earliest experience of family our brains and ourselves are configured to be connected. Heidegger believed there was no such thing as an individual, there are only individuals connected to others and to their worlds (Mitchell, 2009). To see and treat people as if they were isolated individuals is not just unfair but narrow-minded. We don't think alone, we don't feel alone and we can never exist alone – we are definitely 'not islands'. We are defined relationally.

## Systemic approaches to supervision

In a chapter entitled 'Systemic Approaches to Supervision', Peter Hawkins (2011: 167ff) defines and describes the tenets of systemic supervision. He applies his definition to coaching, so I have widened it here to include other professions (and slightly adapted his definition):

> Systemic supervision is the supervision of an individual or a team which:

- is informed by a systemic perspective;
- is in service of all parts of the system learning and developing;
- attends to the client in relation to their systemic context(s);
- includes and reflects upon the supervisee and the supervisor as part of the systemic field.

Using this description as a springboard means that our supervisory minds (both supervisors and supervisees) think systemically, analyse what is happening systemically and consider interventions as systemic interventions. Working with individual supervisees and individual clients doesn't mean we isolate them or ignore them in the light of systemic thinking, but continually consider them and their issues in the contexts in which they live and work. Thinking systemically means that we have the ability to hold individual and organisational needs together and don't commit prematurely to one path rather than the other. Thinking systemically means looking for systemic as well as individual explanations for what happens.

### Example

Howard works with Leah in a coaching arrangement. Leah also works with two other managers from Howard's department. Leah is being supervised by Hayley. In supervision she talks about a culture of bullying that has been part of this department for some time. None of the three managers wants to be responsible for blowing the whistle but all three are considering asking for moves from this department, and if that doesn't happen then thinking seriously of resigning. Leah has worked with them to try to support them individually, but not much has changed. She and Hayley wonder what they can do at a more systematic level to help the individuals involved, the department and the organisation.

This example highlights how individual interventions alone are not always satisfactory in resolving organisational problems. In fact, trying to help Howard stand up to the bully could make matters worse for Howard. This is an organisational issue that needs an organisational intervention. Kusy and Holloway put this very clearly:

> Toxic people thrive only in a toxic system … some of the solutions … require rolling up your sleeves and getting into the muck of the systems where toxic personalities thrive … toxic personalities are part of a complex system, which is the source of their power. (2009: 10)

David Smail points out how easy it is for us to blame individuals for what happens to them, rather than see responsibility in a wider context:

> If you run over a pea with a steamroller, you don't blame the pea for what happens to it, nor, sensibly do you treat its injuries as some kind of shortcoming inherent in its internal structure, whether inherited or acquired. Similarly, if we place the literally unimaginably sensitive organisms which human babies are in the kind of social and environmental machinery which we seem to be bent on perfecting, it can be of no real surprise that so many of them end up, as adults, as lost, bemused, miserable and crazy as they do. (1987: 76)

Kusy and Holloway (2009) and Smail (1987) ask us to turn our gaze towards dysfunctional systems that cause problems rather try to 'sort out' individuals from within themselves.

We can talk about *supervising organisations* (what De Haan (2012: 65) calls *organisation supervision*) or about *supervising in organisations*. Supervising organisation means, in the first instance, a managerial type of supervision which involves holding the organisation and its needs in overview. Leaders and managers are asked to do this. If they get too involved lower down the organisation they can easily miss what is happening in the bigger picture. Their supervisory eyes need to be strategic and comprehensive as they manage all aspects of the organisation.

Supervising in organisations is the kind of supervision we are considering here. We supervise individuals and teams that work within organisations and our supervisory role can be either part of that organisation or external to the organisation (for more details on this, see De Haan, 2012; Hawkins and Shohet, 2012; Hawkins and Smith, 2007).

Organisational interventions can include areas such as culture change for organisations, strategic change, whole-system interventions, team development and organisational development (OD). Supervision creates reflective space for individuals and teams who work in these areas to consider mindfully their practice. What supervision means here is not different from what it means elsewhere (see Chapter 1), but the focus of intervention will be much wider. More organisational awareness is needed than in other forms of supervision where organisations are not involved in the change process. 'Supervision is much more complex, multi-layered and diverse,' writes De Haan and Birch (2012: 66) of this kind of supervision. Supervisors here can be one of two kinds:

1. The supervisor, who is not a member of the organisation or of the consulting team, but has an understanding of the organisation, provides supervision where the focus is the work.
2. The supervision of individual consultants and their work where the supervisor is outside the organisation and may know little about it.

The supervisor may or may not be paid by the organisation for whom the individuals or the team works. Examples include:

- Supervising an employee who works in an organisation as a member of the organisation staff. This employee could be a counsellor or a coach or an internal OD consultant. There are various ways in which this contract can be set up, such as being paid by the supervisees directly where there is no contract with the organisation as such or being paid by the organisation for providing supervision to the designated individuals or teams.
- Supervising a team within an organisational setting. This team could be a specific team (e.g., the counselling team, the coaching team, the HR team) and again can have the same contracts/relationships as the supervision above which involves individuals. The Board of Directors would also be the focus of the supervision contract.
- Supervising individuals or teams who are not members of the organisation but are employed by the organisation to work with them (as outsiders), for example coaches who work with individuals or teams in the organisation and are only employed by the organisation in this capacity.

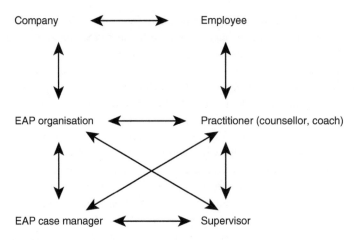

FIGURE 7.1    *The stakeholders in organisational supervision*

There can be a complex web of relationships involved here. Figure 7.1 outlines the subsystems and the potential relationships between them and individuals in them in an example of an Employee Assistance Programme (EAP) associate engaged in counselling with an employee from an organisation.

Figure 7.1 presents six subsystems within the arrangement an EAP might have with an organisation. Company X contracts with an EAP provider. The EAP provider supplies counsellors to work with individuals from Company X. These counsellors have an internal case manager to whom they are accountable and a clinical supervisor who is external to the EAP and is paid by the individual counsellor.

Already the number of relationship involved, the contracts devised, the expectations engendered and the way the various parties relate to each other is complex. Questions arise such as:

Who is responsible for whom?
Who says what to whom?
How do these sets of relationships affect each other and in particular the individuals coming for counselling?

## Some issues

What are the issues that supervisors, supervisees and organisations need to heed in setting up and maintaining a credible supervision system within an organisational? Here we briefly present eight considerations:

1.   Organisations and their understanding of supervision
2.   The supervisor and his/her organisational DNA

3. The supervisor as buffer
4. Ethical issues in organisational supervision
5. Looking after self in organisations
6. Supervision despite the organisation
7. Parallel processes in supervising in organisations
8. Embedding supervision in an organisational culture

## 1 Organisations and their understanding of supervision

We cannot take for granted that organisations understand what supervision means. For many it is still linked to overseeing, managing, risk management and training. It has sometimes earned the nickname 'snoopavision' in organisational settings. While we see those connections, we are also keen to add the developmental, reflective, nurturing, learning and supportive sides of supervision. Towler reviewed supervision from within a police service and indicates how it was viewed there: 'Rank, uniform and hierarchy pervade all aspects of police culture ... the notion that external authority is necessary for internal disciple and order is central ... managers will tend to pull rank to ask for confidential information and there will be pressure to perform well' (1999:189). Mann presents the issue from within religious organisations: 'Perhaps the most significant hazard to obviate is that of unrecognised countertransference' (1999). 'Tact and diplomacy' are the words used by Margate Tholstrup (1999: 121) when advising supervisors how to work with counsellors in educational settings, and Penny Henderson reviews the demands of working in medical services:

> In the pressurised and busy setting of general practice, an issue is the acknowledgement and management of fear and powerful feelings; this parallels the GPs pressures as they deal with issues of life and death, and the projections on to them of omniscience or expertise. (1999: 97)

These short statements from those who work within these particular organisational settings alert us to the fact that the culture of an organisation can be at odds with what we mean by supervision. Their understanding of supervision can be very different from ours, and in some instances almost adversarial to what supervision can mean.

Supervision is about 'taking time out' from front-line work to reflect on and review that work. For many organisations 'time' is a valuable commodity and 'time out' may not be high on their values list. It may go further and be seen as countercultural to fast-moving companies.

A major task for supervisors and supervisees is educating organisations as to what supervision means so that we are working together to support supervisees do their work professionally, ethically and to the best of their abilities.

On-going and frequent contact between organisational representatives, supervisors and practitioners helps keep each informed and allows time for potential conflicts to surface and be dealt with before they become problems.

## 2 The supervisor and his/her organisational DNA

Rarely considered in supervision or other organisational interventions is the person of the supervisor and his/her relationship with organisations. We all connect to, enter and engage with the various organisations in our lives in a somewhat characteristic manner reminiscent of how we first entered and engaged with organisations in our past. An organisational template or blueprint (or DNA) is fashioned by our early experiences of family and becomes the medium through which we later view organisations. Many years ago I heard the psychologist Cary Cooper remark that 'we re-create our family of origin at work'. Quite a statement, and one that stayed with me. Reflecting on this made me realise how I enter organisations, what I think of them and how I make connections. Why is that important? Because when I understand my organisational stance and the organisational stance of others I begin to realise that my actions and behaviours conform to a pattern.

I grew up in a large family system of two parents, nine children and an occasional grandmother. I learned (as second eldest) how to play the system to my advantage and how to use the sources of power within it. As a result, and a bit to my embarrassment, I am very good at playing systems and not getting caught. I am chameleon-like in my ability to change colours as the environment changes, and to adapt to what is needed for survival. I could well be recognised as a marketable personality – I am good at assessing what is needed and changing myself to conform. I am quite conformist by nature, and since conflict was largely avoided and suppressed in my family of origin, I learned quickly to be a quick peacemaker. These organisational signatures of mine mean I have to be very careful when working in organisations and when supervising individuals and teams in organisational settings to ensure that I keep my integrity and do not collude.

In supervision training I ask participants to answer these questions:

1.  What is your organisational DNA?
2.  Can you see traces of it from your family of origin?
3.  What do you have to attend to in order that aspects of your organisational DNA don't blind you to what is happening?
4.  How can you harness your own early experiences in systems to inform your work as supervisor?

## 3 The supervisor as buffer (the supervisee as toxic handler)

Building a space of containment and safety is crucial within organisational settings for supervision. Many who come for supervision come because they play 'buffer roles' within their organisations. They stand 'between' individuals and organisations, they soak up the emotions that cannot be expressed within organisations, they listen to and experience the shadow side of organisations (the opposite of what the organisation is supposed to do) and they work at the interface between individuals and organisations. Frost and Robinson (1999) coined the term 'toxic handler' to describe such people and outline some of the results of being a toxic handler – how over time toxicity builds up until it can poison the individual and the system. Supervision, in turn, can become a buffer between the supervisee and his/her organisation (Towler, 2005). Supervisors have to be careful they don't get pulled into playing the supervisory games that can result from this: 'You and me against the organisation' or 'Let's talk about how horrible the organisation is' and so forth.

## 4 Ethical issues in supervising in organisational settings

In our book on ethical maturity (Carroll and Shaw, 2013), we include a chapter entitled 'Organisations, Context, Ethics and Maturity' and review some of the major studies on 'conformity'. These include research by Zimbardo (2007) and Milgram (1974) to mention but two. All these studies reveal how contexts can overshadow and overcome individuals' character when individuals are faced with making moral decisions. The tendency, when in doubt, to observe and then copy what the majority of others are doing seems to be a fair indicator of what individuals do in organisational contexts. Of course, this leads to collusion, conformity, 'groupthink', and obedience to authority and to the group. This has, at times, disastrous consequences (e.g., the Enron Corporation). A 'collective madness' can take over (Harvey, 1996), resulting in a number of situations (Carroll and Shaw, 2013):

- Ordinary people can behave in harmful and immoral ways if the context supports it.
- Contexts can override individual characteristics at times.
- Novel situations, in particular, are powerful in getting us to do what we would not normally do.
- When people feel anonymous they can be induced to do what they would not usually do.
- It is easy for the human need to belong to slide into conformity, compliance and in-group behaviour.
- Sometimes there are *absolute* ethical codes that allow no degrees of freedom, and no room for extenuating circumstances or individual (ethical) adaptation – these codes drive behaviour towards cruelty because of their inflexibility.
- It is possible to take a stand against situational and contextual influences to act unethically.

These and the emergence of the shadow side of organisations in both work and supervision often create ethical dilemmas for supervisors and supervisees.

## 5 Letting off steam/detoxifying and looking after self in organisations

Those who work in organisations often deal with highly emotional issues. Some are issues of life and death, as in medical settings. Uniformed branches are often directly in the line of fire. Employees frequently have to deal with unreasonable deadlines and unmanageable people.

Supporting supervisees to look after themselves and remain aware of how working within organisations affects them holistically is a key role for supervisors. Being valued is a constant organisational theme that emerges in organisational supervision. Three areas (Towler, 2008) emerge: supervisees valuing and feeling valued by their supervisors; supervisors valuing and feeling valued by supervisees; and supervisors and supervisees valuing and feeling valued by the organisation.

## 6 Supervision despite the organisation

There are instances in which organisations are not prepared for supervision, do not really understand what it means and yet ask that it be introduced into the system in some way. At times supervision can be counter-cultural to the organisations within which it works. Supervision values such as taking time out, setting up reflective environments, creating dialogue, asking questions and being curious may not sit easily with some organisational cultures. There are many reasons why organisations introduce supervision: organisations don't want to be left behind and have heard that other organisations are providing supervision; they are obliged to provide it for auditing and quality control purposes and do so without much knowledge of what they are doing; individuals have requested and been granted supervision provision; or organisations researched the value of supervision and decided it adds value to who they are and what they do.

A good rule for supervisees is to know your organisation and the way it works, and the mists and fogs it creates that permeate everything. Lawton-Smith (2011: 160) presents one model that might be helpful to supervisors and presents four ways in which organisations can be framed:

- The structural frame: organisations as factories where efficiency and effectiveness are the norms.
- The human resources frame: organisations as families where the needs of employees are addressed. Participation is the order of the day.
- The political frame: organisations as jungles where power, authority and decision making are hierarchical.
- The symbolic frame: organisations as carnivals or temples where meaning making is important and rituals, values, vision and play may come to the fore.

These four are not exclusive and can be useful as a lens through which we make sense of what is happening or not happening. Lawton–Smith applies these frames to how supervisors might work:

- To ensure that supervision meets the needs of the sponsor knowing which frames are valued by the organisation.
- Each frame can create its own language and model for discussion in supervision.
- The frames can also be used as a focus for the seven eyes outlined by Hawkins and Shohet (2012).

I would add to this that knowing the frames valued by the organisation can help supervisors know whether or not they can be supported in integrating supervision into the organisation. In one organisation dedicated to drug and alcoholic rehabilitation, I was supervising two counsellors. The organisation frame they espoused was family, while in reality the political and structural frames were the frames in use. As a result the two counsellors were exhausted, burnt out and came to supervision to express their feelings of despair and abuse. Supervision was a vale of tears. I was doing supervision despite the organisation but knew I couldn't do that for long. With their permission I got back to the organisation to tell them that supervision was not fulfilling what they wanted (making them strong and effective in the jungle) but helping them find a new family where they could grieve.

## 7 Parallel processes in organisational supervision

The organisational issues played out on a day-to-day basis will be reflected in supervision as a parallel process. Supervisors expect this and are slow to diagnose what is happening in supervision as issues belonging to supervisees alone.

### Example

Jack arrives for supervision. He is an internal coach and manager. He talks at a great pace, incessantly rushing along in response to a crisis situation that needs immediate and urgent attention by his coachee. When stopped and slowed down he again re-iterates the time issue. Gently the supervisor gets him to stop, breathe and begin to get some distance from the urgency of the situation. Jack was doing to the supervisor what had been done to him. Neither Jack nor his coachee had had time to stop. The supervisor did that for them. They both realised that this was a strong characteristic of this organisation – there was no time to think, doing was all important.

Parallel process can play out in attendance, time keeping, boundary holding, the use of authority and power in the organisation, putting on a strong front, problem solving, short-term solutions, fear, hiding feelings and many other areas. Stopping to monitor what is happening to the supervisee and what is taking place between the supervisee and the supervisor can uncover parallel processes that are major sources of information.

### 8 Embedding supervision in an organisational culture

Supervision usually finds its place on the fringes of organisation's. Rarely is it invited into the heart of what is happening. Organisations are, however, increasingly asking if supervision could play a bigger role in helping create a culture of curiosity, questioning, reflection and dialogue. While space here does not allow thinking this through in detail, some strategic indices are set out below. Leaders are required to:

- actively support supervision by aligning it to the organisation's purpose and mission (they personally engage in it too);
- move beyond individuals and think of team and organisational supervision;
- start with external supervision consultants and supervision for top people;
- train internal supervisors and set up a cascade model of supervision;
- embed supervision in HR, performance management, appraisal systems, training and so on;
- adopt supervision as part of managerial style – reflective, curious, open and creative;
- build supervision into what we do with others (the client group); and
- engender collaborative learning.

(Hawkins, 2012a, has written a book entitled *Creating a Coaching Culture* which presents stages and steps of how to embed coaching in an organisational setting. His book, while not on supervision, contains many suggestions which are very applicable to building a supervisory culture in organisations. The steps above have been adapted from his book.)

## Supervising organisational practitioners

There are a number of tasks supervisors perform when supervising those who work within organisations (Carroll, 1999: 144):

- Be aware of and manage the administrative side of what supervisees do in the organisation (records, statistics, reports, invoices, arranging rooms etc.).
- Build working models of organisations to help understand some of the dynamics involved and how these affect supervisees.

- Evaluate how the work of the supervisee can be supported in the learning, growth and development of the wider organisation.
- Enable practitioners to work and live with the organisations of which they are a part, so that they can remain ethically mature and alert. (There are a number of natural tensions between supervision and organisational culture that need to be kept in mind. Gonzalez-Doupe (2001) outlines five of these: time out v. reduced time; reflect v. respond; individual pace v. crisis/urgent pace; share with others v. self-reliance; and private v. public displays of work.)
- Help supervisees control the flow of information and be able to manage the sheer volume and sensitivity of such information.
- Be aware of multiple relationships and roles and be clear when these fit well together in service of the task, and when different roles clash. 'Wrestling with relational boundaries' is a term used by Towler (2008: 39) to show the struggle needed here at times.
- Create and clarify contacts and ensure that all parties are clear about roles, responsibilities and boundaries. (In one organisation it was only towards the end of the first year that supervisors were contacted to submit their reports. This was first they had heard that supervisor reports would be required. The organisation assumed it would be part of the supervisory requirement without it being included in the written contract itself.)
- Ensure that clear boundaries are negotiated, set up and agreed by all. This can be particularly difficult around confidentiality in organisational settings.
- Watch for parallel process as it weaves its way through individuals and relationships into the supervisory room.

## Conclusion

Supervision can work with and for organisations in many ways. One of these is to make the organisational system the foreground in supervision and see practitioners' work through the lens of the system itself. The other is to see the individual as foreground and review the system through that lens. Both can work well and when alternated can work best: that is, effective supervisors can work with individuals in the system, and the system in the individual.

Our challenge today is to move organisational supervision from the periphery to the centre of organisations. It has much to offer. Stopping, stepping back, reflecting, being curious, creating reflective dialogue, learning from experience, transferring learning into actual practice – all these are the domain of supervision. What would it be like if our modern organisations took those characteristics of supervision on board?

# Eight

# Learning from Supervision

**Chapter summary**

This chapter picks up a theme central to supervision: the process of learning from experience. Practice/experience is at the heart of supervision but often ignored or relegated to second place when put alongside theory or influence from others. This chapter asks how practitioners can trust their own experiences and interpret it in ways that bring insights and change to their work. The experiential learning cycle is presented as the most effective model for practice learning, and four levels of learning are reviewed with examples to illustrate how learning from experience can be deepened. Transformational learning is the deepest form of experiential learning. Supervision is one method of such learning. The chapter ends with a short summary of how to engage with experiences to result in transformational learning.

One of the most difficult tasks in supervision is helping supervisees trust their own experience. What supervisees experience in their work is often the most valuable and useful information they have. They choose to ignore that rich source of help for all sorts of reasons. I did that too, and had to learn to trust my experience myself – it didn't come naturally to me. Quite the opposite. My upbringing and background did everything possible to ensure that I didn't trust my experience. I was taught that others, adults, knew better and their experiences were much wiser than mine. My priest, my church, my father, my teacher, my doctor, my lawyer were all fonts of wisdom where I should come to drink and I remember my father telling me that if I trusted them and their wisdom I would not go far wrong. When there were any differences between my experience (I find church boring) and their experience (church is good for you) they won. Their experience was to be preferred over mine, always. It was too risky to trust my experience. It might put me in conflict with traditional wisdom which had stood the test of time. Worse, it would lead me astray.

I don't think it's only the bygone days that exalted inherited wisdom over personal experience. Today it happens too. Evidence-based practice, manualised methods of treatment, clearly defined routines can so easily make us lack trust in what is happening to us, and ask us to put our faith in the manual or the theory.

We trust others rather than ourselves when it comes to experience with the result that we become passive automatons doing it by the book, rather than responsible individuals who trust relationships to guide them.

---

### Example

'So, what was happening to you as you sat with your client?' I asked Claire.

'I could feel his sadness,' she replied, her eyes already growing moist, 'it was as if he was swimming in a huge pond of sadness, unable to get out.'

'And you shared this with him?'

'No, of course not,' she quipped. 'He had talked about coming to terms with his son's suicide at the age of 19, and how involved he was in helping other families where there had been a suicide. He said he had dealt with it and was getting on with his life; but I didn't know how much of this sadness I was feeling was my own stuff. I know what it's like to lose a loved one.'

'And if you were to share this with him, if you were to trust your experience of what was actually happening in you and between you, what would you have said?' I asked.

When Claire had started talking about her client, the same sadness that had pervaded the counselling room filled the supervision room. I felt it, and I trusted it as it worked its way through my body. Someone was despairingly sad. My next task was to help Claire trust her experience of what had happened in that other room.

Later, as we looked back at what had happened, we both realised how Claire had not allowed herself to trust what was happening to her in the counselling room. She felt she had no permission to talk about the sadness, she felt she would make the client very uncomfortable if she brought it up, and it was not why he had come for counselling. Just as her client had argued himself out of grieving, so Claire had argued herself out of what was really happening to her, to her client and in their relationship. It would have been so easy for all of us to miss what was most important.

---

De Haan (2012: 84) uses a thoughtful phrase, *l'esprit d'escalier*, which is indirectly about learning from our experience. The term itself means the 'spirit of the staircase' and refers to the moment we have begun walking down the staircase after a meeting or a conversation. It is that moment when we know what we *should* have done, or *should* have said, in the meeting. On the staircase we get in touch with what was really happening to us back then. Of course, it is too late then to do much about it.

Supervision is a kind of *l'esprit d'escalier* experience. We remember what was happening to us, we recall what we thought and felt, we get in touch with what we *should* have said or done, we capture our experiences and wish we had trusted them at the time and used them more effectively. However, it's not too late. De Haan puts it well: 'A new realisation about a relationship or a conversation is, therefore, by definition, a new chapter in that relationship or conversation' (2012: 86). Supervision is the forum where we learn how to trust our experience so that the walk down the staircase can become one of congruence and satisfaction rather than regret.

Throughout this book we have presented 'practice' as the central focus of supervision. It is what makes supervision supervision. We bring our practice to another, the supervisor, formally or informally, individually or in groups, and we hope that supervision will help us learn from studying that practice. In supervision we chew the cud of our own experience, learning from that 'chewing' and transferring that learning back into our work, short-term and long-term. Through reflective dialogues our practice is held up to the light. *Learning from experience* through reflection is what supervision offers the practitioner.

## Leonardo, supervisor of the Middle Ages

The patron saint of *learning from experience* is undoubtedly Leonardo da Vinci. I consider him a great supervisor. He has all the traits of a man who facilitates learning. Curious himself, he creates curiosity in others. He was remarkable in that he questioned the accepted wisdom of his day when it was thought that knowledge was certain. He lauded experience, knowledge through the senses, curiosity, artistry and experiments as excellent ways of knowing. Above all, he saw experience as the mistress of all learning: 'My works are the issue of simple and plain experience which is the true mistress' (Gelb, 1998: 78).

Leonardo would suggest his students cultivate perception and attention. He would send them to paint a fish in a pond. When they returned he would often look at their painting and then he would suggest they go and 'look again … and again … and again'. There was always more to be seen and noticed. Very gradually his students learned to perceive more carefully and became experts in noticing, giving attention to, listening intently, gazing deeply and not taking anything for granted. Trust your experience, it never errs, was Leonardo's advice to them. He was wise enough to know we all can err in our interpretation of our experiences; but he was a strong believer in starting with experience as the first port on the learning journey.

'The greatest deception men suffer is from their own opinions.' Leonardo constantly questioned his own conclusions, theories, beliefs and assumptions and suggested others do the same. While experience was the main teacher of knowledge and wisdom, Leonardo recognised that we could also learn from the experiences of others. He called this 'learning by proxy'. Furthermore, he had a vast library and consulted with the finest minds of his day. He was not solely reliant on his own interpretation of his own experiences; learning from mistakes was also high on his agenda of learning. He was willing to try and fail as a process of learning. And fail he did, many times. Working from his principles that 'obstacles do not bend me', his experience of failure was itself a springboard for new learning. He was a true supervisor.

## Stay with your experience

Just as Leonardo would have advised his students to stay with their experiences, so supervisors work with supervisees in the same manner.

### Example

Alex works as a trainee counsellor in a youth agency. It is his first placement and he is excited about the prospects of working with real clients. But his first year training as counsellor doesn't prepare him well for his very first client, who upsets and disturbs him. Sent by his teacher because of his disturbing behaviour in the classroom, 16-year-old Patrick is sullen and resentful. When he does talk he swears a lot and his attitudes are highly racist and sexist. Alex feels his anger rising when Patrick talks about the 'Pakis' in his class as if they were second-class citizens, and a 'queer' that he and some of his chums beat up. There is such a wide gulf between everything Alex believes in and what Patrick thinks, that already Alex is wondering if he should ask for Patrick to have a different counsellor who might be more attuned to his ways of thinking. He is unsure what to do about the bad language and the prejudices he has just experienced. Should he point this out to Patrick, should he tolerate it for now or should he accept that this is the way it is for some people and get on with it? He lets it pass in the first session.

He is clearly shaken when he has his first supervision session with Jenny, who listens to him recount the details of the first meeting with Patrick and hears his dismay about the wide disparity in their value systems.

Jenny is very understanding and points out to Alex that this is his first experience as a counsellor with a client a) who doesn't want to be in counselling; b) who has values very different from Alex's; and c) who generates strong emotions in Alex. Alex has no prior pool of wisdom to call upon to guide him just yet on what to do when faced with such issues. She asks him to stay with his experiences of what has just happened. At the end of the session Alex has outlined some of this learning/questions from his experience with Patrick:

*(Continued)*

*(Continued)*

- Many clients come for counselling resentfully and uncooperatively. They haven't committed themselves yet to counselling.
- Individuals have all sorts of attitudes and beliefs that will be in stark contrast to those of counsellors.
- The first meeting is the beginning of a journey.
- Sometimes people put you on trial in a first session to see how well you accept them (dirty laundry syndrome).
- Can he make sense of Patrick's behaviour from the contexts in which he lives and goes to school?
- Can Alex begin to create shared and acceptable boundaries in the counselling room?
- He will need to decide what is acceptable and what is not in working with Patrick.
- What do you do when you have no prior experience to call on?

Alex's very first session is a master class in learning from the experience he has just had: learning about himself, about others, about relationships, about boundaries, working out what is negotiable and what is non-negotiable. Jenny gives him no theory or framework to make sense of his experience – rather she simply asks him to stay with it and find explanations from within the experience itself. Later she will share with him some of her own work counselling clients with very different values than her own; she will point him to reading that looks at how to work with clients who come with different value sets and cultural backgrounds. For now, she wants him to let his experience be his teacher.

## Whose experience is it?

Learning from experience is our most frequent and in-built human form of learning. All animals, humans included, learn in the first instance from their experiences. Life teaches as we live and experience life. For many animals their own experience and watching others are the only sources of their learning.

Our cat is a good example of learning from experience. He has learned not to enter the garden three doors down; there is a large black dog there which is not partial to cats entering his territory. The experience of travelling through that garden has taught our cat well. He either avoids the garden or, if in mischievous mood, will sit on the fence out of reach of danger, teasing the poor dog below. He has learned that too. Similarly, events occur and we humans learn from them automatically, store the learning and then access it when we need a way forward in a similar situation. Our forefathers had to learn that way; they had no collective wisdom or books they could consult to access the previous learnings of those who went before them. Often they learned through tragedy. Not knowing that a particular foodstuff is poisonous resulted in death for one, and, hopefully, learning for another. New information was now available for the following generation as learning from experience was handed down in oral tradition. Gradually that learning found its way into language, books, classrooms and training.

Many people don't trust their own experience and prefer to trust the experience of others. Survival may depend on trusting the experiences of others at the beginning of life. Our caretakers guide our faltering steps based on their experience, which becomes the guide for our decisions in the early part of life. We are, at that stage of life, followers. As we move through life we begin to question the wisdom we have inherited and often begin to trust our own experience as a more reliable guide. The more we know, the more we learn to trust ourselves and our own decisions. There is still a tendency to trust the experience of others above our own, especially when we are in new situations – we trust experts and those who have more knowledge.

## The first learning from experience can be traumatic

A child puts his hand on a hot stove and learns quickly and painfully not to do that again. We all look back at the events of our lives and how experience taught us so much. We remember our early days at work with some embarrassment about what we did as novices. No doubt Alex will recount his own experiences with Patrick later in life – maybe even as a supervisor supporting another novice counsellor working with young people. Once learned, these lessons are filed away in memory to be called upon when needed. This is both good and bad. While prior experience and learning can guide us about what to do in new situations, it can also lock us into ways of acting that can easily become mindless. Learning from prior experiences can block our learning from what is happening to us just now; we rigidly read the new experience through the filed-away learning rather than be alert to our present experience.

### Example

Mabel had great difficulties learning that feedback was helpful to her in supervision. She came from a shame-based family system where she was put down if there was any hint of her 'getting beyond herself'. Praise was scarce and criticism frequent. Negative feedback still propelled Mabel back into that place of shame and embarrassment. When her supervisor gave

*(Continued)*

*(Continued)*

her some feedback on her tendency to move into rescuing mode, Mabel was mortified. It was as if she had been 'found out' for a charlatan and publicly denounced. Her early learning was a complete hindrance. She had now to learn how to listen to feedback with an open mind and harness it for the next stage of her learning. It was quite a journey as she tried to unlearn some lessons from the past that were blocking her way forward.

## Experience calls on experience to guide it

Like Mabel, our present experiences call on our past experiences to be their guides. We look on what is happening to us in the present for echoes of the past, and then we connect the two. Memory helps us make sense of the present through the past. We couldn't get by otherwise. Seeing a red light automatically makes us put a foot on the brake. Past experience (brake when you come to a red traffic light) impacts the meaning of present perception (red light ahead) and moves us into action (brake). So much of our lives are lived in this 'automatic' manner. We create and learn habits as shortcuts to knowing what to do in everyday situations. These habits, or automatic ways of working, are both the brain's way of conserving energy – we don't have to find a new solution to each daily challenge – and our fast-track way of decision making.

Our strategy in problem solving, in explaining what has happened, and in meeting new people or situations, is to access our memories. Memories store our stories of past events and are a reservoir of our wisdom. It makes sense that we first go there to make decisions and solve problems we face. It means we don't always stay with the present but come from the past into the present with our wealth of already existing knowledge, information, skills and experiences. New information is fitted to old information by the brain; if that doesn't work, then we are faced with a new situation that calls for a new solution – which, when found, is then placed in memory for future recall.

Valuable as this is, it means we approach today and tomorrow with the templates of yesterday, and use yesterday's answers to solve tomorrow's problems. It also means we don't always trust our own experience, especially when it seems to contradict memory.

## Example

Julian was a very committed person-centred consultant. His person-centred theories and skills were part of himself, and he used them very effectively. In one instance he found his approach was not working. In supervision he asked his supervisor to monitor with him what he was doing wrong. If he wasn't providing the 'core conditions' he had been taught and he believed in, then it wouldn't work. Very slowly and gently, he and his supervisor worked towards the conclusion that in this instance person-centred approaches were not the most effective. How could this experience help him find another way of working with this particular client?

Memory versus experience. His experience was telling Julian rather strongly that his normal method of engaging with clients was not working; his memory was telling him it should work. He trusted his memory. His supervisor's job was to help him stay with his present experiences and allow those experiences to teach him through the dissonance they were causing.

The problem with accessing memory is that often we miss the new in the present, or the *new in the now*. Memory and experience conflict at times.

There are learning drawbacks to habits and automaticity.

## Example

Carmel listened carefully to her client, Anita. Anita's husband had decided to take four months off 'to find himself' and was heading for an ashram in India. He claimed there was no one else involved and that this was not about the relationship between him and Anita, but about his need to discover who he was. It wasn't the first time Carmel had heard those words in her years of couples' counselling. She knew the meaning. 'Heading off to find yourself' was a male code for another partner on the scene. She smiled inwardly, knowingly. How could she help Anita deal with this, and not be so easily duped by the pretence of her husband 'finding himself'?

Carmel's conclusion, based on past experience of working with couples, may be true. But it may not be. She has moved from a few instances to a general application. She has drawn a conclusion based on beliefs she has developed from past experience. Carmel's task is to stay with her client and what she is saying, rather than move too quickly into her own memory to resolve the issue. There has been helpful research done on how similar issues can result in doctors making medical decisions on behalf of their patients and moving to false conclusions by not trusting their own experience and staying in the present with their clients (Groopman, 2007).

When there is no prior experience to guide us, then most of us watch what others are doing and do the same ourselves.

In new situations we have no prior experience to call on to guide us. We may still try to make connections to the past, and attempt to squeeze present experience into past explanations, despite the poor fit. Staying with the present can sometimes help us acknowledge the past without letting it control us.

## Example

Gerald felt strongly about abortion and was very much on the 'pro-life' side of the argument. He would refer someone who wanted an abortion rather than work with the person himself. He realised he was not the best counsellor to work with particular individuals at times. His world was torn apart when his 19-year-old daughter was date-raped at a party. This traumatic experience for him didn't fit neatly into the right/wrong categories that he had used effectively in the past. He was very supportive of her decision to use the morning-after pill and realised that he had changed some of the ways in which he thinks.

## The many meanings of experience

Raymond Queneau wrote a book in 1947 which was translated from French into English as *Exercises in Style*. It recounts on the first page a two–paragraph vignette that is pointless and ordinary; he then proceeds to tell the same story in 124 different ways, changing the language, the style of writing and the meaning of the event. The point Queneau is making is that any event, any happening, can be 'proliferated almost to infinity' (1998: 4): there are innumerable ways of telling it depending on who is telling it, their point of view, what they notice and don't notice, what they choose to pay attention to, and from which perspectives they opt to make sense of the event. An event that has no deep significance can be interpreted in a multitude of ways depending on a number of factors: what you saw and heard, what you allowed yourself to see and hear, the background you come from, how you have learned to make sense of things in the past.

Experiences, events, happenings in life have a wonderful ability to be viewed and interpreted in so many different ways. We all know the story of the six blind men and the elephant, each explaining the elephant depending on which part of the elephant they were in contact with. This has been called 'the Rashomon effect', after an oriental film by the same name in which a crime is witnessed by four individuals who recount it in four substantially different and contradictory ways. The Rashomon effect testifies to the individuality of perception and our idiosyncratic interpretation of reality.

What does this say about experience?

- There are lots of ways of interpreting experiences and lots of ways of interpreting the same experience, even by the same person.
- This is not a matter of right or wrong, true or false, but ways of perceiving.

- *How* you perceive is as important as *what* you perceive, but we do not often review our meaning-making perspectives (how we perceive).
- How we perceive depends on a number of factors; some present, such as our emotional state; some past, what we have been taught to notice etc.

Supervision is a forum where we retell the stories and events of our practice and begin the journey of making sense of them. We tell our supervisory story from within our own understanding and then we try to get outside our own understanding to look at other ways of interpreting that event. You could think of supervision as a series of lenses through which you look, with zoom-in and zoom-out lenses, and wide- and narrow-angle lenses. We tell the story, then we retell it from other angles and perspectives and points of view and styles. In the retelling we understand more and more, and we go back to our work wiser, with more insight, with better understanding. Though Queneau never uses the term, his book is about different ways of making meaning, which is also what supervision does.

Supervision is the forum par excellence to learn from practice. It is a reflective-practitioner's oasis. In supervision, practice is the teacher, reflection is the method of learning, and supervisors facilitate that process.

## Experiential learning

Reflection fits within the larger picture of experiential learning (Kolb, 1984). Marsick and Maltbia (2009) have used the ORID model – Objective, Reflective, Interpretative and Decisive Data – as a way of illustrating how experiential learning works. I have added a further section to this model, an integrative arm. Table 8.1 outlines the process under a number of headings.

Experiential learning is the engagement between the outer world of the environment and the inner world of the person. The senses pick up data that is processed by the brain, which then makes sense of it. Experience is the royal road to wisdom.

TABLE 8.1   *The ORID model of experiential learning (Marsick and Maltbia, 2009)*

| ELC | Process | Focus | Method |
|-----|---------|-------|--------|
| *Action* | Objective | What happened? What is happening? | Observe facts, events. Notice, give attention. |
| *Reflection* | Reflective | What am I feeling? What is my reaction? | Monitor and articulate reactions. |
| *Reflection* | Interpretative | What does it mean? | Utilise critical thinking. |
| *Learning* | Integrative | What have I learned? | Assimilate into new learning. |
| *Application* | Decisive | What do I do? | Implement decisions. |

Learning is the process whereby knowledge is created through transformation of experience (Kolb, 1984: 38):

- *Action* (I engage with my client and he reacts to my challenge).
- *Learning* through reflection (I realise I moved too fast in challenging him before he was ready and before the relationship was strong enough to carry the challenge).
- *Transfer* (I go at his pace rather than mine and continue to build up trust and rapport between us).

Experience of itself is not a teacher; experience has to be worked on and processed in order to mine out its learning for us and for others.

## Learning from experience can cause disequilibrium

Learning often takes place most effectively when there is a gap between what we know and what we are experiencing. When our experiences do not fit neatly into the explanations we already have (as in the example of Gerald above), then we are left in some sort of dissonance – a place of uncertainty. It needs resolution. We can either squeeze the new experience into the old explanation or allow the new experience to challenge the old explanation. Staying with disequilibrium is an important element in learning from experience, but it does require some degree of psychological safety to stay with the discomfort.

## Experience sometimes fools us

Experience doesn't lie, but it can fool us if we interpret it wrongly. We make causal links from our experiences that become embedded in our thinking. To quote da Vinci again: 'Experience never errs; it is only your judgement that errs in promising itself results as are not caused by your experiments' (Gelb, 1998: 79).

It worked once, it should work again, is the thinking here. This process easily becomes a prison that confines us. Experiences always happen in contexts and make sense in contexts; change the context and everything changes. 'We have always done it this way' is not a very helpful statement when we are trying to learn from experiences. It often means we thoughtlessly adopt the same actions even when they no longer fulfil the purposes they were first designed for. We make false conclusions from experience and then let these conclusions become general principles that guide us. Experience and reflection together sometimes release us from getting stuck in past experience while using it to make sense of what is happening in the present (see Chapter 9 on reflection).

## Transformational learning from experience

Learning from experience can transform our lives and dramatically change our practice – if we allow it to.

### Example

Many years ago I worked for a year with a young woman who suffered from an eating disorder. At that time little was known about eating disorders, their origins and how to work with them. I asked a counselling psychologist to supervise my work because of her knowledge in this area. I was leaving the agency in which I worked and the town I lived in. I told the young woman I would be leaving but that we had two months before I did and time to work through to an ending or a referral should she desire it. I still see her reaction. She was traumatised by what I said and walked out, never to return. My first defensive reaction was to claim that I had done everything in a proper manner – given her plenty of time to prepare for the ending, arrange for a suitable referral if needed, say goodbye in a clear and clean manner. In supervision I realised how much I had underestimated how important I was to her and how insensitively I had told her of my departure. For me this was a transformational moment in supervision. It put me in touch with my assumptions about endings, the importance of relationships and the need to see events from other perspectives.

Holding up our experience to the light helps us look at:

- who we are in the work we do – the person, the professional and the person in the professional;
- how we relate, engage and use power in relationships;
- our understanding of and our assumptions about the clients who come to see us; and
- our sensitivity to contexts and how they impact on what we do.

There are a number of learning levels in supervision, from zero learning to transformational learning. How can supervision be harnessed to be a vehicle for transformational learning?

We will look at four levels of learning from experience, using the work of Scharmer (2007) and Carroll (2011):

- *Single-loop learning:* recycling (downloading: I-in-me learning).
- *Double-loop learning:* curiosity and open mind (I-in-it learning).

- *Triple-loop learning:* from within the system (I-in-you) learning.
- *Transformational learning:* courage to change perception ( I-in-now learning).

Learning from experience can take place at the level of knowledge/skills, or an intellectual level where understanding is changed, at an emotional level where relationships and systems are reconfigured, or at a transformational level which changes perception and how we view life and reality (Carroll, 2011).

## 1 Single-loop learning

Single-loop learning can be thought of as recycling or downloading learning: closed mind, closed heart, closed will.

Downloading is a form of learning where old learning is projected onto new experiences. Existing models and frameworks are sifted and stretched to make sense of and accommodate new learning. Listening, seeing and hearing take place from within an existing story; the new is made to fit the old. Originating in the need for security, perception is limited, new insight is restricted and learning is at a minimum.

Also called *I-in-me* learning (Scharmer, 2007), experiences are not used to learn anew but recycled within the existing 'me'.

### Example

Hussein is angry when he comes for supervision. He is a counsellor in a large GP surgery in a deprived area of a large town. He works with disadvantaged clients and a constant frustration for him is their helplessness. He brings yet another woman to supervision who is the victim of domestic violence. This is the third time she has come to him, each time promising to leave the abusing husband and never doing it. 'What's the point of counselling?' he asks despairingly. 'It's not working! Why can't these women understand that nothing is going to change till they take charge and leave?' Bernard listens carefully and acknowledges the anger and frustration in Hussein's work. He asks Hussein to look at some of assumptions underpinning his thinking. Hussein elaborates his understanding of what is happening. Some men are violent by nature when they don't get what they want; they abuse their partners because they are weaker; nothing will change till the partner leaves, and even then it won't make much difference. His recent client confirms all of the above.

This type of learning is based on the past rather than the experience of the present. It is a change in information or an increase in information that stays at the level of information. I may learn some new facts or my experience may validate what I already knew:

> This is the realm of 'knowledge and skills', so-called, well known to all who are exposed to a largely bureaucratic approach to questions of truth and its transmission, i.e. training or education. What is being transmitted here is the knowledge of fact and methods. The teacher functions as an expert of discipline-specific knowledge and as a guarantor of its currency. The personal attributes of neither the teacher nor the student come into this. As we said earlier, no-one is necessarily changed as a person by this process of learning. (Prall, 2010, personal communication)

Hussein will continue to see and review his domestic violence clients in the same light and from the same theory. The script is almost definitive and the outcomes pretty certain. Hussein will download his next experience to fit the categories already in existence.

## 2 Double-loop learning

Double-loop learning can be thought of as open-minded learning: curiosity and distance.

This level of learning from experience has been called *I-in-it* learning (Scharmer, 2007). Moving away from certainty and recycling (and me), experience is now viewed from a distance and a dialogue initiated with that experience. A sense of interest, wonder, debate enters the scene. Other values, other opinions and other perspectives are viewed. This may cause some cognitive dissonance or discomfort as new thinking contrasts with old thinking. This form of learning from experience can often stay at a purely intellectual level.

### Example

Hussein listens carefully to Bernard, his supervisor, as he asks him to move into the shoes of the abused women he works with. With difficulty at first, he slowly begins to see their lives and partners from their viewpoint. He hears himself say, 'It so difficult to be a woman on your own with children without support. I know it may seem stupid to you but a violent man is better than no man. And the violence is not all the time. When things are good they are good.' Bernard goes further and asks him to put himself in the minds of men who are violent towards their partners. This is even more difficult for Hussein. Again, slowly, he makes the link. He realises he is not condoning their violence, or their wives' collusion with the violence, but allowing himself to stay in and make sense of behaviour in a particular context.

Double-loop learning stays in the present (rather than the past) and takes the very experiences that are happening as *information under inquiry*. By trying to see it from other perspectives supervisees allow themselves to learn how to work with meaning-making, rather than just deal with the content of problems. Double-loop learning moves from problem solving to dealing with meaning-making perspectives.

## 3 Triple-loop learning

Triple-loop learning can be thought of as viewing experience through relationships and systems with an open heart.

This third stance is *I-in-you* learning. We listen to ourselves reflectively and listen to others empathetically and with compassion (the I-in-you). We move from open mind and an intellectual curiosity to emotional connection with an open heart as well as an open mind. Can I begin to see it from other perspectives, and engage with those perspectives emotionally? This is the bridge to new learning. I take risks. I interrupt my own stories. I leave my comfort zone. I feel unsafe. I can now reflect on this: I have the ability to allow you, your thinking, your ideas and your values to be an *open* subject for me.

In triple-loop learning we also face ourselves and our shortcomings as learners from experience. We ask key questions:

What am I denying to myself?
What am I pretending not to know?
What am I hiding?
What feedback am I not giving to me?
What conversation with myself am I avoiding?
What I am colluding with myself over?
What feelings am I not expressing?

This type of change could be called reformation. We reform *who* we are in the light of experience reflected upon with a trusted other.

### Example

Hussein tries to connect emotionally with his client. He imagines being in the room with her, seeing how she sees, and supporting her to think, feel and see differently. He is working on her self-image, her self-esteem and her self-worth. He respects who she is and what she tries desperately to be. Slowly she finds her voice. Hussein is very conscious that his way of engaging and his use of power will not contribute to making his client feel hopeless and helpless. He is aware that his previous anger towards her, and his emerging need to guide her, are both subtle forms of abuse. He stays with respecting what she is trying to do and be.

## 4 Transformational learning

Transformational learning is to do with courage (open–will learning).

This fourth stance is *I-in-now* learning, learning that focuses on what is happening or has happened, and staying in the present to make meaning of it: 'In the field beyond right and wrong, I will meet you there' (Rumi, the Persian poet).

Transformational learning is an ancient concept that looks at radical change coming from within. The Greek word *Metanoia* (change of heart) captures it well. With transformational learning comes a radical shift in perception which results in a fundamentally different way of acting. All is seen differently: oneself, others, relationships.

In this type of learning we will stop talking and listen more. We will be open. We will be prepared to see the prejudices, mind sets and mental maps that keep us where we are. We will see the thinking behind our thinking, the learning behind our learning. We will try to see the bigger picture. We will reflect, and reflect more, and then even more. And we will be courageous enough to go where the experience is taking us. We will see ourselves as part of the problem and part of the solution. We will let go of pet theories and well-worn dictates.

Mezirow and associates (2000) talk about the processes needed to begin the journey towards transformational learning. Usually a disorientation event happens which unbalances or throws us into some form of dissonance. The theory I worked from no longer works for me. From this disorienting event comes a process of self-examination which uncovers the unhelpful assumptions underpinning our stances.

Abrashoff puts it well: 'When I could not get the results I wanted, I swallowed my temper and turned inwards to see if I was part of the problem … I discovered that 90 per cent of the time, I was at least as much a part of the problem as my people were' (2002: 33).

### Example

Hussein has changed his way of thinking. He has let go of his feelings of anger and frustration in considering the helpless cycle of domestic violence. He has let go of his own helplessness and guilt about not being able to help more. He has faced up to the limitations of what he can do in one small part of a violent system which is handed on from generation to generation. He has realised that his way of thinking has been a part of the problem. He is no longer afraid for himself or for the outcome. His client catches something in his attitude and suddenly is stronger.

### Four approaches

The four types of learning above can be connected to four approaches to supervision – from both supervisee and supervisor perspectives:

- I have the meaning and the answers *already* in my past, and in my memory; I only need to access memory to find the solution.
- I am allowing myself to engage with other ways of thinking and talking about what this might mean. I look at other meanings and other solutions.
- I am open, emotionally, to what is happening now in the wider system and in the relationship. I trust new happenings will occur.
- I am prepared to look at how I make sense of my experience and uncover some of the assumptions that underpin that process. I want to try to see differently in order to make meaning differently.

## Steps towards learning from experience

The following is a seven-step process by which learning from experience can take place:

1.  *Moving into 'learning from experience' mode*

    o  Being curious (rather than evaluative).
    o  Being vulnerable (open to my own limitations).
    o  Indifferent to the outcome (let's go where it takes us).
    o  Courage – what is the price I may have to pay (loyalties)?
    o  Honesty – can I stay with the experience?

2.  *Creating emotional and psychological safety*

    o  Am I safe to begin looking at my experience?
    o  What do I need to review in the context in which I am to ensure my safety?
    o  Can I listen to the diverse and challenging voices around me?
    o  Can I create safe environments for others to learn from their experiences?
    o  Staying with feelings and thoughts.

3.  *What is happening to me emotionally?*

    o  What disjunctures/dissonances or disorientations am I facing?
    o  Where are the contradictions?

4.  *Making meaning of experiences*

    o  Noticing and attending to aspects of my experience.
    o  Considering various meanings.
    o  Discussing meaning and getting information.

5.  *Choosing a meaning for myself*

    o  Can I choose the best meaning for me from the various options?
    o  How can I 'own' my own meaning?
    o  How can I share the meaning I have made?

6.  *Integrating that meaning into my life*

    o  What steps do I need to take to live my new meaning?
    o  Who do I need to help me?

7.  *Understanding my way of making meaning from my experiences*

    o  What are my prisons?
    o  What are my strengths?
    o  Do I understand my LEDNA (learning from experience DNA)?

## Conclusion

Many of us look towards the experiences of others to guide us in deciding what we do. When uncertain about how to act we tend to look at how others act and comply. It's so easy for us to give up our power of managing and directing our own lives and allow others to do that for us. Books, theories, frameworks and models contain and explain how others see and communicate *their* experiences. This is valuable information and worth accessing. It is always good to know how others view life and make their decisions. But it is not enough. While the experiences of others may well connect to my experiences and may indeed provide explanations of what happens to me, they also may not. Starting with them often results in my imposing them on other contexts and on other people.

In this chapter we have looked at how supervisors can support and help supervisees trust and use their own experience as their primary teacher. It entails 'getting out of the way' at times and allowing supervisees to make sense of their experience in their own ways rather than impose pre-existing meanings and methods on them. This is so easily done when we are already committed to a theory, a way of life, a religion or a wisdom tradition. We see from within these, rather than from what is happening, and can so easily impose their meaning on events rather than let the events speak for themselves. Theory can be made more important than either experience or people. We put on the spectacles of meaning offered and unthinkingly allow them to direct our lives and our thinking.

Supervision helps supervisees take responsibility for the experiences that happen to them in their work and supports them as they make sense of that experience. Oscar Wilde was partially right when he said that 'Experience is the name everyone gives to their mistakes'. In supervision experience can also be our best teacher.

# Nine

# Reflection and Critical Reflection in Supervision

**Chapter summary**
This chapter and the next focus on the theme of reflection in supervision. Reflection is presented as the learning methodology of supervision so this chapter asks what it is and how it takes place. It then proceeds to outline eight steps in the reflective process. Critical reflection and critical self-reflection make up the final section of the chapter, where hunting down and changing assumptions are seen as central to reflection in supervision.

Reflection is the life-blood of supervision; it is the process par excellence through which we learn. We talk about reflective practice as being the highest form of engagement in our work. Working without reflection ends up as mindlessness: the routine process of producing the same things over and over again without thought. Reflection on its own can so easily become self-indulgent navel-gazing that leads nowhere. That can become dangerous, as Thompson and Thompson point out: 'It is dangerous to allow our practice to be based on habit, routine, mindless following of procedures, simply copying what others do' (2008: x).

Together reflection and practice create a wonderful team called *praxis*, which is the essence of supervision. Other animals live mindless lives driven by instincts and lacking the ability to reflect on why they do what they do. We are the only animals that have learned to reflect. My attempts to teach our cat Cami the rudiments of reflection end in frustration for me and cat-alepsy for him. He has no ability to make sense of his life or ascribe meaning to why he does certain things. Why kill little birds when he is well fed? The simple fact is he *cannot* change his behaviour through a process of reflection. Cami has no ability to hold his life up to the light and ponder its meaning. He cannot access his 'inner kitten' and work on his self-awareness. The reason he cannot reflect is because he has a very small prefrontal cortex – the part of his brain from which these abilities emerge. Unlike humans who have much larger frontal cortices (human brains), Cami is condemned to living the unreflective life, criticised by Socrates as 'not worth living'. The prefrontal cortex is also known as the human or executive brain, and seems to be central to reflection.

Reflection is our human way of pondering on experience and making sense of it. Reflection is the process we use to *make meaning*. Reflection stands between the input of information or experience and the output of making sense of that information or experience. Meaning doesn't exist on its own – humans create it and compose it. We often tell stories as a way of making sense of our experience. Narratives capture the meaning of events for us and others. Reflection is the bridge between information and wisdom; more, it's the process that turns information and knowledge into wisdom. Through reflection and critical thinking the events of our lives can make sense for us. We can choose from different meanings rather than entertain meanings that are chosen for us by others. We can also prudently outsource our meaning-making abilities to others and allow them to 'make sense' of our lives and behaviours for us.

## Example

Gerald is really curious about what has happened in his work with Josh. Josh just stopped coming to counselling despite the fact that he had said several times he was finding it helpful. It was difficult to make sense of – there was no obvious reason for his unexplained absence, and despite several attempts to contact him there was still no word from Josh. In supervision Gerald wondered out loud if he had done something he was unaware of that had disappointed, hurt or upset Josh. His supervisor is equally puzzled, and together they look at a range of possible explanations to make sense of this unexpected behaviour.

Gerald and his supervisor are recounting various stories as possible explanations for a notable incident in Gerald's work.

Supervision is a story-telling methodology for learning, a process of narrative inquiry (see Chapter 11 where we connect the brain and storytelling). How we construct and tell those stories is as important as the content of the stories themselves. Our ways of making meaning can be very narrow and rigid. Some individuals have only one way of making meaning; for example, interpreting everything that happens to them through a victim stance (Gerald could easily lock into the fact that he is a newly qualified counsellor and wasn't experienced enough as his only explanation). Others have diverse and multiple ways of making sense of events in their lives; for example, they interpret fluidly and creatively, entertaining possibilities without committing prematurely to them. In the example of Gerald's supervision above, he might have been helped to consider several different possible explanations for why Josh had not returned for counselling: he was ill, he had got what he needed from the sessions he had attended, he was finding the counselling too painful, too difficult and so on.

Helping strategies often involve us in supporting others to find different or new meanings to the events in their lives. Counselling and other talking therapies are ways of changing the meaning of events. What has previously been interpreted as tragedy can be re-interpreted and given new meaning. For example, the traumatic experience of divorce can shift from tragedy to opportunity, as the client sees a new start or a new way of appreciating life. Coaching, too, helps coachees adopt new perspectives on who they are and what they do. Supervision is particularly strong on helping supervisees look again at their work and see it from other perspectives. It's a process of looking at what we do with *super-vision*: with new eyes, new perceptions, new visions we see things differently. Reflection is dependent on *perception* and *attention*. Supervision is about a new way of looking, a *super* way of *visioning*. With new visions come new perspectives and new meanings. We notice new things. Supervision is always about the quality of awareness. With reflection comes meaning at different levels. If I step outside my comfort zone and take an open stance, without judgement or shame, without blame or assumption, and I remain open and indifferent to the outcome, what will I allow myself to think and reflect upon? Can I look beyond, beside, beneath, above, below, against, for? What will happen if I look at myself, my client, our relationship, the organisation in other and different ways?

Supervision is about paying attention to our practice. We stop doing; we pull back from our work; we start thinking/reflecting. We move from subject, where we are identified with or attached to our work, to object, where we can take a meaning-making position outside of ourselves. We move from reflection-in-action to reflection-on-action to reflection-for-action. Supervision is a strategic withdrawal to meditate, contemplate and think about our work. In the attention *to*, and the reflection *on*, we learn how to do our work better. Supervision is a 'respectful interruption' of our work to set up reflective dialogues through which we learn from that very work: we sit at the feet of our own experience; we allow our work to become our teacher (Zachary, 2000). The medium we do this through is reflection – reflection becomes the method through which we learn. Reflection is the discipline of wondering … what if?

Supervision is the relationship where we weave our sense of meaning making with someone else's sense of meaning making and together we make the best sense possible of what we are considering. Reflection is one of those words that is hard to pin down and communicate exactly what we are talking about. *We* know what *we* mean by reflection but find it hard to explain to someone else. For those interested in entering that discussion, see Moon (1999). My intention here is to skip through the distinctions and the theories and move towards a theory of *usefulness* for reflection in supervision.

## The process called reflection

There are a number of steps involved in the process of reflection:

1.  Stepping outside ourselves
2.  Adopting a curious and compassionate stance
3.  Focusing, noticing, noting
4.  Using different reflective lenses
5.  Considering different meanings
6.  Opting for the best meaning
7.  Building that meaning into practice
8.  Reviewing the process (meta-reflection)

Few people go through this process in a logical format – reflection for most of us just happens. But slowing down the process and taking reflection apart can help us review our own methods of reflection. This eight-step process is outlined below.

### 1 Stepping outside ourselves

Getting distance is a requirement of reflection. Being caught up in events, emotions, experiences can hamper reflection. Even reflection–in–action needs some internal distancing in order to make sense of what is happening. *Self-distancing* is a term that has been used to describe this process. *Self-immersion* is the opposite – where we are so involved or emotionally caught up with something that we cannot separate and view it from outside (Kross and Ayduk, 2011).

### Example

Michelle is finding it difficult to be objective in supervision. She failed her counselling accreditation viva despite the fact that she and her supervisor had prepared for it well, her supervisor even giving her a mock viva. Noreen had carefully pointed out some of the weak areas of Michelle's work and had suggested taking another year before putting herself up for the accreditation dialogue. Michelle thought she was ready for it. Now she is 'gutted' by the result, and very angry. She feels many aspects of the accreditation have been unfair and she wants Noreen to help her formulate an appeal. Noreen is very aware that Michelle is thinking this through from within her own sense of failure, embarrassment and rejection. She is hurting badly. At this stage Noreen

*(Continued)*

*(Continued)*

knows there is little hope in her taking a wider and more comprehensive view of what has happened in the accreditation. She will have to wait a little longer, until Michelle is able to reflect in a wider way and review whether or not there is important learning for her in the accreditation process.

Michelle is reflecting from within herself and from within her emotions. It would be easy to get trapped in this one lens of reflection. This sometimes happens when individuals are highly committed to a theory, a cause, a way of life or to gaining accreditation, as in Michelle's case. Their commitment, if they are not careful, can become a prison that funnels their way of thinking and reflection in that they have reached their conclusions before reflection begins.

Having been raised in Belfast, Northern Ireland, I am aware of how easily all actions of the 'other side' can be interpreted in the same adversarial light – even when the actions are not negative. Limits can be set prematurely on reflection, which skews the outcome from the very beginning. This non-negotiable stance is not bad in some instances – we all have values that are not open to reflection or negotiation, and these values have stood us in good stead throughout our lives. I have a friend who refused to work in Saudi Arabia because, until recently, they refused to allow women to vote; I know consultants who don't work with tobacco companies because of their views on the harm caused by smoking; and others who don't engage with arms manufacturers. These are chosen, non-negotiable positions that need little reflection. Like all absolute stances they need review as situations change; for example, women have recently been granted the vote in Saudi Arabia. Working in environments and contexts where things are not as black-and-white, it helps to widen our ability to reflect in other ways – we could be missing multiple meanings. Asking 'Can I take the stance of what I oppose?' is often a good way to reflect from truths other than our own.

Langer (1989) talks about 'premature cognitive commitments' – commitments we make on the basis of a certain amount of information that then doesn't allow us to think differently. She gives the example of the Ugly Duckling, who 'prematurely' decided he was a duck until a disorientating event opened his eyes. Eye-opening events happen all the time and make us review the cognitive commitments we have made. We have reflective habits, well-established methods by which we filter how and what we reflect on. These viewpoints are usually developed early in life and form the basis of what we sometimes call 'core beliefs' or 'cognitive schemas'; for example, men cannot be trusted, women are weak and need protection. Such beliefs are often hidden from us and even when articulated can become very difficult to shift and change.

Bolton (2001) uses the term 'self-spectatorship' to describe what happens when we become, in so far as we can, objective viewers of our own work. In *spectator-ing* we re-create and re-imagine our practice in order to give attention to, notice, focus on and consider aspects of what we have done in order to learn from it – from an outside perspective, as well as from an internal one.

Reflection is a process where we get 'outside ourselves' while still remaining 'inside ourselves' and move back and forth between them as we consider ourselves as 'other'. We intentionally make ourselves objects so that we can study ourselves and learn from our own behaviour. Subjectivity and proximity can impact on what we see and how we make sense of what we see.

## Example

Janine is upset and hurt. Tears flow in supervision as she explains how terrible she feels. Her client walked out of the session saying it wasn't helping her and she wondered why she ever thought of coming for counselling. Janine wonders why she ever thought she would make a good counsellor.

At this moment, in supervision, Janine is reading and making sense of her experience through her emotions, feeling hurt, rejected and useless. Her 'am I good enough' driver is activated in her – an old pattern from the past when she tried desperately to live up to her more 'successful' elder sister and never quite made it. Her supervisor acknowledges how she feels and stays with those feelings as Janine connects them in the different stories of her life. Very gently, she nudges Janine away from her emotions – asking her to step outside herself and be a more compassionate observer of that moment when the client walked out of the counselling room. What did she see? What did she notice? Janine's eyes lit up; of course, she said, she sees in her client the pattern of her own life! She always rejects others first so that they don't reject her. Just before walking out of the room the client had shared a particularly painful moment when she felt ashamed. Certain Janine would reject her for her failure, she jumped first and rejected Janine. Together Janine and her supervisor decided to write the client a letter of acceptance and understanding, and inviting her back to work through the issues. They also looked at what Janine could have done in the session that might have held the client more securely as she shared her shame. Could Janine, even in that cauldron of emotion, get some emotional distance to make sense of what was happening, and react appropriately?

It is not always easy to get into an observer or spectator position. It is often our emotions that trap us inside ourselves (e.g., shame, injustice, anger, rejection). Where these have been part of our upbringing and education they become strong triggers that trap and cage us within ourselves.

## 2 Adopting a curious and compassionate stance

The next step is the attitude with which we look at the self. Reflection is a bit more than just getting outside ourselves; it's also about *the way in which we look* at the self and the work as object (i.e. objectively). Can we view ourselves and our work with curiosity, empathy, compassion, understanding and honesty? Our norm may be to stand outside ourselves and defensively justify what we did; we may be used to standing outside ourselves and blaming ourselves for the disasters that took place; but can we stand outside ourselves with compassion and curiosity and consider what happened as a way of learning from it? It is so easy to begin reflection judgmentally and close off avenues of curiosity.

Janine did that. She blamed herself immediately and used that blame to put herself down and question her ability as a counsellor. Even if it was her fault that the client had walked out, being more compassionate towards herself, her limitations, her humanness and so on would be a more helpful stance in reflecting on what happened and learning from it.

Curiosity is our starting point in supervision. As curious beings, we wonder and ask why. 'Premature cognitive commitments' (Langer, 1989) are conclusions that lock us into the prison of one meaning, like Janine believing she shouldn't be a counsellor. Curiosity gives us room for movement in making sense of what has happened and allows us to at least consider other possibilities. We ask questions of ourselves and of our practice in order to learn. Can we move from instant evaluation to contemplative curiosity? We can evaluate later. For now we stop and wonder. And we do that with kindness and compassion. Not a kindness and compassion that denies what has happened, or becomes overly optimistic, but one that allows for human frailty, understanding and acceptance.

## 3 Focusing, noticing, noting

With some useful tools to hand (distance, curiosity and compassion installed), we now focus on the *content* of our reflection. This will mean using memory to access what has happened and then allowing our narrative ability to retell the story of our work. Inevitably we focus on certain aspects of the work; we notice some things and leave other things aside. We make note of specifics. The seven-eyed process model of supervision (Hawkins and Shohet, 2012) can direct us at this stage as supervisees, and supervisors, and both together tell and retell the story from different perspectives:

- The perspective of the client.
- The perspective of the interventions used.
- The perspective of the relationship.
- The perspective of the practitioner; what was happening to him/her.
- The perspective of the supervisor.

- The perspective of the relationship between supervisor and supervisee.
- The perspective of the systems involved.

It is usually the supervisee who begins the story from their perspective. This inherently informs the supervisor about which perspective is being used, and how it is being used to make sense of the meeting with the client. The supervisor may notice a missing perspective and ask about it (I notice you haven't talked about how this client has affected you; I get the sense you have some strong feelings about what happened). Perhaps there is a perspective that goes unnoticed most of the time (the systems viewpoint, what is happening to the supervisor)?

Noticing how we notice, realising we focus a lot of the time on one aspect rather than another, helps us widen our ways of perceiving. Often our training will pull us towards one aspect of what is happening rather than others: a psychodynamic counsellor will notice different aspects than will a CBT counsellor. Their eyes will go immediately to what their training has taught them to look for.

## 4 Using different reflective lenses

There are different reflective lenses through which we can look to make sense of events. These lenses will be created by experiences from our past, education, culture, race, gender, age and so on. These affect how we reflect. (Chapter 10 presents six such reflective lenses through which we examine what happens in our practice.)

## 5 Considering different meanings

Supervision relies for its effectiveness on the quality of awareness of both supervisors and supervisees. Awareness in supervising results in waking up, noticing, giving attention to and focusing on the many facets of practice. Reflection enhances awareness and is the human mechanism that gives meaning to our work.

The human face

has a third eye,

not just 'I see',

but 'I see why'. (Hunt, 2010: 155)

Supervision and reflection in particular ask *why*? Asking why of events is about making sense of them or giving them meaning. There are many possible meanings in every event and humans have the ability to look at, review and choose one meaning from many as their preferred way of making sense of an event.

---

### Example

In supervision Jim is considering why his client didn't appear for their session. Even after a telephone message left on the client's answering machine and an email follow-up, there has been no response from the client. This is quite unusual for this client who until now has been very good at keeping in contact and responding to communication. Jim's conclusion is that in their previous counselling session he had challenged the client about contradictions in his behaviour around the area of integrity. It was clear during the session that the client was deeply disturbed by this challenge and came back to it several times. Jim thinks he may have been too confrontational too soon, and his client is punishing him for that by staying out of contact and not attending their arranged session two days ago.

---

Clearly this is one way of making sense of a series of events that Jim has connected up to create a plausible scenario. There are a number of other possible explanations:

- The client was called away at the last minute to deal with an emergency situation overseas (which has happened before).
- The client couldn't make their session and had asked his secretary to cancel but the secretary forgot.
- The client was taken seriously ill and has been kept in hospital.
- The client had indeed taken the challenge badly and was still processing the issue.
- The client had thought deeply about the challenge and realised that Jim was quite right and had put his finger on a deep issue he had had to face. He was embarrassed to be 'caught' out and his deep embarrassment had made him skip the last session, conveniently forgetting to let Jim know.
- The client was punishing him for confronting him about one of his values.

With some imagination, I am sure we could come up with a number of other possible explanations for the client's behaviour. As mentioned above, locking into one meaning closes the dialogue and commits us to one way of action. Langer (1989) uses a telling example. She holds up a pencil and asks her class what it is. Inevitably they all answer, 'It's a pencil'. 'What else could it be?' she inquires of them. Back comes a range of suggestions: it could be a stirrer for tea, a weapon to defend yourself with, a stalk to hold up a flower, a wedge to hold open a door and so on. When you ask a similar question in regard to something important (What is a family? What is a person?) you will often discover some locked-in meanings (a family is a mother, father and children) which restrict your possibilities. Until Jim's client gets back to him and offers his explanation for his absence, Jim and his supervisor are left guessing. Outlining as many explanations as possible means we keep an open mind and remain curious. Locked-in meaning commits us to 'putting all our eggs in one basket'. Some people make sense of their lives from the stance of 'being a victim' – whatever happens to them is explained in the context of how horrible life is *to me*. Religious people will attempt to explain events through the eyes of their god. If this is their only explanation then they tend to be left with unhelpful contradictions, such as how can a loving God allow such suffering? The ability to create multiple explanations is a high-level reflective skill.

## 6 Opting for the best meaning

From the many meanings considered we now zone in on what might be the most plausible meaning just now. *Just now* are important words here. A more accurate meaning might emerge later when we have more details or new information. We can then change the meaning of events in the light of the present. From the six possible meanings in the example with Jim above, he and his supervisor decide that the best possible explanation, in the light of all the information they have, is the fourth; that the client had indeed taken the challenge badly and was still processing the issue. Taking this as the best option then allows them to think through what they need to do next. They could be wrong, and if future knowledge shows that to be the case, then they will have to change their interpretation of events. But for now they go with their best interpretation.

## 7 Building new meaning into practice

Imagination is a key faculty in reflection. We access our previous practice through memory, we ponder and reflect upon it in the present, and we prepare for our future work through imagination.

From reflection comes learning; learning what to do in the specific situation we are facing. For instance, in the example above, Janine decides to write a letter.

But there is wider learning from reflection. We can widen our application from specific situations to general principles of service, practice and policy. There is also more general learning about self, relationships, systems and clients.

### Example

Ernest looked back with his supervisor at the past year. Asked by her to review what he had learned, he remembered how difficult it had been for him to end sessions. He just couldn't say goodbye and had promised his clients to be available should they need him in a crisis. Audrey (his supervisor) had

*(Continued)*

*(Continued)*

helped him look at this and together they had broken some old habits around abandonment, rejection and attachment. It was still difficult but by the time he was saying goodbye to his fourth client he was watchful and alert to making it a clear and clean ending. He had learned over the course of the year, through his reflective dialogues with Audrey, to stay with the pain and the difficulties of endings in his work. His practice, he felt, was much the better for it.

Applying learning from reflection to practice is key if appropriate shifts are to take place in our work. Articulating the learning and building intentional bridges to practice is one way of doing this. Planned transfer of learning ensures that it happens.

## 8 Reviewing the process (meta-reflection)

Besides the content of reflection – what is reflected upon – there is the method and structure of reflection used. If reflection itself involved one step back to perceive practice from an observer perspective, then meta-reflection takes two steps back to look at how reflection itself is taking place. We have our own particular ways of reflecting, which are a sort of reflective style that is *ours*.

### Example

Esme notices that her supervisee James tended to blame himself when anything went wrong in his life. His critical eye turned first to himself, without taking much else into consideration. He was doing it now with a client who was stuck and asking him desperately what he should do with his life and career. James was stuck too and looked almost despairingly at Esme. 'What am I doing wrong?' he asked.

Esme replied, 'I notice, James, when everything is not going according to how you planned it in your mind, that you tend to blame yourself for that ... have you noticed that?'

'I do that all the time,' James replied. 'I think it's my fault because I am meant to be the expert.'

James' reflective style pushed him towards a self-blaming reflection as his first port of call. It was his innate reflective style. By becoming aware of this he now has the possibility of changing his style.

We all have an architecture or structure to our way of reflection that not just influences but largely determines the outcome of that reflective process. Getting in touch with that structure enables us to liberate ourselves and move towards a more open, wider and friendlier way of reflection. (*Drivers* and *scripts* from transactional analysis provide one useful way of helping us see the reflective styles and filters we have built into our lives; see Carroll and Gilbert, 2011: Ch. 7.)

## So what is reflection?

Can we gather together our thoughts on reflection? A common image that comes to mind when the word reflection is reviewed is the image of 'mirror'. Mirrors show back what is put in front of them. Their value is that they make an objective image of what is placed before them. As I look in the mirror I see an accurate image of myself (unless it is a trick mirror or I project onto the image something that is not there). But for the moment, in reflection we get some distance from ourselves or our experience, and we review self and experience from that distance. So I look at myself in the mirror and I see myself there – I am an observer of myself. I notice that I am somewhat rounder in the middle than I used to be and make sense of this by deciding that I'm putting on some weight. That is my explanation for what I see, and as a result I make a decision to go on a diet.

In a sense, reflection is holding up a mirror to life and reality and then interpreting what we see in the mirror. In brief then, the definition of reflection used here will be: 'Reflection is mindful consideration of what has happened, what is happening or what might happen' (Hewson and Carroll, In press).

The key words in that description are 'mindful consideration'. *Mindful* means that the kind of reflection (consideration) we are talking about in supervision is intentional. Much reflection is not intentional in the sense that we do not set out to do it, it just happens automatically. We reflect unintentionally all the time – about life, events and happenings. Making sense is inbuilt and natural to us, and so 'just happens'. The reflection looked at in supervision is mindful in so far as we set it up as a learning process. Having done our work, having got some distance from it (physically, emotionally and psychologically), the intention is to use that experience of our practice as a springboard for learning.

### Example

Jim thought back to the moment with his client when he challenged him. He recalled what he said and noticed again the reaction of his client. He could access his memory and remembered, just before he spoke, a shadow of doubt crossing his mind. Was this the right time to challenge? 'You know,' he shares with his supervisor, 'I have always had the tendency to blurt out things and have often got into trouble for my directness. I do not always pace it right and the person I am talking to is often not ready. I wonder, has that happened here? I think his reaction is saying it did.'

The second important word in the definition above is *consideration*. Consideration involves a number of steps and stages:

- *Positioning myself as observer*: but knowing there is no such thing as totally neutral observation.
- *Stopping and recalling*: stepping back and accessing memory.
- *Noticing*: giving attention to the bigger picture of the event.
- *Focusing*: from the many aspects I notice, what will I focus on that will help explain what happened?
- *Thinking, feeling and intuiting*: as I sit with the event in front of me I allow my thoughts and feelings expression.
- *Explaining (individually, systemically)*: I begin to see the event in its contexts, each of which may add to its meaning.
- *Probing with incisive questions*: from myself and from others.
- *Making meaning*: I make sense of what happened (from many possible explanations).
- I choose one meaning that seems to be the best explanation for me *at this time with the knowledge I have.*

To complete reflection:

- I share my meaning with another (supervisor).
- I listen to their reaction to my explanation.
- We discuss and dialogue about it.
- We come to a joint decision on what it means.
- We devise a plan to integrate this into my work.

After reflection (meta–reflection):

- I look at how I reflect.
- I name assumptions and uproot and replace them if needed.
- I polish my reflective lenses.
- I integrate my reflective learning into my practice.
- Over time this becomes habitual practice and tacit knowing.

## Reflection-in-action (creating an internal supervisor)

Reflection–in–action is mindful consideration of what is happening as it is happening. It is fast-track consideration, not having the luxury of time. Thinking on your feet or thinking on the run is what we mean by reflection–in–action. It is the ability to engage in practice and at the same time create sufficient space to reflect on that practice even as it is taking place. It is the quality of work that comes only with experience. As the work unfolds so the practitioner remains open to possibilities, rather than locking in too quickly to one way of thinking or doing. We create reflective space for ourselves even as we work. Bolton called this 'the hawk in the air' (Bolton, 2001).

   This is not easy to do: to engage and be disengaged at the same time; to be involved and yet sufficiently distant; to be self-supervising. It demands focus and review as part of the engagement.

## Example

Some years ago, a lawyer was 'sent' to me for coaching support. Albert had been off ill with severe depression for a number of months and was on his way back into work on a gradual basis. His HR director asked if I would meet with him once a week for the first few months of his return-to-work programme, to be a confidential support outside his work environment. I agreed and a date was set for our first meeting. That was the first mistake I made. When he arrived he brushed past me, sat down, took out a notebook, turned his side profile to me and demanded to know my qualification. Reflection-in-action took over just then. With this question hanging in the air it was as if time stood still, though there was a frenzy inside my head! I was thrown off-balance momentarily – this is not the way most of my clients engage with me in the first moments of our relationship. I was making meaning rapidly of this unusual behaviour. My first emotional reaction was one of feeling attacked and I could feel irritation turning to anger and anxiety. In those few seconds I knew I had a crucial choice to make: to answer the question, or go beneath the question to the communication. A huge amount of internal dialogue took place before I heard myself say, 'It sounds like it is quite difficult for you to be here with me.' I was hearing, rightly or wrongly, that he didn't want to be with me in coaching, and that he was taking control of the situation and putting me on the back foot. He was looking for some justification for deciding I was not the person to be with him. I *felt* more than *thought* that he was out to sabotage our relationship before it even started.

This reflection–in–action is an example of what happened when I self-supervised at a critical moment in a coaching relationship. I could have reacted immediately from my thinking (let me give you my qualifications) or from my emotions (why are you so aggressive?). I think neither would have helped the situation. Choosing instead to pause and reflect led me to sense that behind the bluster and the aggression was a fearful man who was used to getting his own way. I decided to focus on this fear but used a milder, less direct form of enquiry to signal that I understood – and also that I was in control of the situation.

Reflection-in-action generally develops over time. Beginners find it difficult to do. There is so much to hold together in the mind all at once: the words, the processes, the feelings, the body language, the tone of voice, the theoretical wisdom, past experiences, the context and the other person. It amounts to what Gladwell calls 'thin-slicing' – that moment of insight and intuition that comes with experience – and describes what this means: 'Thin-slicing refers to the ability of our unconscious to find patterns in situations and behaviour on very narrow slices of experience' (2005: 23).

## Critical reflection

Critical reflection is the ability to move beyond the content of reflection to tracking, unseating and releasing assumptions that underpin our beliefs, behaviours and theories.

Brookfield is one of the foremost thinkers and writers on critical reflection. His work, written in the context of educational theory, is applicable to supervision. He starts one of this books with a section entitled 'How Critical Thinking Saved My Life' (2012: 2). Diagnosed at one stage in his life with clinical depression and embarrassed to ask for help, he tried to reason his way through it and use willpower to overcome it. Then he reached a conclusion: 'What was getting in the way of my dealing with my depression,' he writes, 'was my inability to think critically about it.' He went in search of his assumptions and discovered that there was a series of them which kept him from managing his depression. Some of these were the assumption that:

- depression was a sign of weakness;
- depression should be hidden from others;
- if I was a real man then I should be able to deal with my depression and over-come it; fully functioning men (like Clint Eastwood) are clear headed, deter-mined and tough, and overcome obstacles such as depression;
- depression is caused by external circumstances, and since his external circum-stances were good he had no right to be depressed;
- effective 'self-talk' (come on, get a grip and sort yourself out) would move the depression along;
- a *normal* individual doesn't get depressed;
- professionals don't let feelings of worthlessness or shame dominate their lives; and
- real men don't need help or counselling or psychiatrists; drugs are acceptable for women, but not for real men.

He went through what he called a process of 'ideological detoxification', a way of unearthing, challenging and discarding multiple assumptions that kept him impris-oned in this thinking and behaviour.

For Brookfield, critical reflection is about hunting down and changing unhelpful assumptions. Assumptions are guides to truth embedded in our mental outlooks (2012: 7).

Assumptions underpin everything. They are sets of opinions embedded in our thinking that colour how we think and how we reflect. Supervision is the place par excellence to help us uncover and review the assumptions that infiltrate our work.

### Example

Jay knew he was wrong even as the words came out of his mouth. His client Marie was going through a rough patch at work, struggling with stress, lack of self-confidence and assertiveness. As she sat in front of him, tearful and silent, he heard himself suggest that he would contact her boss and explain how rough things were for her. 'Would you?' she said gratefully, tears welling up once more in her eyes, 'that would make such a difference.'

With the help of his supervisor, Jay was able to articulate the assumptions that underlay his decision to intervene directly in the life of his client. Some of these assumptions were that:

- she could not handle this on her own;
- her boss was amenable to his calling;
- he would not create dependency by taking this action; and
- as a woman she needed a man to defend her.

## Process of assumption-tracking in supervision

Some of the steps that take place as we track down assumptions are:

- *Examining assumptions:* hold them up to the light to examine them (particularly with others who will give us some feedback on them).
- *Changing assumptions:* try to change or adapt them to more useful and workable assumptions.
- *Integrating new assumptions:* embed new assumptions into our practice.
- *Servicing assumptions:* review our assumptions occasionally to ensure that they continue to be helpful.

## Critical self-reflection

Critical self-reflection is the process of critical reflection applied to oneself. It's the process of holding one's own theories and processes of reflection up for examination. What assumptions about me and myself do I bring to reflection? There are lots of myths regarding the nature of professionalism.

> ## Example
>
> Neasa is looking at herself and the way she makes meaning of events in life. She has uncovered some templates through which she looks as filters in her meaning-making processes. One of these is her 'not good enough' filter, which in the past has pushed her to read more, do more courses and get more qualifications. None of these has quenched the thirst to be better. In her most recent supervision session she once more put herself down for missing something her client had said. Her supervisor picked up on this and asked her to take a different stance. 'What would the good-enough Neasa say about that?' she inquired. Neasa laughed. 'That's what she would do,' she said, 'she would laugh at repeating this old pattern. But she would go back quickly and see it from the other perspectives too. This is good work!'

Neasa had hunted down, named and unseated a basic assumption in her life: that she is not good enough. Her critical self-reflection has reached a stage of monitoring what happens to her and being able, like an archaeologist, to trace where it comes from and uproot it. She can catch herself out when old habits and old assumptions emerge to control her thinking and reflecting.

## And finally – the problem with reflection

Reflection is one of the best gifts we have as humans. It allows us to delve deeply into meaning making in regard to our actions, lives and relationships. It allows us to question, to wonder, to be curious. We discover that there are many ways of making sense of even a single behaviour.

As with many gifts there is, however, a shadow side. When not balanced, reflection can be underused or overused. Underused we have talked about earlier, in looking at the lenses of reflection. It was what Socrates meant when he remarked that the *un-reflected life is not worth living*. To not reflect, or not reflect sufficiently, is to allow others to make our opinions and decisions for us. We become sheep when we don't reflect: our lives are driven by instincts, emotions and the will of others. Lack of reflection often ends up in mindless routine and locked-in thinking.

Over-reflection is equally dangerous. It can result in rumination and obsessional thoughts that impact on our lives and imprison us in our inner world, rather than equipping us to live in the outer world.

## Example

Julio is a trauma psychologist. He works a lot with post-traumatic stress disorder. Recently he worked with a policewoman and fireman who attended a horrific multiple pile-up on a motorway. A number of children had been severely injured and five had died. The policewoman and the fireman had found this incredibly difficult to deal with and it had got through their usual protective, professional armour. Both of them were unable to sleep at night as the pictures of these injured and dead children invaded their minds. Julio was finding their vivid descriptions and accounts of what they had seen, heard and smelled haunting him too. Last night he had lain awake for several hours trying to evict the unwelcome pictures that refused to let him sleep.

Julio, the policewoman and the fireman are all suffering from post-traumatic stress disorder, one of the symptoms of which is over-reflection – not being able to turn off reflection when they need to. Memory is also a gift that can turn into a prison when we are not able to forget what it would be helpful for us to forget; it feels impossible to liberate ourselves from our thinking and our reflection.

Supervisees also get invaded with thoughts, pictures and questions about clients and their work. These uninvited guests are difficult to get rid of, and most practitioners know what it is like to 'take their clients home with them'.

O'Leary calls this the 'curse of the self' and points out how self-awareness and the ability to reflect can create a host of problems 'by allowing people to ruminate about the past or imagine what might befall them in the future' (2004: vi). He points out that we live in two worlds: the internal world of reflection, thoughts, feelings, fantasies; and the external world of objects, people, events. We move back and forth between them, unlike other animals which tend to spend their lives in the external world. As O'Leary says, 'they [other animals] do not spin introspective webs of self-related thoughts.' The problem for humans arises when being preoccupied in our inner world blinds us to what is happening in the outer world.

## Example

Jamie is sitting opposite his client, who is sobbing. It has been an incredibly difficult time for her personally and at work, and she is overwhelmed. He is not sure what to do and his inner world is working overtime. Would it be appropriate to move across and sit beside her? Perhaps reach out a hand and allow her the option of holding it? Maybe give her more tissues to soak

*(Continued)*

> *(Continued)*
>
> up her tears? Or just sit and wait and let her believe she can deal with this and come through it? Absorbed in his thoughts about what he ought to do, he fails to notice that she has gone silent and stopped sobbing. His supervisor asks him what would have happened had he ignored the chattering in this head and just stayed with his client in the outer world of what was happening. What if he had responded intuitively without going into reflection-in-action modality?

At times, 'just do it' is the best intuitive and most humane response. Occupied with our thoughts and plans, caught up in our ruminations, imprisoned by our compulsive reflections we often miss our *outer world* lives as they pass us by. 'Too much inner dialogue can be detrimental,' O'Leary suggests (2004: 31). Sleep disturbance and sexual dysfunction can be examples of how our inner world affects our outer world negatively. How to get the balance right? Is there a time to *just do it*? Or is there a time to think about doing it? Sports people are good at reminding us that the time for reflection is before you perform and after you perform; reflection during performance can adversely affect the performance. Can we create a reflective switch to turn it on when it is needed, and turn it off when it is likely to get in the way?

Several suggestions have been made about ways of being still internally and quietening the self. Meditation is one way of calming and controlling our inner worlds and stilling our thoughts (see O'Leary, 2004: 47–52). Recognising and managing self-talk is another. Noticing how we talk to ourselves can support us in changing the conversation. A third is our ability to manage worry, which can be a form of over-thinking about the future. Part of over-reflection is the use of imagination – our human way of anticipating and planning the future. Sometimes allowing our imagination free rein is unhelpful to staying in the present.

> Joe is, as he says, dog-tired. He has had a long autumn semester as a counsellor in a busy university setting. Holidays start tomorrow and already he is beginning to plan his break. He has to forcefully pull himself back from the imaginary future into the present with his client. Christine is talking about her difficulties in going home for Christmas and the horrible family dynamics she faces. Joe's mind is already picturing Christmas day with Jill, the two boys and his parents. He sees the wide eyes of little Eamonn gazing in awe at the new bicycle he has asked Santa for, and Aaron ... He quickly pulls himself back into the present, noticing that Christine has started to cry. He shakes his head as if to dispel these distracting thoughts, lovely as they are.

We are faced with decisions. When is the time for reflection, for deep reflection, and when is the time to stop reflecting? When is reflection our friend and when does it become our enemy, or as O'Leary calls it our 'curse'. Sports coaches and psychologists suggest that reflection is our best friend before we perform, and afterwards as we think back and learn from the experience. Reflection during action, they point out, is often unhelpful, and focusing on our performance reduces its effectiveness.

## Conclusion

In this chapter we have reviewed what reflection means and the stages and steps to go through in order to make meaning from our experiences (from our practice). Reflection is not a given, and we cannot assume that supervisors and supervisees can reflect in honest, open questioning and curious ways that lead to meaning. We reflect, and we reflect on how we reflect, to ensure that our reflective processes are in good working order. Critical reflection moves from focusing on the content of reflection to unearthing the assumptions that underpin our ways of thinking and reflecting. Critical self-reflection puts oneself at the centre of reflection and seeks to track down and challenge the assumptions about ourselves that have become directors of our behaviours. Finally, in this chapter we have noted the shadow side of reflection: what happens when we reflect too much or too constantly. Reflection can easily turn from being a human gift and blessing to being a burden and curse. While we have treated reflection as if it were a personal internal process, reflection optimally takes place in conversations. The next chapter will look in detail at reflective dialogues.

# Ten

# The Six Lenses of Reflective Supervision

**Chapter summary**

This chapter continues the reflection in supervision theme. It suggests six different reflective lenses through which practitioners can review and learn from their work. Each of these six is then individually examined. The chapter concludes by looking at the skills needed to use each lens effectively.

Reflection is not an all-or-nothing activity. It is not a matter of being able to reflect or not being able to reflect, as in the difference between humans and other animals. Humans have the ability to reflect, to ask the question why, while other animals do not have that capacity. However, there are many rooms in the reflection mansion. There are levels of reflection (surface reflection or deep reflection); there are focus points of reflection (content, process, self); there are time spans in reflection (reflection *on* action, reflection *in* action and reflection *for* action – past, present and future).

Reflection and learning are always closely connected and changes in one automatically activate changes in the other (Moon, 2004). Different terms have been used by different authors to describe types of reflection; some authors use the term *stage* to describe a developmental process within reflection (King and Kitchener, 1994; Torbet, 2004); others use terms such as *level*, which again indicate various depths of reflection (Carroll, 2009; Hawkins and Shohet, 2012); *tones, modalities, scales* are words used by De Haan (2012) to capture a less developmental view of reflection while sustaining the myriad ways in which it takes place; reflective *phases* is used by Rogers (1958), who traces the stages individuals go through as they move from rigid non-awareness to trusting themselves through reflection in counselling.

The words we use to describe reflection are heavily nuanced. Words and phrases may smuggle values in with them; using the term *level* to characterise reflection can imply that some levels are deeper than others, and that the deeper levels are more valuable; *stage* can also imply that expertise or wisdom that comes with later stages is missing from former ones.

Whatever the term used, reflection is seen here as *a progressive journey in the service of learning*. My belief is that we can learn to reflect and we can deepen and widen our ability to reflect. Educationists see learning as moving through phases from zero learning (nothing is learned) to transformational learning (a major shift in perspective and behaviour takes place). Such phases also occur in reflection. Jason is an example of a counsellor who begins to reflect in a deeper way on the work he was taking for granted.

> Jason's wake-up call came in his work with Maureen. He thought they were doing a great job in helping her deal with some problems at work. But ten sessions into their counselling arrangement, not much had happened. They were going round in circles. It was when his supervisor challenged him to listen carefully to Maureen that he realised he had been problem solving. Maureen brought her problems, Jason helped her resolve them or at least find strategies to contain them. To his astonishment he realised he saw Maureen as a 'problem to be solved' and like a good tradesman he dipped into his toolkit to find the perfect solution. Widening his reflections on the way he worked even further he discovered that this was his approach to life: clarify what the problem is and then fix it. Jason was quite shocked to learn how much this fix-it approach characterised who he was – he had always thought he was much more relational than that.

In this chapter I am going to use the term 'lenses' to describe our human ability to reflect from within a number of viewpoints. The word 'lens' contains or implies the idea of an ability to widen the perspective to get a bigger picture, or to narrow it to focus on a particular aspect of the scene; it also suggests the idea of changing and changeable lenses which allow us to perceive our experiences from different viewpoints. Like life. Life provides us with changing lenses – we can see from the viewpoint of a child, an adolescent, a parent or an elderly person. These are stages we go through as we grow older and become more experienced, and with those stages come specific knowledge and skills. We don't expect children to be reflective but we do hope adults can be. Because something is described as developmental does not mean it happens automatically. We cannot not age, that is a given; but we can age without growing up emotionally and psychologically. Our ability to reflect in deepening ways depends on a number of factors – how safe we feel, the context in which we live, our experiences in life, our relationships, our need for security and so on. The environment in which we live and work has a major impact on how we reflect and how deeply we allow ourselves to be curious and question our inherited wisdom. Reflection moves through stages, sometimes chronologically, where knowledge is viewed in more complex ways, where abstraction allows for wider thinking and where there is a realisation that answers are not just given, but have to be *worked out* through this process called reflection.

TABLE 10.1   *Lenses of reflection, stances and connectivity*

| Lens | Ability for reflection | Stance/attitude | Connection quality |
| --- | --- | --- | --- |
| 1 | Zero | Me | Disconnected |
| 2 | Empathic | Observer | Intellectual connection |
| 3 | Relational | You and Me = Us | Emotional connection |
| 4 | Systemic | You and Me + Others | Contextual connection |
| 5 | Critical self-reflection | Me (internalised) | Transformational connection |
| 6 | Transcendental | Other (universal) | Universal connection |

I have been working recently on how to understand reflection (Carroll, 2009) and in particular how to help supervisees use reflection to its maximum. As a result I have devised six modes or levels/lenses of reflection that allow us to look at the same event from six perspectives and make meaning in six different ways, using reflection as the medium of learning. Choosing six levels was somewhat arbitrary – other people may chose more or less. By adopting six different viewpoints, however, we can get a holistic 360° perspective which gives us insights to create the best informed interventions. Table 10.1 gives a brief summary of the six levels. I will provide examples to illustrate how the six levels can be used later in this chapter.

## The six lenses of reflection

Each lens is examined using the nine general categories listed below (the italicised words represent the paragraph headings used):

1.  *Description* of the lens.
2.  What kind of *learning* this particular lens is connected to.
3.  The *TA stance* pertinent to this lens (transactional analysis).
4.  Typical *statements* made from this lens position.
5.  What the end *result* might be if using this lens to reflect.
6.  The sort of *strategy* that characterises this reflective stance.
7.  *Positives and negatives* in this lens.
8.  The *blocks* to moving to the next level of reflection.
9.  An *example* of reflection using this lens.

### Lens 1: Zero reflection (me stance, disconnected)

**Description** Lens 1 is a non-reflective stance; it could be described as zero reflection or as a pre-reflective stance. *Imprisoned* reflection is another term for this because it is reflection confined to rigid ways. Being right, being certain, being fundamentalist in viewpoint puts one in this kind of position. Reflection only takes place when there is some uncertainty or ambiguity; when there is none, when certainty rules the roost, then reflection is dismissed. This reflective lens finds it difficult to look inside or outside, at wider pictures or bigger systems. It has a very black-and-white stance. Making sense of events is based on a theory of causality that is very simplistic: this caused *that* to happen and *that* is all that is needed to know. There is no awareness of circular causality here, of where cause and effect intertwine. The answer we seek is also usually quite straight forward – if you would only change, my life would be easier. An example of this kind of reflective stance is the comment made about a teacher who claimed he had 20 years' experience of teaching. After listening to him at a job interview one interviewer reported that the teacher had had one year of experience, repeated 20 times over.

**Learning** Here knowledge is viewed as absolute and predetermined and there is no room for other views. There is a right answer and once that answer is found then there is no need for further seeking or for reflection. Beliefs and facts are not distinguished. Scharmer (2007) calls this 'zero-thinking' or 'I-in-me' thinking where new knowledge is filtered through old certainties and does not change the underlying beliefs. A further step in this category, but still within it, acknowledges other beliefs but sees them as wrong. Authority keeps us right.

**TA stance** I'm OK, (maybe not OK), you're not OK. A position of blame is often adopted as people are categorised into those who are right and those who are wrong. The 'chosen people' syndrome often occurs here where one group sees itself as special and having the truth – with the result that other groups are not chosen, and do not have the truth. When bad or difficult things happen to people in this stance they often interpret it from a victim perspective – see how badly the world treats me! I have called this the 'me stance (external)' because it focuses on the actor/person but from an external perspective – there is little consideration for how I might be part of the problem or contribute to it. By and large at this stage *you* are the problem, *I* am the solution. There is disconnection from others. Principles/rules/regulations can be more important than individuals, with the result that humans may be sacrificed to theory or principle.

**Statements** The kinds of statements that emerge from this lens are: this client is resistant; this coachee is not committed to the process; this manager wants to get her own way; this leader cannot delegate because of his issues with power; because it is obvious; that's the way it is. Statements tend to place the problem outside the person and onto another.

**Result** Being stuck, strong feeling and resentment. Individuals here often stay solely at the content level of issues and have a simplistic answer to life. However, there is not always a feeling of 'stuckness' from within even though from outside being locked into one way of thinking is obvious. Individuals and groups will often feel confident and even arrogant that they have the truth that will not be negotiated.

**Strategy** Telling or asserting as if it were totally true: this is what you will do or should do. The conversation is one of monologue. Withdrawal or defensiveness can be strong positions.

**Positives and negatives** The positive of this stance is about holding strong, non-negotiable values, ideas and positions. Commitment can be very strong and lasting within this stance. The negative is the other side of this; there is no negotiation, no reflection when it would help to have it. At its most negative, individuals and groups are locked into one way of viewing their lives and experiences.

**Blocks** Being certain, being right, very strong feelings, fear of giving up control and power, fear of change. Fear and shame are further blocks at this level.

## Example

Phil is managing director of the investment branch of an international bank. He has trained as an executive coach in order to integrate coaching with his management style, and if appropriate, to take on some coaching in his organisation. Lisa is his supervisor and she is external to the organisation. Eager to get started and try out his new skills, he reviews his staff to see who might be suitable for coaching from himself. Phil suggests he coach Marian who has joined his branch of the organisation as the new director in charge of training. She is new to his department, they have no prior history and she is keen to learn. He will be both mentor and coach to Marian as she finds her feet within the branch. Marian is pleased with this suggestion and they set up a coaching arrangement.

Having seen Marian for three coaching sessions, Phil comes to supervision very anxious. It hasn't quite worked out as he had thought. Amongst his directors he has noticed that Marian is viewed as a sort of 'favourite'. She herself has not helped the situation by her attitude towards the other directors and himself. She seems to flirt with him in a subtle way, even when they have formal directors' meetings, and has used the coaching arrangement to ask for some favours regarding financing her section of the department and some external training for herself. This has not gone down well with the other directors and he has heard rumblings of dissatisfaction. He feels that she has used her coaching arrangement with him to gain some credibility and he senses she has used her relationship with him as leverage with others outside the department.

Using Lens 1 as his reflective position, Phil is angry and upset with Marian for misusing the coaching arrangement. He feels abused and manipulated by her, and sees what she is doing as taking advantage of his generosity in offering her coaching. His solution is simple: he will end the coaching arrangement with her and if need be get her another coach from within the organisation or externally. He will discuss this with the HR director. Lisa gives him time and space to vent his feelings and get in touch with what has happened and begin to reflect upon it.

## Lens 2: Empathic reflection (observer stance, intellectual connection)

**Description** Lens 2 reflection sees the reflector beginning to become more of an observer with the ability to get outside self and start to see things from other perspectives. This stage may start with an intellectual appreciation that others might have some value in their points of view. There is empathy for the other person's perspective or for other perspectives in general. A more compassionate interpretation allows for insights into what is happening to the other. This could be called *intellectual* reflection or *empathic* reflection.

**Learning** The learning base of this lens has been called *quasi-reflective thinking* (King and Kitchener, 1994) and moves from absolute knowledge to understanding that uncertainty exists – there are some problems to which we do not have exact solutions. We begin to allow ourselves to consider other possibilities. Scharmer calls this the 'I-in-you' stage where there is some ability to consider knowledge from other stances and beliefs.

**TA stance** I'm OK (could still be I'm not OK) and realising you might be OK (but not yet). You are still the problem and I am still, by and large, the solution. A position of blame plus understanding (some empathy) is most common. Throughout there is movement from 'ignorant certainty' to 'intelligent confusion' (Kroll, 1992, quoted in King and Kitchener, 1994: 225).

**Statements** I can understand why the person does this though that does not excuse it. I must be more understanding but I must also hold the line. I can be somewhat accommodating now that I understand what is happening. The problem is still out there.

**Result** More understanding and loosening of response. The certainty that comes with Lens 1 has begun to unfreeze a bit, at least intellectually.

**Strategy** I still tell/force as my way of helping others change. Conversation can be discussion, debate or monologue but will tend to be intellectual in content without a lot of emotional engagement.

**Positives and negatives** The positives in Lens 2 are that this stance allows the person reflecting to become more of an observer, get outside his/her own thoughts and ideas, and begin the journey to understanding the viewpoints of others. The negatives are that it can lead to collusion with others or too easily and readily devolve one's own authority to others.

**Blocks** Not believing I contribute to this, not wanting to give control and power to others. It uses simplistic causality thinking. Still elements of being certain, right and of having found the answer. Rumi suggests a way forward: 'Sell your certainty and buy bewilderment' (Frackston, 1999). While there may not be bewilderment, some intellectual confusion is allowed.

## Example

Phil is still hurting in his supervision session with Lisa. She acknowledges his hurt and sense of betrayal by Marian. Very gently, she helps him get some distance from his negative feelings and reactions and begin to see it from Marian's perspective. Flattered to be offered coaching by her boss and chosen as the only one from the department to get it, she is clearly using it as a springboard to declare her sense of being the favourite. Phil sees what has happened and begins to understand what she has done from within her perspective. However, he knows this cannot continue and still blames Marian for creating this difficult situation for him and for the team. He feels she was not mature enough to build in suitable professional boundaries to protect the coaching.

## Lens 3: Relational reflection (you and me = us stance, emotional connection)

**Description** Lens 3 often follows a dialogue (internal or external) where we begin to share the issues and start to see that many of the problems are relational (now I see that it's about you and me and how we are getting on together). We realise that the problem is relational rather than simply inherent in one partner. While we both bring our personal histories into this shared space there is awareness that we create a relational dynamic for which we both have some responsibility. We can work out a way of working together. This could be called *emotional* reflection.

**Learning** With this stage comes the understanding that knowledge is not a 'given' but must be constructed and is always open to new evaluation and new interpretation. Context and evidence make a difference here. Here individuals take on the role of inquirers – those who are actively involved in creating and constructing knowledge with others. Learning takes place in relationships.

**TA stance** We are OK if we can talk about it. Position is one of collective responsibility: an 'us' stance. We have a problem; we have the solution.

**Statements** Let's talk about this. How do you think we both contribute to the issue/s? What can we do together to make this situation more manageable for both of us? How can I begin to see this from multiple perspectives? Where are the connections? How do we 'make' this problem together?

**Result** Movement from projecting and blaming and seeing the problem located in another, or out there, to seeing that we co-create the issue and we all take responsibility for it.

**Strategy** We talk honestly and openly about ourselves, our needs and our relationship. Self-awareness allows other information into the system (e.g., my need to control). Reflective dialogue (where together we begin to think about and talk about the issues) is used.

**Positives and negatives** Positively, there is a movement away from blaming others totally for the situation and a realisation of how easily we co-create issues in the dance of relationship. The negative is that we can abdicate personal responsibility and not see our own part in creating problems and issues.

**Blocks** No awareness of psychological patterns in my life; denial because of the work I would have to do if I believed there is another level of reflection. The problem is in the relationship. There may be little awareness that the wider systems to which we belong impact on us and co-create the problem with us.

## Example

In supervision Lisa asks Phil to look at what has happened from within the relationship between himself and Marian. 'Think of it as a dance you created,' she suggested. Phil was honest. He found Marian attractive and was excited about trying out his new coaching skills. Marian was eager to learn and advance herself in the organisation. 'Gosh,' said Phil, 'we have been using each other to get what we want; me to become an experienced coach, her to get on in the organisation. We have set up a relationship based on usefulness.' Lisa wonders if Phil could bring this back into the coaching conversation to help both of them learn from what has happened, and help both take responsibility for their individual behaviours in creating this relationship and problem.

## Lens 4: Systemic reflection (you and me + others stance, contextual connection)

**Description** This is the systemic reflective stance that looks to the system and the various subsystems involved and allows us to reflect on the situation from these wider perspectives. It is the helicopter (or satellite) ability to see the various small and large systems that affect our lives and our behaviours. Lens 4 reflection looks for the connections between the 'you' and 'me' that create a larger 'us' extending beyond our immediate dyad, team or group to the shared resources and history that shape and influence our choices and values. Lens 4 can extend our reflective inquiry into ancestry, heritage, community, culture, ecosystem and so on.

**Learning** Learning through systemic lens considers knowledge as created together, within communities and contexts. Learning takes place between and amongst people. This learning can be for better or worse – for better when we create collective wisdom and learning cultures, for the worst when we involve ourselves in 'groupthink' or collusive learning. Learning in this lens takes place through dialogue with others, with teams and with organisations.

**TA stance** We're OK. Position 4 is one of systemic responsibility. We ask: how is it all connected and how can we see and reflect from these multiple perspectives?

**Statements** How do we all contribute to creating a common culture around values that may or may not be conscious but which have immense power to influence our behaviour? Can I see patterns and themes that impact me, my relationships and my life in the small and large systems to which I belong? How does our communal stance create this kind of situation?

**Result** Taking a larger view that considers the various systems levels (culture, politics, values, gender, discourse and dominant narratives etc.) and realising that some issues, problems and situations need to be viewed within a systems perspective to make sense.

**Strategy** Reflect on system as it impacts behaviour. What do we need to change in order for this situation to be different? Create external generative dialogue that results in action. Move to upstream helping rather than downstream resuscitation (i.e. seeing the system as a problem and not just the individual).

**Positives and negatives** The positives of viewing issues in a systemic way are that we see the bigger picture and how connections interweave in subtle ways. We can also view individuals in their contexts and understand how context impacts behaviour. Negatively, it can be a way of avoiding personal responsibility and it's very easy for individuals to get sacrificed to and for the system.

**Blocks** See the big picture but forget about individuals.

---

### Example

Phil and Lisa look at the systems side of what has happened in the coaching arrangement with Marian. Phil realises he had not thought through the implications of coaching Marian, a member of his own team. His excitement in setting up his first coaching arrangement had blinded him to the possible systemic implication of what might happen. The members of his department are quite competitive and there has always been a lot of jockeying for position and credibility – he forgot to take this into consideration. Individuals are very sensitive to favouritism from those in authority. The system is reacting to the coaching arrangement and aware that Marian is trying to take advantage of it. Phil has naïvely ignored this part of his work. He did no preparation for how the system might receive coaching and his choice of one of the directors to be his coachee. On reflection it would have been better for him to find coachees outside his own managerial remit, where there was less possibility of negative reactions.

## Lens 5: Critical self-reflection (me (internalised) stance, transformational connection)

**Description** This is the self-transcendent position that means I begin to look at me and how I can so easily set up these situations with which I find myself involved (Gosh, it's actually about me!). It looks at how insight and awareness by me on me can result in ways of working that mean changing my mind-set and my meaning-making perspectives. I can change and if I change, then others have the opportunity to experience the situation differently. Thinking inter-subjectively (relationally) but in a way that helps me see my part in this. This could be called *transformational* reflection.

**Learning** Learning and knowledge here revolve around self awareness and knowing oneself often seen as the most difficult of all ways of knowing. Individuals look inwards to review who they are, how they learn and what meaning-making perspectives colour their processes of learning. Besides looking inwards introspectively to discover themselves they also look outwards to others to tell them who they are through feedback, dialogue and relationship.

**TA stance** I'm OK, you're OK. Position is one of personal responsibility. The me-stance (internal). I have issues and problems I need to resolve. Unlike Lens 1 which is also a 'me' position but external to me and sees problems outside myself, Lens 5 goes internal to articulate my own patterns and themes that contribute to the way I engage in life and relationships. I am therefore part of the problem as well as part of the solution.

**Statements** What is my contribution to this? Can I see patterns in my life whereby I end up here a lot? How does my way of thinking result in this kind of situation? What strategies did I develop back there that still impact my here-and-now behaviour?

**Result** I become self-aware – of myself as person, myself in relationship to others, myself at work. I look for more awareness and insights into myself as agent and try to articulate the themes and patterns in my life that contribute to keeping me where I am.

**Strategy** Reflect on self-as-agent. What do I need to change in order for this situation to be different, and for a psychological pattern to be broken? An internal dialogue? I look for the assumptions I bring to life and work. I review my meaning-making processes. I change the thinking behind my thinking.

**Positives and negatives** This stance is positive in that it looks inside to help individuals understand how the patterns of their lives, their scripts and ways of being impact on behaviour and others in major ways. It assists increased self-awareness and transformational learning. Negatively, it can result in blaming oneself in the first instance for anything that goes wrong – it's always me. It can also result in shame and fear in individuals who focus on this lens to the exclusion of other lenses.

**Blocks** Navel-gazing. So caught up in my own development that I forget others. Over-reflection that results in rumination and obsessions. Our inner defences can also become an obstacle to further reflection.

---

### Example

Lisa asks Phil to look within himself and see if he can articulate what he has brought to the table and what personal learning he can take from this experience with Marian. With some embarrassment, Phil admits he could have handled this situation much more delicately had he given cognisance to the system he worked in and been more aware of the implication of his actions. He looked within and realised that he had chosen Marian because she was new, she was attractive and he quite liked the 'adoration' she gave him. He was also like a child with a new toy – so eager to try it out that he forgot to think though the implications of who he 'played with'. He liked that he was mentoring someone inexperienced who was open to his wisdom. He realised he had not drawn up a contract with Marian or with the rest of his team. And he had learned about how open he was to manipulation. From these growths in awareness Lisa helps Phil get in touch with the implicit and explicit assumptions underpinning how he thinks and acts, and supports him in changing them for healthier assumptions.

---

### Lens 6: Transcendental reflection (other (universal) stance, universal connection)

**Description** This is the reflective stance that sees beyond – to what makes, and gives, meaning to life. It transcends any particular relationship, person or situation, opening into a larger construct that is inherent in all relationships, people or situations. For many this can be a religious or spiritual stance that helps reflect *from* a philosophy or a system of meaning that already exists (e.g., Christianity, Judaism) or one that I create (my philosophy of life). It can be seen as what gives meaning to life, people and behaviour (e.g., that God loves us, that suffering exists, that individuals have value in themselves). It adopts an existential position on life and is often called transpersonal or transcendent reflection. It can be theistically based or not.

**Learning** Learning and knowledge here builds on metavalues and ways of being together that transcend or subsume individual difference. This way of knowing asks individuals, teams and groups to suspend individual ways of knowing and find communal knowledge based on beliefs they can share with integrity. It is not a demand to give up individual knowledge but a courageous way of going beyond individual learning in the service of the whole.

**TA stance** There is a higher or larger perspective that helps me make sense of life and purpose (humanistic, atheistic, denominational religion etc.). I find meaning by subscribing to this existential position and I attempt to live the current situation through this expanded perspective, recognising my own personal limitations of perception, but with the clear intention to expand my 'little self' and embody more of the qualities of transcendence that guide, teach and inspire me. I am willing to adopt this expanded view/state of being, even though it may require me to enter a space of 'not knowing' and may engender a profound restructuring of my mental constructs.

**Statements** From within this viewpoint (my philosophy of life) how can I make sense of this event? What are the real values that I believe in? Behind our choices lurk our values.

**Result** Building my behaviour on principles I believe in, that go beyond myself and others as individuals and even systems.

**Strategy** Reflect on life, people and behaviour from a spiritual and transcendent purpose that is bigger than we are. How do I/we reflect from a wider purpose bigger than us all? We find humility, curiosity and reverence helpful here. Finding the overarching context that makes sense of how I/we make meaning.

**Positives and negatives** Positive reflection here can help see and view life and reality in an even bigger picture than that based on values. These values tend to be more than just personal values but deep principles and communal values. Negatively, reflection here can become an end in itself where action is ignored. It can get out of touch with reality when principles and values are more important than people.

**Blocks** The block here is that individuals can become 'so heavenly minded that they are no earthly good'. Get lost in philosophy or transcendental (rather than an incarnational) theology or spirituality. Get overwhelmed by the vastness of perspective and disconnect from the ordinary delights of daily living. Lens 6 can become a flight from reflection, and indeed a way of avoiding reflection.

## Example

Lisa asked Phil to go wider again and look at himself and his values. Phil had been strongly Buddhist in his beliefs and practice and wanted to call on that as a way of reflecting on what had happened. How to be compassionate towards himself came high on the list. Then compassion for others. Acceptance of his limitations and his learning. He realises the limitations in his life, and works towards letting go his negative feelings towards Marian and himself.

## The skills needed for each lens

Running this example briefly through the six lenses of reflection helps us see the focus of each stage and the strategies that emerge from reflection using these different perspectives. Obviously new skills are needed in order to have access to different lenses. For example, the move from Lens 1 (zero reflection) to Lens 2 (empathic reflection) requires empathy and the ability to separate somewhat from one's one point of view. This can be taught and may need some practice times to become fine-tuned. Moving from Lens 2 to 3 and 4 requires the ability to think relationally and systemically, and understand systemic relationships where behaviour can be seen to be a result of those relationships. It also requires the skill of dialogue.

Self-awareness skills, insights, awareness, openness and some courage is needed at Lens 5 as we begin or continue the journey of insight into ourselves and our interpersonal and intrapersonal styles. Lens 6 is based on a belief of something beyond or further and often takes place when we are able to move beyond ourselves to principles that guide and support us. It would seem helpful to train or coach individuals and teams in the abilities needed to access all six levels of reflection.

Table 10.2 illustrates the skills needed to make best use of each lens.

TABLE 10.2   *Skills needed for each reflective lens*

| Lens | Skills needed |
| --- | --- |
| 1 | (None) |
| 2 | Empathy/self-distancing |
| 3 | Dialogue/emotional intelligence |
| 4 | Thinking systemically |
| 5 | Self-awareness/listening to feedback |
| 6 | Transpersonal thinking/values clarification |

## Learning from the six lenses of reflection

A number of factors emerge while working with the six lenses of reflection. First of all, while we started and moved through the lenses systematically, from 1 to 6, it is not always necessary to do so in that order. Many individuals go directly to Lens 6 and review their situation through the values they hold dear, others move quickly to lens 5 and ask how they are contributing to the relationship. Reflection does not have to be sequential, as presented here.

Second, all lenses of reflection are good. While lenses sometimes gives the impression that the deeper I go the more valuable it is, the most helpful stance is being able to use all six lenses as and when needed. Lens 1 can be an invaluable asset during times when I don't want to be empathetic, dialogic or negotiate: 'That is not acceptable behaviour – I do not want to listen to you – you will need to change what you are doing' is a valid response in some circumstances. Being non-negotiating is not bad at times.

Third, each reflective lens brings valuable information pertinent to its own stage. Observing which lens is used can help supervisors learn about how the supervisee impacts on people in the outside world. Lens 1 and 2 reflections give valuable information on the interpersonal world of the other. It will also help supervisors see how the supervisee's history impacts their interpersonal scheme (e.g., take up a persecutor, rescuer or a victim stance). Lens 2 will offer supervisors an idea of how people can be empathetic to others but still remain at a relationship distance. Lens 3 is important for the reflector to achieve if they are to do good work with the other person. Lens 4 gives good insights and information on the organisational and systemic contexts in which we work, and sometimes ignore to our peril. Our own learning comes in Lens 5, which we can feed back into Lens 3 and 4.

Fourth, it is important not to get fixated with any of the lenses, especially 4 or 6, where we can over reflect or become disconnected from the more grounded aspects of life. Being able to move back and forth through all six lenses (when appropriate) is the most helpful stance. It is not helpful to conversations or relationships when someone is stuck in one level and cannot reflect from within other levels. It is like having a camera with only one lens; accessing or changing lenses provides greater choice and multiple perspectives. Difficulties arise when there are different levels of conversation and reflection in the same room (e.g., someone using Lens 1 one can be certain of what they say, but it will be difficult to have an open conversation if someone else is coming from within Lens 4). The supervisor must, however, allow themselves to reflect back some of the areas important to supervisees (e.g., helping supervisees review their work through the lens of their religious beliefs).

Fifth, the skill of moving amongst these different lenses of reflection is not just an individual competency but applies to couples, teams and organisations. It is legitimate to ask which reflective lenses are available to a team or an organisation. Individuals, couples, teams and organisations have characteristic reflective lenses that they move towards automatically; under stress they often revert to 'lower' levels of lens. Contextual and external influences can impact dramatically on our ability to use different lenses.

## Example

Paulo is normally calm and easy going, with a relaxed and open interpersonal style. He is reflective and sensitive to his clients. However, three crises in the space of three weeks has thrown him. His daughter has hurt her neck in a car accident and is still off work and in pain; his mother has been

*(Continued)*

*(Continued)*

diagnosed with senile dementia and is no longer safe on her own; and he and his wife have reached the decision to spend some time apart to decide if they want to remain together. Without noticing it, Paulo has become tense and somewhat impatient. With one of his long-term clients he heard himself say, to his own horror, that it was time 'to pull yourself together and stop wallowing in self-pity'. Paulo realises in supervision that his ability to access all of the reflective lenses is greatly diminished, and his empathy seems to have disappeared as his personal problems have grown.

These reflective lenses can be used in both life and work. Decision making can rely on one level or many. Ethics and religion can be seen from within each level and the types of ethics practised (ethics of duty, ethics of trust, relational ethics, systemic ethics etc.) can differ radically depending on which level is used to access it. There can also be blocks to reflection, as we have indicated above, some particular to each level. Sometimes we need to ask at what level of reflection we need to be in order to resolve a particular problem we are facing. Perhaps problems don't get faced or resolved because we are not looking at them from an appropriate perspective (e.g., environmental issues and problems often need a systemic and collaborative strategy rather than simply an individual response).

At times some levels may not be appropriate to use. Asking someone who is been bullied or harassed at work what contribution they are making would be very insensitive and could easily make them feel responsible for something outside their control.

These lenses of reflection can be connected to different levels of learning (single-, double- and triple-loop learning). As we move down the levels we move away from content (Lenses 1 and 2) into process (Lenses 3 and 4). Issues of how power is used (power over, power with, power through and power within) can also be applied to different levels (e.g., power over is more of a Lens 1 feature, while power with is more focused on Lenses 3 and 4). Power within can come with Lenses 5 and 6. The movement through lenses is not simply a cognitive one but a fully emotional one that involves the body as well as the mind. Moore (2008) presents on reflective processes that involve enhanced and deepening self-awareness, or what he calls *emotional knowing* as part of supervision reflexivity. Individuals often reflect in and through their bodies. Consciousness raising takes place as we are able to access deeper levels (Kegan, 1994).

Supervisors consider which is the appropriate level of reflection that best connects to where the supervisee is, and yet challenges them to move towards their next level of reflection and learning.

## Conclusion

For a long time we have presented 'reflective practice' as an ideal to be attained. Reflecting on our work leads to insights and shifts that change practice. There is little to help supervisors learn how to reflect or how to deepen their reflection so that they might in turn hand on this ability to their supervisees. This chapter not just presents reflective lenses but hopefully also provides ways in which supervisors and supervisees can learn how to access and use all of the lenses as an integral part of supervision.

# Eleven

# The Storytelling Brain and Supervision

**Chapter summary**

Storytelling is our human way of communicating our experiences. We wrap our experiences in stories as a way of making sense of them and then communicate them to others in story-like formats. But not only do we tell stories, we also have a particular and unique way of telling our stories that is founded and based on our early life experiences – our storytelling signature. This signature is hardwired into our brains and often out of awareness. In this chapter we use Cron's insights to look at supervising, storytelling and the brain and how we can get in touch with how we tell our stories and why we do it the way we do.

As far as I know, animals other than humans don't tell stories. We know they have forms of communication, and some of these are quite astonishing – as when elephants communicate through the ground and dolphins and whales sing to one another. I have even learned the communication patterns of our cat, who leaves me in no doubt about what he wants. But telling stories seems to be unique to humans. Why is that? Why do we cluster together and create stories? Is it the camaraderie of sharing news or gossip? Or simply the sheer enjoyment of using the human gift of language? It seems to be all of these. Knowing *why* we package experience in story formats and knowing *how* we do it is of interest to supervision; supervision is a story-telling methodology. Supervisees tell the stories of their work in supervision. They weave their practice into narratives that explain to themselves and to those who listen what happened with their clients.

## Example

Gerry glances at his notes. 'Today,' he says to his supervision group, 'I want to talk about Elsie. I saw Elsie for the first time yesterday. She is tall, rather overweight and dresses in very dark and rather dowdy clothes. I noticed immediately how little eye contact she made when I met her at the door. And even though I knew she wanted to be in counselling with me, I found it hard work. I had to do a lot of the running. But let me back up a bit. Elsie is in her early 40s ...'

In the next ten minutes Gerry presents Elsie to his supervision group. His presentation will be a mixture of facts (she is in her early 40s), of interpretation (she is shy and uneasy around people), of conjectures (that her unease with him shows her unease around men in general) and speculation (her way of dealing with the world is very embedded and short-term counselling may not help). For good measure Gerry will throw in his own experience of being with Elsie (it was very difficult to engage with her emotionally; she kept me at a distance) and explain his theoretical understanding of why she is the way she is (her attachment style is avoidant, as illustrated in her first meeting with him). All of these elements will be contained in the *story* he tells of his first meeting with Elsie.

His story doesn't end there. His supervisor and other members of his supervision group will hear the story he recounts, and they in turn will create other stories, incorporating his story and adding their own touches.

## Example

Brigid listens carefully as Gerry recounts his first meeting with Elsie. She processes what she hears through her own experience of working with women, and wonders if Elsie was abused as a child. A lot of what Gerry tells the group about Elsie seems to fit into that pattern.

Noel listens carefully too. He wonders if counselling will be of help to Elsie. What she seems to be missing are social and emotional skills. He wonders if being part of a woman's group might help Elsie better, and he is about to suggest to Gerry a group therapist who runs such groups.

Pat, the supervisor, has heard the story and two things have crossed her mind. Why is Elsie coming to counselling just now – has something happened to make her decide to come to counselling? Why choose a man as her counsellor? She is thinking of how Gerry told the story of their first meeting; it was delivered in a very rational, logical, non-emotional manner. She was curious about how their first session story could be re-told from an emotional perspective.

What story would we hear if Elsie was to narrate her account of what happened in that first session? Actually she did, to her best friend, when they met in the evening after that first session.

> ### Example
>
> 'I didn't like him,' Elsie said. 'When my GP said they had a counsellor as part of their practice and suggested I see him, I went along with it. I would have preferred to see a woman, actually. I wasn't sure if I needed counselling or career guidance. This bout of low energy and this dreadful flu are, in my view, more about being in the wrong job. But I went along anyway. I found him cold. He was very professional with that counsellor-face you see at times in films. It was all deadly serious and intense. At the end of it he suggested I come back for five more sessions to see if we can work on my depression. He just didn't get the message that I didn't want to share my thoughts with him. I'm not going back.'

How many stories, all different, are contained in the episode of Gerry meeting Elsie for the first time in a GP counselling service? It reminds us of Queneau's (1998) little book we referred to in Chapter 9 about the same incident being re-counted in over a hundred different ways.

## Stories and supervision

We wrap up and package our experience in stories. Narrative is our way of making sense of what happens to us and our way of communicating our sense of that experience to others. Hence the many different stories above – each makes sense of what happened in his/her own way; stories are told about stories. Stories are less about objective truth, what actually happened, and much more about how we interpret what happened. Creating the story and communicating the story are what makes us human. Our executive brain allows us to do what other animals cannot: make sense of our experience. Our wonderful imaginations weave that sense-making into stories.

## Signature stories – how the big story influences the little stories

In the example above it is Gerry who is telling the story of his first meeting with Elsie. Were it someone else, they would probably tell the story differently. We tell stories from *who we are* and from *where we are*. Stories are not just facts; they are as much about the way individuals meet, notice and recount facts as they are about facts. We all have a story-making mould that influences how we tell the story.

Our stories are constructed around scaffolding that is particular and peculiar to us. We each have our own story-telling modality. Being aware of it helps us know how and why we tell stories the way we do; it also helps us change the way we construct our stories.

Like so much else in our lives the why, how, when, what, where aspects of the way we create and tell our stories have their roots in childhood. Our induction into family, community and wider contexts of life brings with them a way of seeing, reflecting on and interpreting the world. These influence the way we construct our narratives. We develop a story-making style. Largely inherited, our first thinking and reflective lens is fashioned on the anvil of our childhood experiences which we embed in life strategies. Transactional analysis practitioners call this 'a life script' and show how it determines how we see, think and express ourselves. It has also been called an 'organising statement ... summaries of our lives condensed into a single phrase or sentence – that's our autobiography in a nutshell, that's how we see the world' (Luxmoore, 2011: 108).

This organising or signature statement contains a characteristic way of thinking, of doing, of relating and feeling and could be summarised in statements such as: I wasn't wanted; I am special; I have ADHD; I always come second; I am invisible; I don't deserve anything; I don't exist; I have dyslexia. It is a powerful statement that *defines* the person. The power of these organising statements is their ability to colour, influence and determine both how we see reality and the lens through which we reflect on the reality we see. A coaching colleague of mine recalls a pivotal moment in his life when he heard his father say to his mother, 'That boy never finishes anything'. Presumably his father had caught accurately the signature of his life. My colleague will tell you how that phrase, and the stance behind the phrase, guided his life and career for many years.

Wilson (2002) calls this a 'distinctive behavioural signature' which colours behaviour deeply. It works on the *if ... then* causal pattern. *If* I am unwanted by my parents *then* in a situation where I am given negative feedback I feel a deep sense of rejection and abandonment. I internalise the criticism that was meant for my work. My story will always be tainted with an abandonment or rejection theme. You can fill in for yourself the *if ... then* sentence: If I am shy, then ... what? If I have little confidence, then ... what? If I never finish anything, then ... what? There is a clockwork kind of quality about this. It happens subconsciously. Freud wrote many years ago that we cannot hide who we are – it manifests itself in many ways.

The 'distinctive behaviour signature' has a 'scanning pattern' or template that selects pertinent information and data that supports its own story. It notices things and interprets them according to the dictates of the signature. It is constantly alert for certain types of stimuli: rejection, criticism, dismissal, praise, admiration.

What that signature does is hardwire us into habits so that we live unconsciously most of the time – our 'learned pre-packaged routines' (Engle and Singer, 2008:10). Rock puts it well:

> Our habits are literally unconscious to us; we don't 'have in mind' what we are doing. You might take this further and say that once people have done a job for some time, they are unconscious much of their workday. (Rock, 2007: 13)

Practitioners in the helping professions perform much of their work on autopilot, and the more experienced we are, the more the tendency towards automaticy occurs. Just as we have mind habits and action habits, so we have story-telling habits. Supervision is a wake-up call to pay attention to the work we have been doing without much thought. It is an invitation to trace and expose the habits that have become second-nature to us. In doing so, we give ourselves an opportunity to hold them up to the light, reflect on them and decide whether we want to maintain them or trade them for more appropriate habits.

Many of our habitual processes are unconscious and generally inaccessible through introspection. Looking at our behaviour, rather than analysing ourselves, and asking others for feedback is much more helpful in illuminating for us these behind-the-scenes ways of thinking and reflecting. As we do our work, we make moment-to-moment decisions about how to proceed. Reflection in action helps this. Reflection in action reviews the decisions made and feeds back into skills development.

## Example

Eleanor asks Sandy if he would write her a note to confirm she is in counselling with him, and working on her authority issues. She wants to bring this note to her forthcoming appraisal session which she hopes will be a springboard for a promotion. Sandy takes a moment to reflect on the request. It is only the second session and he is still forming the relationship with Eleanor. He wants to please her, and show how accommodating he is. He agrees to do so there and then, but later, with his supervisor, he reflects back on what has happened. In the less-urgent and more conversational context of supervision he feels that his decision had been hurried and he had 'given in' to a request without thinking through its implications. While he couldn't renege on his promise, he decided for the future that he would not do so without having time to think it through. In particular he would not be pressurised by what he hoped the client would think of him.

Sandy realises from this example that he has a tendency to please his clients and seek to be liked by them. This was activated by Eleanor's request and he responded spontaneously without much reflection. Later he became aware of what had happened to him, and his insights helped him prepare for the future when similar requests are made.

Signature stories can be about our lives, our world, our worldview or about others. Indeed, *story* has become synonymous with the contours of individuality that mark us out: 'What's his story?' When we ask that question we are looking for facts, but not just facts – we want both the story and what it means.

Counselling rooms throughout the world are populated by people whose story has been stolen by abuse, neglect, trauma, bullying or bad parenting. A plant which is overshadowed is deprived of the light it needs to grow and a person who has been overshadowed has been deprived of the room to grow into their own story. Individuation has been hampered by a domineering parent or sibling. In such cases it feels like the person's story has been stolen. The function of counselling could be said to be the restoration of the right of the client to tell their own story. Supervisees can have their stories stolen too – by supervisor and supervision groups that impose a different story or disrespect their story or shame them when they have told their stories. In this respect *story* is very close to what we mean by *voice* in Chapter 9. Stories are fragile: they carry with them much more than words, communications and explanations – they carry identities.

## Conscious and unconscious story-telling

In summary, the human brain learns and then consigns learning into the unconscious so that we can respond to external situations and stimuli *without* thinking or awareness. This creates habits which save enormous amounts of brain energy and allows us to work speedily. It has been estimated that more than 40 per cent of our actions aren't actual decisions, but habits (Duhigg, 2013: Location 148 of 7929). Our brains create patterns of automaticity in our lives (automatic pilot) whereby we respond quickly and easily to the day-to-day situations that arise. Activities such as driving a car, getting dressed in the morning and using a computer are automatic gestures for the most part. It means we live most of our day mindlessly. We also have a hidden method of telling stories that is also habitual.

Faced with a new situation, the brain rapidly trawls memory for the solution, an earlier story. What you have done before is the normal guide to what you will do now. We tend to react to present situations in the way we have reacted to past situations; it is still a recognised psychological principle that past behaviour is a fair predictor of future behaviour. When you recognise a friend coming towards you from the crowd, your memory has successfully matched this image with the image installed in your memory. You meet your friend 'from memory' and rarely 'from the experience of the present.'

### Example

Jemima was talking with her supervisor about her problem in ending with a particular client in her counselling work. She shared how she had been putting off terminating the relationship even though he was happy with what

*(Continued)*

*(Continued)*

they had done, and had talked of moving on. Jemima's supervisor, Harbrinder, remembered Jemima talking several times about her childhood and the feelings of abandonment around her father who had died when she was two and her elder sister who had died when she was six. Abandonment had been a key issue for Jemima throughout her life and she lived with an expectation that important people in her life would leave her. Harbrinder made the connection and asked, 'Do you think your reluctance to end with Eamonn is connected to your on-going fear of abandonment?' 'I suppose it must be. That would certainly explain it,' Jemima replied. 'But let me just stay with this a bit longer.' As she and Harbrinder talked in some depth about the client they both realised that while there were connections to her past, Jemima was also picking up that her client had not quite finished what he had come to counselling for. She was picking up two messages simultaneously from him: it's time to move on; and I want you to challenge me about what I need to do before moving on. Harbrinder had made meaning from the past without considering that there could be an explanation from the present.

We all too quickly move to the past, and our memories, to provide explanations rather than stay in the present to make meaning. The fact that I know my boss is moody and gets distracted can all too readily come to mind when I notice that he is a bit volatile and withdrawn. Rather than realising that he is actually preoccupied just now with an issue that is worrying him, I interpret his behaviour through the lens of my prior knowledge of him. I have explained his behaviour from memory rather than from present experience. Past explanations (you always do this!) may be unhelpful in present situations (I wonder why you are doing this?). Previous stories we have to ourselves can be helpful or unhelpful in creating the story of the present.

Gazzaniga (2012: 85) recounts a social psychology experiment that illustrates how we perceive through what we already know. Subjects in this experiment had make-up artists draw a very real looking scar on their faces. They were told that the experiment would look at how other people responded to their very visible scar. Those to whom they were talking wouldn't know that the scar was false. The subjects were asked to take note of any reactions they considered took place as a direct result of the scar. At the last moment, unbeknown to the subjects, and under the guise of adding a bit more make-up, the scar was removed. The subjects went to meet people thinking they had scars on their faces while in reality they did not. After their conversations they reported that they had been treated badly by the others. When shown a video of the person to whom they talked they readily recalled their reactions, attributing those reactions to the scars. They read the reactions of others through the (mistaken) information that there was a scar on their face, even when there wasn't. They constructed their stories accordingly.

From this experiment we can make some inferences: that all of us make sense of our experiences from within the information we already have and the memory-stories we have created in the past – we rarely allow experience to teach us on its own. Experiences in life are met from within, and interpreted through, existing knowledge. Our new stories are being formed in the stories we have already created. Being given information becomes a self-fulfilling prophecy; we explain it from within information we already have. Our experiences are being constantly hijacked by our existing knowledge and squeezed into pre-existing mental models and frameworks.

Isaac (1999) talks about trying to meet people we know as strangers. This helps move from our knowing them from memory to meeting them fully in the present. Meeting someone as if you were meeting a stranger implies that you don't 'dump on them' all the existing knowledge you already possess and through which you make sense of current experiences with them.

Storytelling is a movement from mindlessness to mindfulness – we bring to mind what we are doing and capture it in words. Before we begin telling our story we recognise that we already have built up a *reflective process* through which we make sense of experience and capture it as meaning-making narrative. We don't tell isolated stories, rather we *recount* them selectively:

- through values we have already in place;
- from assumptions underpinning our lives and from which we move outwards;
- from limitations on what we have/haven't permission to reflect (perish the thought that I could be a selfish person); and
- from within communities of practice.

Critical self-reflection is the process by which I come to know the template behind my way of telling a story. It is the very individualised way that my reflective house has been designed and constructed. Think of the way you reflect as an assembly line. In comes the information, ideas, impressions, then they are processed in a predetermined and fixed manner.

## Example

Julie is pregnant and doesn't want to be. She has two children already and just been offered promotion to a long-sought job in her company. Having another baby at this stage in her life is not only inconvenient but would also put paid to the plans she and her husband, Eustace, have for the next few years. Julie sits down to reflect on her situation and review what might be the best decision for herself, her family and the unborn baby. She knows herself well enough to realise she will not be impulsive – it's not her. Neither will she be just accommodating the needs and wishes of others: Julie has spent a good deal of time working on her assertiveness and is able to hold the needs of others and her own needs in good balance.

We pause for a moment to look at the reflective process that Julie has installed as her way of reflecting. She is 'pro-choice', which means she is not theoretically or morally against abortion, and so she allows herself to give attention to abortion as one choice amongst others. She notices when she does this that she relaxes and feels easier about the future and her family. She knows she has existing assumptions about what being a woman and a mother means, and having an abortion would not damage her image of either of those. She knows that she and Eustace will spend time on this decision. Money could be tight if they decide to have the baby but money has never been a major factor in their decisions together – it is given space, but not allowed to dominate any decision.

Or take a different stance: Julie is morally opposed to abortion as a choice for herself. Her reflective assembly line starts from that position. Abortion is just not an option from a values point of view, so she is restricting her reflection to decisions that do not include that possibility.

A *holding space* is a moratorium we create when we are unsure, uncertain, puzzled. When we have no obvious answer we go into *on-hold* mode while we sort out thinking, feeling, intuiting and sensing. We go into a process of consideration to see if we can come to a decision.

The 'see, I told you so' story is a common one and we may stick with it whatever. This locked-in story of ours becomes the template for creating other stories. Information is squeezed into this mould like meat into a sausage machine: I tell a story to make sense of my experience; the story I tell is created from within my particular story-making mould which has itself been created from my early life. Can I be liberated from this circular way of making stories and learn to tell them differently?

Supervision is an internal journey to find out *how I tell stories* as well as an external journey to look at the possibilities of telling other, new stories so that we can arrive at the 'best story for now'.

## The brain and stories

Lisa Cron (2012) summarises what we know about our brains with regard to storytelling and story writing:

- We think in story which allows us to envision the future.
- The brain uses stories to simulate how we might navigate difficult situations in the future.
- When the brain focuses its full attention on something it filters out all unnecessary information.
- Emotion determines the meaning of everything.
- Everything we do is goal directed.

- We see the world, not as it is, but as we believe it to be.
- The brain is wired to resist change, even good change.
- The brain is hardwired to make causal connections (if this, then that).
- Since the brain abhors randomness, it is always converting raw data into meaningful patterns.

## Example

Stacey is a couple's counsellor. She meets Chloe for the first time. Within minutes Chloe is in tears, sobbing. Through her tears she recounts how she didn't for a minute see it coming – her husband of 25 years has suddenly decided he needs 'to find himself' and is going to an ashram in India for two months. She is feeling totally rejected and isolated. Their only child, a daughter, is in Australia, travelling. Chloe is certain there is another woman involved and that this is her husband's way of breaking the news more gently to her. Since telling her a week ago, he has moved out to stay with his best friend. She is exhausted, emotionally distraught and can't think of anything else. She is telling and retelling the story in different ways: What if ...? In particular she is worrying about facing the future on her own and is already rehearsing scenarios about what life would be like after marriage.

This event illustrates how Chloe's brain is making sense of what has happened. Processing it through Cron's statements on the brain illustrates how the brain creates stories. We think in story which allows us to envision the future (Chloe has created a story from the events that have happened and already has envisaged a future without her husband).

Question: What other possible stories are there besides this one?

The brain uses stories to simulate how we might navigate difficult situations in the future. (Chloe's imagination has already fashioned scenarios to deal with possible futures.)

Question: How might imagination create different future scenarios?

When the brain focuses its full attention on something, it filters out all unnecessary information. (Focused on her current situation, Chloe cannot get outside what is happening to her and she might miss relevant information that might help interpret things in other ways.)

Question: What information is being missed and not attended to that could make a difference in the narrative?

Emotion determines the meaning of everything. (Chloe, at this moment, is caught in a cauldron of emotions that are dictating her thinking and her actions. Later she will be guided, rather than ruled, by her emotions in making decisions in respect of her husband and the future.)

Question: What emotions need be considered deeply and how can distance be created from emotions that are overwhelming or imprisoning just now?

Everything we do is goal directed. (Chloe is already thinking of the future and while her thinking just now is short term, her long-term thinking processes will click in eventually.)

Question: What is needed short term and what is needed long term?

We see the world not as it is, but as we believe it to be. (Chloe's world is being created from behind her eyes as much as from what is in front of her. Her beliefs and values impact what she perceives and sees and she filters out information that does not conform to scanning pattern; e.g., the possibility that there may not be another woman involved.)

Question: How might others see what is happening? What other interpretations might there be?

The brain is wired to resist change, even good change. (Chloe cannot think that what has just happened might be an invitation for her, her husband and their relationship to change. Perhaps later she will.)

Question: What are these events challenging me to think about, to feel and to change?

The brain is hardwired to make causal connections. (Already Chloe has constructed and connected up what she knows to create a coherent account of the information she possesses; she concludes her husband has another relationship and is finding a way of telling her about it so that she can be let down more easily.)

Question: What assumptions are being made and can they be articulated and questioned?

Since the brain abhors randomness, it is always converting raw data into meaningful patterns, the better to anticipate the future. (Chloe's antennae are focused now for every scrap of information that will fit into her story; even when material is not connected, she will find a way of making it consistent with the story she has created.)

Question: Can the story be unravelled and can randomness be tolerated for a while?

How helpful is it in counselling and supervision when we understand how the brain creates story, and when we look in detail at the processes we are going through as we create our stories? Such knowledge and insight gives us more control over our stories and more awareness of the methods, helpful or otherwise, we employ to make sense of our experiences.

## Conclusion

This chapter has looked at how our human brains, unlike the brains of other animals, are structured to tell stories. This human ability has two main functions: to make sense of our experiences to ourselves; and to communicate our experience to others in ways they can understand. Stories wrap facts in imaginative boxes. Opening the boxes becomes a compelling adventure. Stories are about journeys. They move from the outward to the inward. As I face the characters in the story, so I begin to face myself. Who am I in the story? What part do I play? I can be raconteur, witness or central character, and occasionally all three? The story won't let me settle for neutral observer status – it almost always demands more. It insists I identify with and find myself in the characters. Stories are more about the listeners than they are about the characters that appear in them.

All good stories pluck the heartstrings. A story is meant to provoke emotions, to engage feelings. For a long time the West ignored feelings and saw them as distractions, irrelevant or subordinate to rational thought. That has all changed and the modern task-oriented world of objectives and deadlines knows that feelings and emotions are of paramount importance as the *motive* force behind actions. Stories 'know' that intuitively. Each story enfolds us in an emotional world. Story is our way of making sense of what life delivers to us, first emotionally and then cognitively.

Stories are the 'stuff' of supervision. Understanding them as a medium of communication, understanding the storyteller as an architect of meaning, understanding the supervisory relationship as the context in which one story becomes a shared story is what makes supervision fascinating and ever fresh.

# Epilogue

I started this book by suggesting we take a walk across the supervisory landscape, stopping occasionally to notice and dwell on some key themes within supervision. Thank you for accompanying me on the journey. You may well have chosen themes other than the ones I did. Mine are ones that have chosen me and wormed their ways into my practice both as supervisor and supervisee. Choice inevitably limits, and one of the limits of this book is that it is not comprehensive, making no attempt to cover all aspects of supervision. I have chosen to present a 'philosophy of supervision' rather than the 'nuts and bolts' of how supervision works. Other excellent supervisory texts do that. I have pointed you towards the ones I have found helpful as we have meandered through the supervisory field.

Working with people, in any form, creates the potential to be 'extremely dangerous', as Mike Ellis points out when he writes: 'I know just enough about clinical supervision to be extremely dangerous' (Ellis, 2010: 112). Relationships truly are for better or for worse. The danger in relationships is often about how power is distributed, shared, used and abused. It's far too easy to enter into 'guru' or 'expert' status (in one's own mind, of course) and begin to think one knows more or better than others, especially supervisees. Power is forever at work in relationships, unbalancing them and tipping them imperceptibly towards abuse. Over the years I have noticed how easy it is for my needs (to be needed, to be admired, to be depended upon, to be strong, to be a supervisory Robin Hood or Attila the Hun) to spring to the surface and hijack supervision. Those are the times I am 'dangerous'. Humility, awareness and acceptance of my own limitations, being prepared to admit how little I *really* know, are the best tools in my supervisor's toolkit. They help keep some of the dangers at bay. These qualities keep my feet on the ground and my head close to reality. They help me put supervisees and clients where they truly belong: at the centre of supervision. True wisdom is knowing how little we know and rejoicing humbly in the knowledge we have and the skills we possess. I wish I were able to do that more consistently and more often.

For me Socrates is the supervisor par excellence. What makes him such an icon for supervisors is his attitude to himself, his life and his work. What might he say to the supervisors and supervisees of today? These are the principles I imagine he would suggest that we follow:

- *Know how little you know:* No matter how much you know or how many books you have read, there is so much more that you don't know. Be aware of your ignorance and don't get complacent. Uncertainty is the beginning of wisdom.

- *Be open minded:* There are other models, frameworks and theories that will teach you a lot. Yours is always only a partial truth – move away from 'aggressive certainty' (Armstrong, 2011). Continue to be curious and inquisitive – even after you have made decisions.
- *Contemplation takes time:* Good decisions are not judged by the speed by which they are made.
- *Keep talking to others:* In dialogue, where you are gently truth-seeking together, you will come more easily to what is right for you. Consider what is said or known, and what is not yet said or known.
- *Take responsibility:* While others will help, advise and share with you, you must take final responsibility for the decisions you make. Your decisions reflect your own moral character, so asking yourself what will be right for you as well as right for others is important in delivering authentic action, and then living with yourself later.
- *Use your power wisely:* Do not overwhelm, or force others to believe what you believe, but help them to question. Create an atmosphere of trust where it is safe to be curious and challenge each other.
- *Above all, don't be afraid:* Fear is the enemy of learning and excellence.
- *Act consciously:* Given particular relationships, contexts, systems and timing, there will be times when you choose to obey rules and regulations even when not of your making, and even when you disagree with them. It is important that you do this thoughtfully and in a reasoned way, being conscious of why you have chosen to do this as the best option in the circumstances.
- *Take the initiative:* Don't wait for others to do things.
- *Live what you believe in:* Build bridges all the time, especially between theory and practice.

These strategies, as well as Socrates' love of incisive questions, are good guides for supervisors. Unfortunately, Socrates did not live to a ripe old age seeing out his years in supervisory arrangements appreciated for his wisdom and insights. He fell foul of those who felt his stance on reflection and questioning accepted wisdom was a form of corruption. Sentenced to death, he passionately defended his position and elegantly accepted the verdict. While such a fate awaits few modern supervisors, perhaps we are not in danger because we don't risk enough, challenge what is taken for granted and ask the kinds of incisive questions that create turbulence. If supervision is to be at the edge of learning, then it must ask the questions that everyone takes for granted and befriend the forgotten, the silenced, the ignored and the subtle. Socrates refused to take money for his work so that he could be 'his own man'. Maybe he knew what we may have forgotten or have never known – that money buys not just ideas but people, and when you are bought you so often collude. Collusion is the original and greatest supervisory sin, and collusion to keep supervision safe, acceptable, calm and reasonable is still as big a temptation today as it was in the days of Socrates.

Many years ago I discovered the work of Sam Keen and I am profoundly grateful to him for offering me a 'Spirituality Bullshit Detector' when I needed one. Since then I have adapted his work to supervision and have devised a 'Supervisor Bullshit Detector' along similar lines. This can be applied to yourself as supervisor and to those you choose to supervise your work. As in all aspects of supervision, its aim is to keep you ever open to learning and realising that the best leanings often come from the most unexpected of places, and the most unusual of people. Hopefully the final aim of supervision is to create an 'internal supervisor' that becomes more sensitive and watchful over time. Here are the tenets of the 'Supervisor Bullshit Detector':

Beware of charismatic leaders, unquestioned authorities, enlightened masters, perfect gurus, reincarnated teachers and particularly those who have discovered the only valid form of doing something. You will only end up seeing life and clients and supervision through their eyes and not your own. You will know this kind of person because they will demand that you be like them.

Beware of anyone who demands obedience; they have not discovered that there are 'other' people in the world and want to keep you as a child.

Beware of supervisors who lead double lives. Look carefully at their professional life; are there double standards, are they asking from you what they do not do themselves?

Check to see if your supervisor has friends, peer relationships and a community of equals, or do they have only disciples? Beware of those who have only disciples.

Beware of supervisors who have achieved universal compassion but lack the capacity for simple friendships. Keep in mind what Dag Hammarskjöld once said: 'It is more noble to give yourself completely to one individual than to labour diligently for the salvation of the masses' (1966).

Beware of supervisors who do not encourage difference of opinion, challenge, criticism and discussion. Good supervisors are open to whatever truth comes knocking on the supervisory door.

Beware of supervisors who demand that you put loyalty to them above loyalty to friends or family, especially those who put down others and ask you to take sides.

Test your supervisor to see how much humour and poking of fun about beliefs, slogans and dogmas is permissible. The absence of humour is an almost certain sign that you should pack your psychological bags and get the hell out of there! The first thing deadly serious fanatical rulers and organisations do is to forbid satire, repress the clowns, silence the jesters and kill levity. Supervisors who never laugh or play should be avoided at all costs.

And finally, check the batteries on your own Supervisor Bullshit Detector to make sure it is in good working order. (Adapted from Sam Keen, 1994: 113–114)

Finally, I don't want to end this book on a negative, even if with an amusing account of supervisor bullshit detectors. I want to end it by saying I love supervision,

I love being a supervisor and I love being supervised. Throughout the 34 years I have been involved with it I have not lost my enthusiasm or passion for supervision. It is all I hoped it would be: creative, fascinating, insightful, challenging and demanding.

I started off in the Preface by quoting Brookfield: 'the best teachers are good burglars, contextually attended plunderers – they are always on the lookout for something they haven't tried before that, with a few adaptations, will work with their students' (2012: x). My hope is that you have had lots to plunder in these pages and lots that, for you, are starting points to think about supervision anew.

# Appendix 1
## The Supervisory Journey: A Memoir

I am sure there is a wonderful connection between why individuals become supervisors and their early experiences in life. Joan Wilmot describes this for herself in a chapter entitled 'Work as Transformation through Supervision' (2011). She remembers her father dying in a motor bike accident when she was nearly two years old; she recounts her mother's family history including accidental deaths and family break-ups. Her conclusion:

> I think as a result of this early trauma I have a part of me that is engaged in healing shock both in myself and in other people. Supervision is the conduit by which I do it and help others to do the same. (2011: 78)

What early influences in my life led me to work in supervision? This question uncovers many otherwise hidden connections, associations, motivations, values, aspirations. It is deeply personal. It remains a mine of personal awareness as life progresses and becomes richer the more we excavate!

Let me start my own story by recounting a Native American legend:

> An old Cherokee chief is teaching his grandson about life: 'A fight is going on inside me,' he says to the boy. 'It is a terrible fight and it is between two wolves.' One is evil – he is anger, envy, sorrow, regret, greed, arrogance, self-pity, guilt, resentment, inferiority, lies, false pride, superiority, self-doubt and ego. The other is good – he is joy, peace, love, hope, serenity, humility, kindness, benevolence, empathy, generosity, truth, compassion and faith. 'This same fight is going on inside you – and inside every other person too.' The grandson thinks about it for a minute and then asks his grandfather, 'Which wolf will win?' The old Cherokee replies, 'The one that I feed.' (Traditional)

In every endeavour involving relationships (being present to, being with) it is always worthwhile locating oneself. Where I am, where I come from and who I bring with me are fundamentals in all relationships, including the supervision relationship. The Native American story above locates me somewhat. Not that the two wolves inside me are the wolves of negativity and positivity, though those are there too. The wolves that locate me in supervision are the wolves of reason and emotion.

## The fight

I was born in Belfast, Northern Ireland, in the mid-1940s. I was the second eldest of a Catholic family of nine children from working-class parents. We lived and grew up in the volatile cauldron of sectarian differences and violence; already these two 'collective wolves' had a centuries-old tragic history. Alongside these external wolves, two further wolves also existed in my family. My father was a fairly typical Irish man who was dedicated to his family. He worked all hours possible to put food on the table, and by and large left the dynamics of family life and child-rearing to my mother. He was quite remote emotionally and would have felt awkward with public signs of affection or feeling. In later life he changed quite dramatically and became emotionally present to his children and grandchildren. As the disciplinarian of the family he saw it as his duty to stay somewhat distant and to 'supervise' family life from his pedestal. My mother was quite the opposite – warm, available, emotional, involved – and soft when it came to discipline. The warm relational wolf and the remote rational wolf co-existed relatively peacefully together.

I fed the wolf of reason and discipline and at the early age of 12 joined a junior seminary to study for the priesthood. My journey of cultivating reason began. There was little or no recognition of the role of emotion, feeling or of the physical body in my priesthood training and education. The body existed, as someone said, to get your head to meetings. Nothing existed from the neck down. We know now, as the horrendous results of clerical sexual abuse in Ireland come to light, of the dangers of denying our bodies and repressing our feelings. My studies in philosophy and theology were typical of the modern rational approaches to knowledge and learning. Even my relationships with others were reasonable and rational relationships. I couldn't say I was truly 'in relationship', since much of the emotional connection in how I lived and worked with people was missing. In this celibate, perhaps even sterile, world of discipline and collegial relationships the wolf of reason thrived while the wolf of emotion starved. The resilient emotional wolf would not, however, stay silent, and his persistent cries began to be heard as the life of the rational wolf became more and more unsatisfying. Eventually the emotional wolf demanded recognition and acceptance. As my studies in counselling and psychology evolved (including group work, individual counselling, supervision etc.), I became more and more aware of the one-sidedness of my life. I began the interior journey of feeding, befriending and loving the emotional wolf. It was a journey that led me to leave the priesthood, get married and start a new life of emotional awareness. I learned to critique some of the assumptions of reason, think for myself and allow myself to feel and express my emotions. So, belatedly, I started to see the value of, and immerse myself in, individual reflective practice.

I left my former life, however, with an inheritance. I was still very much influenced by what has been called 'technical rationality' (Schon, 1883: 31). (Technical rationality is an approach that logically finds right answers or methods of applying professional knowledge to practice in a technical or robotic manner.) My religious training had been based on the assumptions of natural law whereby everything, human beings included, can be understood as following definite and fixed laws of cause and effect. This paradigm 'reduces practitioners to the level of technicians whose only role is to implement the research findings and theoretical models' (Rofte et al., 2001: 7). Technical rationality works on the principle that once the theory has been grasped, the practice will follow automatically.

I was learning fast, however, that between the theory and the application is a vast chasm that the practitioner has to bridge. From the lofty heights of what should work according to professional knowledge, to the down-to-earth practice of what did work, there was a whole territory of adjustment, adaptation, interpretation, readjustment and moment-to-moment decision making. Practitioners are not like carpenters with a hammer and chisel; they are more like tailors with their cloth. The answers are not given. They are certainly not as applicable as a sticking-plaster is to a wound.

This is where reflection enters the helping equation. It becomes the bridge that adapts professional knowledge to real-life and real-time situations: 'The reflective practitioner acts as a skilled tailor, using the knowledge base of his or her profession as the cloth from which to cut appropriate solutions to fit the requirements of the specific practice situation' (Thompson and Thompson, 2008: 15).

Supervision became a central and symbolic component in my new life and stands as an archetypal bridge between my past and present. It provides a path for both myself and others to span the distances between past and present and between the emotional and the rational. It is of course a fragile, rickety bridge rather than a solid structure. It represents the abilities to both go with the flow and stand against the current.

My journey in supervision has enabled the wolves of reason (theory, skills, models, frameworks and research) and emotion (relationships, engagement, trust, critical moments and ethical decisions) to find ways of living together and co-existing in harmony. The reasoning wolf is well fed in my avid reading and interest in the supervision literature. The rational supervision wolf is plump and sleek. But I have also been practising supervision attentively – involved, engaged, relating, emotional and connected. The emotional wolf is equally well-fed and sleek. My legacies from my mother and father have combined productively in my supervision. I know I need to feed both wolves. My hope is that this book will show how reason and emotion combine to make supervision one of the most creative learning environments available to us.

## Learning and supervision

At the heart of my interest and passion for supervision is my fascination with learning. It has been an abiding theme of my life and all my jobs have revolved around setting up learning relationships, creating learning environments and facilitating learning in one-to-one, group, team and organisational settings. Learning for me means increased knowledge, new or more finely-tuned skills, capability, competency and change of behaviours, values, mind-sets and mental maps. Simply put: learning = growth = development = change. Being part of the journey of learning is one of the most satisfying and fulfilling aspects of my life. What thrills me most is when I meet someone who was on a programme I directed and they say how that programme affected their learning and their lives. Those transformational moments are what make my work worthwhile. I look back and become 'retrospectively introspective' (Ray and Myers, 1986). Kierkegaard is reputed to have said, 'You live life forwards, you understand it backwards.' He could, of course, have been talking about supervision, which is concerned with making sense of past experiences and past practice. He could have been talking about my making sense of my own learning. I want to gather or glean my learning from experience and see if it resonates with your supervisory learning and experience.

## From the past to the future

I wish I could 'live the mantra' outlined by Shaw and make it a way of life rather than simply a set of skills:

> I have a keen sense of the move towards and away from agreement, of shifts in power difference, the development and collapse of tensions, the variations in engagement, the different qualities of silence, the rhetorical ploys, the repetition of familiar turns of phrase or images, the glimpsing and losing of possibility, the ebb and flow of feeling tone, the dance of mutual constraint. (2002: 33)

My own mantra would include:

> I want to formulate desires and aspirations for myself as both supervisor and supervisee.
> I want to be less knowing.
> I want to stay more with unknowing and uncertainty.
> I want to cherish silence.
> I want to disagree more agreeably.
> I want to listen, notice and articulate the assumptions I make.

I want to accept the discrepancies in my practice.
I want to build authentic bridges between theory and work.
I want to remember that most bridges are rickety.
I want to notice the textures of feeling.
I want to see and hear what I so often overlook.
I want to see my blind spots, speak my dumb spots, hear my deaf spots.
I want to be patient and wait until the insight is ready.
I want the enthusiasm of the beginner and the wisdom of the experienced.
I want to see my supervisors, my supervisees and all our clients as bearing gifts.
I want to be able to distinguish the gifts from their wrappings.
I want to see with the heart as well as with the head.
I want to become real to myself and to others.
I want to be a critical reflector leading to transformational learning.
I want to glimpse the future in the present.
I want to reflect deeply and critically on all of my life.
I want to be supervision-in-motion.

## An exercise

When training supervisors, I often ask them to write their 'Philosophy of supervision' for me and for others. What letter would you like to give potential supervisees that captures for them what supervision means to you? Take lots of time on this and when you have a first draft ready seek feedback from trusted colleagues and friends. I suggest you repeat this exercise every few years as your philosophy of supervision evolves in the light of practical experience.

Here is one that you might use as a starting point:

I want to offer you a space where vulnerability is accepted, where there is respite from perfectionism, achievements and the demand for results, where there is rest, time and space for reflection. A place to stop, to get off the treadmill, be heard and nourished and challenged to be who you truly are, to develop potential. I want you to be safe to push the barriers of your comfort zone, so there can be growth. I want you to have the freedom and spontaneity to shout with excitement and enthusiasm at your success and to acknowledge without shame your worst scenarios. Supervision is an encounter where spirit meets spirit.

When this meeting happens there will be trust, humility, modelling and shared learning; there will be the ancient art of play, guides come to education, challenges present themselves, there is honest and loving feedback. The senses of taste, smell, touch sight and sound, knowing and wonder become sharper and are appropriate channels. There is a real sense of connection, a reservoir of deepening levels of awareness and personal responsibly, a mystery waiting to be explored. An eagerness to meet, a quickening of life forces, magnets which draw teacher to teacher. I want there to be innocence and purity, surprises and creativity. I want to take the risk of being wounded, scared into reality so that you can be healed. You need to feel protected from ridicule, shame and abuse. Bubbles of energy seep to the surface.

Sometimes I am a parent, firm, loving, authoritarian and playful. I am a natural curious child, adapting to whims of play. I am an adult growing towards wholeness, maturity and responsibility. Sometimes I am the student, sometimes the teacher, often the coach, occasionally the judge. I am so wise, I am so foolish, I know a lot, I know nothing. Sometimes I succeed, and sometimes I fall on my face. I will never let it be dull. (Christine Earley, Personal communication)

When you are happy with your introductory letter, go over it with a highlighter pen picking out words and phrases that relate to your personal value systems, beliefs and ethical stances. How much of you is embedded in your statement?

## Conclusion

A supervisor needs a coherent, personalised underpinning philosophy of supervision to inform and shape their praxis. The facilitation of reflective learning from experience is an essential methodological and ethical commitment.

Supervision is a young but rapidly growing discipline with a rich history and many fertile bridges and connections to other disciplines and applications. Each of these 'honoured guests' brings something unique to the supervision banquet.

# References

Abrashoff, D.M. (2002) *It's Your Ship: Management Techniques from the Best Damn Ship in the Navy*. New York: Warner.

Armstrong, K. (2011) *Twelve Steps to a Compassionate Life*. New York: Anchor Books.

Autagavaia, M. (2001) A Tagata Pasifika Supervision Process. In L. Beddoe and J. Worrall (eds), *From Rhetoric to Reality: Keynote Address and Selected Papers*. Auckland: Auckland College of Education.

BACP (2010) *Ethical Framework*. Lutterworth: British Association for Counselling and Psychotherapy. Available at www.bacp.co.uk/ethical_framework/

Barretta-Herman, A. (2001) Fulfilling the Commitment to Competent Social Work Practice through Supervision. In L. Beddoe and J. Worrall (eds), *From Rhetoric to Reality: Keynote Address and Selected Papers*. Auckland: Auckland College of Education.

Belenky, M., Clinchy, B., Goldberger, R. and Tarule, J. (1986) *Women's Ways of Knowing*. New York: Basic Books.

Benefiel, M. and Holton, G. (eds) (2010) *The Soul of Supervision: Integrating Practice and Theory*. New York: Morehouse.

Bernard, J. and Goodyear, R. (2014) *Fundamentals of Clinical Supervision* (5th edn). Upper Saddle River, NJ: Pearson.

Bolton, G. (2001) *Reflective Practice*. London: Paul Chapman.

Bond, T. (2007) Ethics and Psychotherapy: An Issue of Trust. In R.E. Ashcroft, A. Dawson, H. Draper and J.R. McMillan (eds), *Principles of Health Care Ethics* (2nd edn). Chichester: Wiley. pp. 435–442.

Bond, T. (2013) The Ethics of Research. In M. Carroll and E. Shaw (eds), *Ethical Maturity in the Helping Professions*. London: Jessica Kingsley.

Bowlby, J. (1988) *A Secure Base: Clinical Applications of Attachment Theory*. London: Routledge.

Brookfield, S.D. (2012) *Teaching for Critical Thinking: Tools and Techniques to Help Students Question their Assumptions*. San Francesco, CA: Jossey-Bass.

Brown, B. (2010) *The Power of Vulnerability*. TED Talk. Available at www. ted.com/talks

Brown, P. and Brown, V. (2012) *Neuropsychology for Coaches: Understanding the Basics*. Maidenhead: Open University Press. (Kindle version.)

Carifio, M. and Hess, A. (1987) Who is the Ideal Supervisor? *Professional Psychology*, 18 (3): 244–250.

Carroll, M. (1995) The Generic Tasks of Supervision. PhD Dissertation, University of Surrey.

Carroll, M. (1996a) *Counselling Supervision: Theory, Skills and Practice.* London: Cassell.

Carroll, M. (1996b) *Workplace Counselling: A Systematic Approach to Employee Care.* London: Sage.

Carroll, M. (1999) Supervision in Workplace Settings. In M. Carroll and E. Holloway (eds), *Counselling Supervision in Context.* London: Sage.

Carroll, M. (2001) The Spirituality of Supervision. In M. Carroll and M. Tholstrup (eds), *Integrative Approaches to Supervision.* London: Jessica Kingsley.

Carroll, M. (2009) From Mindless to Mindful Practice: Learning Reflection in Supervision. *Psychotherapy in Australia*, 15 (4): 38–49.

Carroll, M. (2011) Supervision: A Journey of Lifelong Learning. In R. Shohet (ed.), *Supervision as Transformation: A Passion for Learning.* London: Jessica Kingsley.

Carroll, M. and Gilbert, M. (2011) *Becoming an Effective Supervisee: Creating Learning Partnerships.* London: Vukani.

Carroll, M. and Shaw, E. (2012) *Ethical Maturity in the Helping Professions – Making Difficult Work and Life Decisions.* Melbourne: PsychOz.

Carroll, M. and Shaw, E. (2013) *Ethical Maturity in the Helping Professions – Making Difficult Work and Life Decisions.* London: Jessica Kingsley.

Cavicchia, S. (2012) Shame in the Coaching Relationship: Reflections on Individual and Organisational Vulnerability. In E. de Haan and C. Sills (eds), *Coaching Relationships: The Relational Coaching Fieldbook.* Farington: Libri.

Claxton, G. and Lucas, B. (2007) *The Creative Thinking Plan.* London: BBC Books.

Covey, S. (1989) *The Seven Habits of Highly Effective People.* London: Simon and Schuster.

Critchley, B. (2010) Relational Coaching: Taking the Coaching High Road. *Journal of Management Development*, 29 (10): 851–863.

Cron, L. (2012) *Wired for Story.* Berkeley, CA: Ten Speed Press. (Kindle version.)

Curran, D.A. (2008) *The Little Book of Big Stuff about the Brain.* Carmarthen: Crown House.

Curtis Jenkins, G. (2001) Counselling Supervision in Primary Health Care. In M. Carroll and M. Tholstrup (eds), *Integrative Approaches to Supervision.* London: Jessica Kingsley.

De Bono, E. (2006) The Scientist-Practitioner as Thinker: A Comment on Judgement and Design. In D. Lane and S. Corrie (eds), *The Modern Scientist-Practitioner: A Guide to Practice in Psychology.* Routledge: Hove.

De Haan, E. (2012) *Supervision in Action: A Relational Approach to Coaching and Consulting Supervision.* Maidenhead: Open University Press.

De Haan, E. and Birch, D. (2012) The Organisation Supervisor: Shadow Consulting in Full Colour. In Erik De Haan (ed.), *Supervision in Action: A Relational Approach to Coaching and Consulting Supervision.* Maidenhead: Open University Press.

De Haan, E., Bertine, C., Day, A. and Sills, C. (2010) Critical Moments of Clients and Coaches: A Direct-comparison Study. *International Coaching Psychology Review*, 5 (2): 109–128.

DeSalvo, L. (1999) *Writing as a Way of Healing*. Boston, MA: Beacon Press.

Dixon, N. (1998) *Dialogue at Work*. London: Lemos and Crane.

Duhigg, C. (2013) *The Power of Habit: Why We Do What We Do and How to Change*. London: Heinemann. (Kindle version.)

Dunnett, A., Jesper, C., O'Donnell, M. and Vallance, K. (In press) *Getting the Most from Supervision (A Guide for Counsellors and Psychotherapists)*. London: Palgrave-Macmillan.

Egan, G. and Cowan, M. (1979) *People in Systems*. Monterey, CA: Brooks/Col.

Ellis, M. (2010) Bridging the Science and Practice of Supervision: Some Discoveries, Some Misconception. *The Clinical Supervisor*, 29: 95–116.

Engle, C. and Singer, W. (2008) Better than Conscious? The Brain, the Psyche, Behaviour and Institutions. In C. Engle and W. Singer (eds), *Better than Conscious? Decision Making, the Human Mind and Implications for Institutions*. Cambridge, MA: MIT Press.

Fine, C. (2007) *A Mind of its Own: How your Brain Distorts and Deceives*. Cambridge: Icon Books.

Frackston, J. (1999) *Signs of the Unseen: The Discources of Jalaluddin Rumi*. Boston, MA: Shambhala Publications.

Frost, P. and Robinson, S. (1999) The Toxic Handler: Organisational Hero and Causality. *Harvard Business Review*, July–August.

Garvin, D. (2000) *Learning in Action*. Boston, MA: Harvard Business School Press.

Gazzaniga, M. (2012) *Who's in Charge: Free Will and the Science of the Brain*. London: Constable and Robertson.

Gelb, M. (1998) *How to Think Like Leonardo da Vinci*. New York: Dell.

Gladwell, M. (2005) *Blink: The Power of Thinking without Thinking*. London: Allen Lane.

Gonzalez-Doupe, P.A. (2001) The Supervision Group As Protection: The Meaning of Group Supervision for Workplace Counsellors and their Supervisors in Organizational Settings in England. PhD dissertation, University of Wisconsin-Madison.

Groopman, J. (2007) *How Doctors Think*. Boston, MA: Houghton Mifflin.

Haidt, J. (2006) *The Happiness Hypothesis: Putting Ancient Wisdom to the Test of Modern Science*. London: Heinemann.

Hammarskjöld, D. (1966) *Markings*. London: Faber and Faber.

Harvey, J.B. (1996) *The Abilene Paradox and Other Meditations on Management*. San Francisco, CA: Jossey-Bass.

Hawkins, P. (2011) Systemic Approaches to Supervision. In T. Bachkirova, P. Jackson and D. Clutterbuck (eds), *Coaching and Mentoring Supervision: Theory and Practice*. Maidenhead: Open University Press.

Hawkins, P. (2012a) *Creating a Coaching Culture*. Maidenhead: Open University Press.

Hawkins, P. (2012b) Keynote address. BASPR conference, Twickenham.

Hawkins, P. and Shohet, R. (2012) *Supervision in the Helping Professions* (4th edn). Milton Keynes: Open University Press.

Hawkins, P. and Smith, N. (2007) *Supervision for Coaches, Mentors and Consultants.* Maidenhead: Open University Press.

Heidegger, M. (1962) *Being and Time* (trans. J. Macquarrie and E.S. Robinson). Oxford: Blackwell.

Henderson, P. (1999) Supervision in Medical Settings. In M. Carroll and E. Holloway (eds), *Counselling Supervision in Context.* London: Sage.

Henderson, P. (2009a) *A Different Wisdom: Reflections on Supervision Practice.* London: Karnac.

Henderson, P. (2009b) *Supervisor Training: Issues and Approaches.* London: Karnac.

Hewson, D. and Carroll, M. (In press) *Mindful Practice in Supervision: The Reflective Toolkit.*

Hitchings, P. (2012) Keynote address. BASPR Conference, London.

Holloway, E. (1992) Supervision: A Way of Teaching and Learning. In S. Brown and R. Lent (eds), *The Handbook of Counseling Psychology* (2nd edn). New York: Wiley.

Holloway, E. (1995) *Clinical Supervision: A Systems Approach.* Thousand Oaks, CA: Sage.

Holton, G. (2010) Wisdom's Garden: A Metaphor for Cross-professional Training. In M. Benefiel and G. Holton (eds), *The Soul of Supervision: Integrating Practice and Theory.* New York: Morehouse.

Hughes, J. and Youngson, S. (eds) (2009) *Personal Development and Clinical Psychology.* Chichester: BPS Blackwell.

Hunt, C. (2010) A Step too Far? From Professional Reflective Practice to Spirituality. In H. Bradbury, N. Frost, S. Kilminster and M. Zukas (eds), *Beyond Reflective Practice: New Approaches to Professional Lifelong Learning.* Abington: Routledge.

Inskipp, F. and Proctor, B. (1993) *Making the Most of Supervision: Part 1.* Twickenham: Cascade. (2nd Edition, 2001).

Inskipp, F. and Proctor, B. (1995) *The Art, Craft and Tasks of Counselling Supervision. Part 2: Becoming a Supervisor.* Twickenham: Cascade.

Isaac, W. (1999) *Dialogue and the Art of Communication.* New York: Doubleday.

Jackson (2010) Nurturing Ministerial Leadership through Supervision. In M. Benefiel and G. Holton (eds), *The Soul of Supervision: Integrating Practice and Theory.* New York: Morehouse.

Kaberry, S. (1995) Abuse in Supervision. M.Ed. Dissertation, University of Birmingham.

Keen, S. (1994) *Hymns to an Unknown God: Awakening the Spirit in Everyday Life.* London: Piatkus.

Kegan, R. (1994) *In Over our Heads: The Mental Demands of Modern Life.* San Francisco, CA: Jossey-Bass.

King, P.M. and Kitchener, K.S. (1994) *Developing Reflective Judgment.* San Francisco, CA: Jossey-Bass.

Kohlberg, L. (1982) *The Philosophy of Moral Development.* San Francisco, CA: Harper and Row.

Kolb, D. (1984) *Experiential Learning.* Englewood Cliffs, NJ: Prentice Hall.

Kroll, B.M. (1992) *Teaching Hearts and Minds: College Students Reflect on the Vietnam War in Literature.* Carbondale, IL: Southern Illinois University Press.

Kross, E. and Ayduk, O. (2011) Making Meaning out of Negative Experiences by Self-distancing. *Current Directions in Psychological Science*, 20 (3): 187–191.

Kusy, M. and Holloway, E. (2009) *Toxic Workplace: Managing Toxic Personalities and their Systems of Power*. San Francisco, CA: Jossey-Bass.

Ladany, N. and Bradley, L.J. (2010) *Counselor Supervision* (4th edn). New York: Routledge.

Ladany, N., Lehrman-Waterman, D., Molinaro, M. and Wolgast, B. (1999) Psychotherapy Supervision Ethical Practices: Adherence to Guidelines, the Supervisory Working Alliance and Supervisee Satisfaction. *The Counseling Psychologist*, 27: 443–475.

Lane, D. and Corrie, S. (2006). Counselling Psychology: Its Influences and Future. *Counselling Psychology Review*, 21 (1): 12–24.

Langer, E. (1989) *Mindfulness*. Cambridge, MA: Perseus.

Lave, J. and Wenger, E. (1991) *Situated Learning: Legitimate Peripheral Participation*. Cambridge: Cambridge University Press.

Lawton-Smith, C. (2011) Organisational Psychology Models in Coaching Supervision. In T. Bachkirova, P. Jackson and D. Clutterbuck (eds), *Coaching and Mentoring Supervision: Theory and Practice*. Maidenhead: McGraw-Hill.

Loehr, J. and Schwartz, T. (2003) *On Form: Achieving High Energy Performance Without Sacrificing Health and Happiness and Life Balance*. London: Nicholas Brearley.

Luxmoore, N. (2011) *Young People and the Curse of Ordinariness*. London: Jessica Kingsley.

Mann, E. (1999) Supervision in Religious Settings. In M. Carroll and E. Holloway (eds), *Counselling Supervision in Context*. London: Sage.

Marsick, V.J. and Maltbia, T.E. (2009) The Transformative Potential of Action Learning Conversations: Developing Critically Reflective Learning Skills. In J. Merizow and E. Taylor (eds), *Transformative Learning in Practice*. San Francisco, CA: Jossey-Bass.

Marzano, R.J., Frontier, T. and Livingston, D. (2011) *Effective Supervision: Supporting the Art and Science of Teaching*. Alexandria, VA: ASCD Publications.

McGuire, J. (2013) Foreword. In J. Clarke and P. Wilson (eds), *Forensic Psychology in Practice: A Practitioner's Handbook*. Basingstoke: Palgrave Macmillan.

Mezirow, J. and Associates (2000) *Learning as Transformation: Critical Perspectives on a Theory in Progress*. San Francisco, CA: Jossey-Bass.

Milgram, S. (1974) *Obedience to Authority: An Experimental View*. New York: Harper and Row.

Mitchell, D. (2009) Responsibility in Existential Supervision. In E. Van Deurzen and S. Young (eds), *Existential Perspectives on Supervision*. Basingstoke: Palgrave Macmillan.

Moon, J. (1999) *Reflection in Learning and Professional Development*. London: Kogan Page.

Moon, J. (2004) *A Handbook of Reflective and Experiential Learning*. Oxford: Routledge Falmer.

Moore, B. (2008) Group Supervision with a Multi-disciplinary Trauma Resource Team in the North of Ireland: A Participative Inquiry into The Application of a 'Process Framework'. D. Prof. dissertation, University of Middlesex.

Murphy, K. (2009). Keynote address. British Association for Supervision Practice and Research Conference. London, July.

Nelson, M.L., Barnes, K.L., Evans, A.L. and Triggiano, P.J. (2008) Working with Conflict in Clinical Supervision: Wise Supervisors' Perspectives. *Journal of Counseling Psychology*, 55 (2), 172-184.

O'Leary, M.R. (2004) *The Curse of the Self.* New York: Oxford University Press.

Oshry, B. (1996) *Seeing Systems: Unlocking the Mysteries of Organizational Life.* San Francisco, CA: Berrett-Koehler.

Owen, D. and Shohet, R. (2012) *Clinical Supervision in the Medical Profession.* Maidenhead: Open University Press.

Pohly, K. (2001) *Transforming the Rough Places: The Ministry of Supervision.* Franklin, TN: Providence House.

Poole, J. (2010) Perspectives on Supervision in Human Services: Gazing through Critical and Feminist Lenses. *Michigan Family Review*, 14 (1): 60–70.

Prall, W. (2010) *Metanoia and the Making of a Psychotherapist* (private publication).

Proctor, B. (2008) *Group Supervision: A Guide to Creative Practice* (2nd edn). London: Sage.

Quantum of Solace (2008) Produced by Eon Productions: Directed by Marc Forster and produced by Michael G. Wilson.

Queneau, R. (1998) *Exercises in Style.* London: John Calder Publishing. Originally published in 1947 by Editions Gallimard, Paris.

Ray, M. and Myers, R. (1986) *Creativity in Business.* New York: Broadway Books.

Roberts, M. (1997) *The Man who Listens to Horses.* London: Arrow Books.

Rock, D. (2007) *Quiet Leadership: Six Steps to Transforming Performance at Work.* New York: Collins.

Rofte, G., Freshwater, D. and Jasper, M. (2001) *Critical Reflection for Nursing and the Helping Professions.* Basingstoke: Palgrave Macmillan.

Rogers, C. (1958) A Process Conception of Psychotherapy. *American Psychologist*, 13: 142–149.

Ryan, S. (2004) *Vital Practice.* Portland, UK: Sea Change.

Scaife, J. (2009) *Supervision in Clinical Practice: A Practitioner's Guide.* Hove: Routledge.

Scharmer, C.O. (2007) *Theory U: Leading from the Future as it Emerges.* Cambridge, MA: SoL Publications.

Schon, D. (1983) *The Reflective Practitioner.* New York: Basic Books.

Schon, D. (1987) *Educating the Reflective Practitioner.* San Francisco: Jossey-Bass.

Shaw, P. (2002) *Changing Conversations in Organisations.* London: Routledge.

Shohet, R. (2008) Fear and Love In and Beyond Supervision. In R. Shohet (ed.), *Passionate Supervision.* London: Jessica Kingsley.

Sills, C. (2012) The Coaching Contract: A Mutual Commitment. In E. de Haan and C. Sills (eds), *Coaching Relationships: The Relational Coaching Fieldbook.* Farington: Libri.

Skovholt, T. (2001) *The Resilient Practitioner.* London: Pearson.

Smail, D. (1987) *Taking Care: An Alternative to Therapy.* London: Dent.

Tholstrup, M. (1999) Supervision in Educational Settings. In M. Carroll and E. Holloway (eds), *Counselling Supervision in Context*. London: Sage.

Thompson, S. and Thompson, N. (2008) *The Critically Reflective Practitioner*. Basingstoke: Palgrave Macmillan.

Torbet, B. (2004) *Action Enquiry*. San Francisco, CA: Berrett-Koehler.

Towler, J. (1999) Supervision in Uniformed Organizations. In M. Carroll and E. Holloway (eds), *Counselling Supervision in Context*. London: Sage.

Towler, J. (2005) The Influence of the Invisible Client. PhD dissertation, University of Surrey.

Towler, J. (2008) The Influence of the Invisible Client: A Crucial Perspective for Understanding Counselling Supervision in Organisational Contexts. In C. Shillito-Clarke and M. Tholstrup (eds), *Occasional Papers in Supervision*. Leicester: BPS Publications.

Tudor, K. and Worrall, M. (2004) *Freedom to Practice: Person-centred Approaches to Supervision*. Ross-on-Wye: PCCS Books.

Vaill, P. (1996) *Learning as a Way of Being*. San Francisco, CA: Jossey-Bass.

Van Deurzen, E. and Young, S. (2009) *Existential Perspectives on Supervision*. Basingstoke: Palgrave Macmillan.

Vespia, K.M., Hechman-Stone, C. and Delwith, V. (2002) Describing and Facilitating Effective Supervision Behaviour in Counselling Trainees. *Psychotherapy: Theory, Research and Practice,* 39 (1): 56–65.

Wall, J.C. (1994) Teaching Termination to Trainees through Parallel Processes in Supervision, *Clinical Supervisor,* 12 (2): 27–37.

Watling, R. (2012) Tension, Trust and Transference: Exploring Key Features in the Early Stages of Supervisory Relationships. Essay for Module 1 ACOS. Berkhamsted: Ashridge Business School.

Westefeld, D. (2009) Supervision of Psychotherapy: Models, Issues and Recommendations. *The Counseling Psychologist,* 37 (2): 296–316.

Whitehead, J.D. and Whitehead, E.E. (1994) *Shadows of the Heart: A Spirituality of the Negative Emotions*. New York: Crossroads.

Whyte, D. (1994) *The Heart Aroused*. London: The Industrial Society.

Wilmot, J. (2011) Work as Transformation through Supervision. In R. Shohet (ed.), *Supervision as Transformation: A Passion for Learning*. London: Jessica Kingsley.

Wilson, T. (2002) *Strangers to Ourselves: Discovering the Adaptive Unconscious*. Cambridge, MA: Harvard University Press.

Woodcock, V. (2012) Offering Normative Supervision. Paper submitted in partial fulfilment of the Postgraduate Certificate in Coaching and OD Consulting (ACOS). Berkhamsted: Ashridge Business School.

Zachary, L. (2000) *The Mentor's Guide: Facilitating Effective Learning Relationships*. San Francisco, CA: Jossey-Bass.

Zimbardo, P. (2007) *The Lucifer Effect: How Good People Turn Evil*. London: Rider.

Zuboff, S. and Maxmin, J. (2002) *The Support Economy: Why Companies are Failing Individuals*. New York: Penguin.

# Index